UNIVERSITY LIBRARY
UW-STEVENS POINT

W9-BEE-575

The State and the City

The State and the City

TED ROBERT GURR

AND

DESMOND S. KING

The University of Chicago Press

Ted Robert Gurr, professor of political science at the
University of Colorado, Boulder, is the author of
numerous books, including *Why Men Rebel* (1970), which
received the Woodrow Wilson Award, and coauthor of *The
Politics of Crime and Conflict: A Comparative History of
Four Cities* (1977). Desmond S. King, lecturer in politics
at the University of Edinburgh, is the author of *The New
Right: Politics, Markets and Citizenship*.

The University of Chicago Press, Chicago 60637

Macmillan Education Ltd, UK

© 1987 by Ted Robert Gurr and Desmond S. King
All rights reserved. Published 1987

Printed in Hong Kong

96 95 94 93 92 91 90 89 88 87 54321

Library of Congress Cataloging-in-Publication Data
Gurr, Ted Robert, 1936-
    The state and the city.
    Bibliography: p.
    Includes index.
    1. Federal-city relations—United States.
2. Federal-city relations—Great Britain.
I. King, Desmond S. II. Title.
JS344, F4G87   1987   320.473   87-5015
ISBN 0-226-31090-6
ISBN 0-226-31091-4 (pbk.)

JS
344
.F4
G87
1987

Contents

v

List of Figures

List of Tables

Introduction

Public policy and private capital have reshaped Western cities and urban systems during the last thirty years at a pace that has no historical precedent. The central objective of this study is to present a general analysis of the role of the state in this process and the evolution of that role during a period of rapid urban change. Our basic premise is that national and local states have their own distinctive interests in cities and have significant autonomy in how they pursue them. Our second premise is that the changing character of cities in advanced industrial societies and the widening discrepancies in the quality of urban life between growing and declining cities are not simply the results of inexorable economic processes but they have been substantially influenced by the decisions and actions of public officials, national and local. These assumptions, articulated more fully in Chapter 1, provide the basis for this book's comparative analysis of urban policies in the United States and Great Britain. We are concerned with how national states' urban interests and policies have evolved, with their capacities to direct and compensate for the stresses of urban change, and with the implications of neo-conservative policies now in vogue around the Atlantic basin for the future of declining cities.

We have two different but reinforcing reasons for taking a state-centred approach to this issue. One is an academic interest in applying new theories about the autonomy of the democratic state to the analysis of one particular area of public policy. It is widely assumed by empirical theorists that modern states and public officials have their own interests, institutional momentum and the capacity to act with relative autonomy: major recent statements to this effect have been made by political scientists, notably Eric Nordlinger (1981) and Roger Benjamin and Stephen L. Elkin (1985); by political sociologists

such as Theda Skocpol and her collaborators (Evans, Rueschemeyer and Skocpol, 1985); and by political geographers
Gordon L. Clark and Michael Dear (1984). Case studies have
shown that these general arguments lead to plausible new
interpretations of subjects as diverse as the formation of US
foreign policy on economic issues (Krasner, 1978), the origins
and growth of social welfare policies in Western societies
(Heclo, 1974; Weir and Skocpol, 1985), and the Norwegian and
American governments' roles in promoting development in the
oil industry (Visher and Remoe, 1984; Feagin, 1985). Largely
lacking in this literature are studies which carefully build
bridges between general theory about the state and the analysis
of particular cases or policy areas. This we attempt to do with
regard to urban policy by identifying the nature and origins of
state interests in cities, then applying the theory in a
comparative analysis of how national and local states in Britain
and the United States have shaped and responded to urban
crisis and decline. Our focus on cities also highlights the
diversity of interests among segments of the state apparatus
and the significance of contention among its national, regional
and local strata. State interests cannot be assumed to be simply
the aggregate of the individual preferences of officials. Nor are
Western states monolithic in interests or action even in a
specific policy area.

Our second reason for undertaking this study is a humanistic
interest for the qualities of city life, qualities which vary
enormously among and within Western societies. The conventional explanations for the stark contrasts between blighted old
industrial cities like Newcastle, England or Newark, New
Jersey and thriving centres of commerce and culture like
Bristol, England or Boston, Massachusetts are economic ones.
Our evidence demonstrates that the policies of the local and
national state can have equal or greater effects on urban
well-being. Regulatory and tax policies shape the environments which attract or repel investors and prosperous
residents; government procurements and contracts stimulate
the private economy; decisions about public investment
determine whether infrastructure and housing will be rebuilt or
allowed to deteriorate; and the allocation of public employment and social transfer payments can keep declining central

cities from becoming sinks of unemployment and social degradation.

Our argument is also intended as an alternative to the economic and ecological determinism which has dominated so much recent discussion of the future of Western cities. There is ironic agreement between the neo-conservative right and the neo-Marxist left in the United States and Britain that urban growth and decline is a function of economic forces. The left attributes urban decay to the migration of private capital in pursuit of greater profit margins and sees in it further evidence of the crisis of late capitalism. The conservatives believe that the fate of cities should be left to the regenerative forces of the market which will save those cities which deserve to be saved. Both left and right acknowledge that the state plays a role in urban growth and decline but minimise its significance: the left because the state is regarded as too subservient to private economic interests to take action that is costly to those interests, the right because the state is regarded as the source of too much constraint on private initiative.

In our view, the parts played by the national and local state in shaping cities have become so substantial and well institutionalised in all Western societies that it is no longer plausible to argue that economic forces are or can be primarily responsible for urban growth and decline. The vitality of some cities and the decline of others are both the results of interaction between public and private decisions. The essential political economy questions raised by present urban realities concern public decisions about what responsibilities to assume *vis-à-vis* cities, whether those responsibilities are vested in the national or local state, how they are to be financed, the kinds of political and official interests that drive those decisions, and the ways in which state power and private economic forces interact in shaping urban environments. Rather than take direct issue with the economic determinism of contemporary Marxists and conservatives, this book is concerned to demonstrate the state's tangible and autonomous influences on the vitality of cities and urban systems. If the case is made effectively, then its implications for simple economic determinism should be clear. Those who hold and use state power *can* allow the fate of cities to be determined mainly in the private economy, but that is a matter of public choice rather than iron necessity.

Our preference for a state-centred approach does not mean that we therefore advocate an expanded state presence as a means of 'saving' declining cities. The effects of state activities and policies in cities are far too diverse to think that they necessarily contribute to some illusory 'common interest' of all city dwellers. Nor do we propose specific policies for specific ends, because the potential effects of policy depend on the particulars of the urban condition, political and social support for state action, and the productive potential of region and society. This book presents a general analysis of the urban interests of the national state and evidence on how they have evolved under the impact of economic and social change. Such an analysis demonstrates that public policy has a more substantial and autonomous effect on Western cities than is acknowledged by many scholars and some advocates. That should be enough for one book.

Chapter 1 offers a general theoretical argument about the nature, structure and interests of the state with specific reference to advanced industrial societies, and builds on it an historically-grounded account of the evolution of the Western state's interests in the viability of cities. Evidence is offered about the capacities of modern states to pursue their interests along with a brief analysis of constraints on state autonomy. Chapter 2 extends the theoretical argument by examining the nature of the local state and the extent to which local states in Western societies are autonomous from the national state and from private economic interests. The analytic distinctions are applied in a discussion of the effects of urban fiscal crisis on the local state's autonomy in Britain and the United States. In Chapter 3 we develop a theoretical interpretation of the ways in which urban decline has increased the political salience of cities for the national state in contemporary Western societies. One of the consequences of increased salience is substantial growth in the range and impact of the national state's activities at the urban level. A comparative analysis of thirteen American cities shows a remarkable range of variation in the size and nature of their public sectors: Boston has become the archetypical public city, with half its population and personal income directly dependent on government spending; Houston is its polar opposite.

Chapters 4 and 5 provide detailed applications of the state-centred approach to specific problems of urban public policy in the United States and Britain. Chapter 4 traces the evolution of federal policies toward US cities during the 1930s and 1960s: in each decade step-level increases in the federal commitment to cities were made in response to urban crises which simultaneously threatened national interests and offered opportunities for programmatic expansion of the federal bureaucracy and electoral gains for the national Democratic Party. We also report results of an aggregate analysis of the political and economic conditions associated with the allocation of federal grants-in-aid among cities from 1960 to 1980 which provides empirical support for the larger theoretical argument. The dynamics of decline in Britain's old industrial cities and the urban policies followed by Margaret Thatcher's Conservative Government are the subject of Chapter 5. The British case highlights the conflicts between the national and local states' interests in the social and economic life of cities. The local authorities of the large conurbations are being deprived of fiscal and political autonomy to respond to the problems of urban decline by a national government committed to the overriding objective of reducing the public sector. The consequences for meeting the national state's minimal interests in the maintenance of public order and acceptance of its authority in urban populations are highly problematic.

The concluding chapter integrates the arguments and evidence of the preceding chapters in an analysis of alternative futures for cities in Western societies. The shifting patterns of urban growth and decline in Britain and the United States are determined by interactions between economic and political forces. Among the four emerging types of city, two are dependent mainly on the private economy, two on the public economy. Of particular concern are the consequences of neo-conservative preferences for reliance on market forces to revitalise cities. We conclude that there are very real political limits to the economic decline and social crisis that can be tolerated in the category of 'welfare cities' which are being abandoned by both private capital and the national state.

The book has benefited from careful readings by a number of British and North American scholars. We are particularly appreciative of readings given to all or major portions of the study by Gordon L. Clark (Carnegie-Mellon), Brian Elliott, David McCrone and Gianfranco Poggi (University of Edinburgh), Alex Hicks (Emory University), Andrew Kirby and William O. Winter (University of Colorado), Kenneth Newton (University of Dundee) and James Simmie (University of London). Helpful comments on particular segments of the study have been provided by Malcolm Anderson, Fred Block, Nigel Bowles, Christopher Chase-Dunn, Paul Culhane, Robert Denmark, Henry Drucker, Edward Greenberg, John Holmwood, Jan-Erik Lané, Eric A. Nordlinger, Theda Skocpol, Jeremy Waldron and Oliver Williams. Essential assistance in the preparation of successive drafts of the manuscript was provided by Rachel Frick.

Institutional and salary support for the project was provided during 1982–84 by the Center for Urban Affairs and Policy Research at Northwestern University. Support during 1985–86 came from the Center for Comparative Politics at the University of Colorado, Boulder, and the Department of Politics of the University of Edinburgh. We also acknowledge the assistance of the National Science Foundation in the form of doctoral dissertation grant SES-8309627.

TED ROBERT GURR
DESMOND S. KING

Acknowledgement

An earlier version of Chapter 2 first appeared in Paul M. Johnson and William R. Thompson (eds), *Rhythms in Politics and Economics* (Praeger, 1985) and of Chapter 3 in Jan-Erik Lané (ed.), *State and Market* (Sage, 1985). Revised versions appear here with the permission of these publishers.

Chapter 1

A Theory of State–City Relations in Western Societies

There are diverse theoretical conceptions of the state underlying contemporary analyses of urban change in Western
societies. Those conceptions, some of them anchored in
democratic pluralism and others in the recent political
economy literature, incorporate assumptions about the purposes of states' urban policies and shape conclusions about
what states can and should do about the social stresses of urban
growth and decline. In the pluralist conception, government
policies tend to promote the general welfare because public
policy results from the interaction of diverse, contending
sectoral interests in the larger society. The specifics of urban
policy decisions and implementation are a function of shifting
coalitions of organised economic, political and social groups,
some pursuing conceptions of general welfare, others seeking to
enhance sectoral and individual interests (see, for example,
Banfield, 1961, ch. 12 and Dahl, 1961; a recent general
statement is Guterbock, 1980, pp. 433–4). To the extent that
there is a self-conscious government objective in urban policy,
it is to enhance the common welfare. Urban economic
development is pursued by American municipal governments
in active partnership with business because growth is widely
beneficial to all urban groups (Peterson, 1981).

The prevailing American view is that the market is the
primary shaper of cities and that policy intervention should
aim at relieving its undesirable consequences, not at intention-
ally redirecting market activities. Bradbury, Downs, and Small
(1982) conclude their study of decline in American cities with
the caution that 'market forces are extremely powerful; so it
would be folly to try policies that ignored their constructive

7

roles in guiding the form and structure of economic change' (p. 296; see also Kasarda, 1980). European urban scholars give the state a more active role. In the Urban Europe project's major cross-national study of urban growth and decline it is assumed that the national government 'will try to reduce to a minimum the interpersonal and interregional differences in well-being, or at any rate to provide for a certain minimum level of well-being for all groups and regions under its care' (van den Berg *et al.*, 1982, p. 22). The state should not accept urban spatial developments as given. Rather, it should attempt to influence the locational behaviour of households, businesses and public authorities 'in such a way that urban development from a welfare point of view will be optimum in the long run' (van den Berg *et al.*, 1982, pp. 105–6).

In sharp contrast to these welfare-maximising assumptions about the state's policies are those of the neo-Marxists, whose essential assumption about the state is captured by C. B. MacPherson: 'an indispensable job of the state in capitalist society is to maintain the conditions for capitalist enterprise and capital accumulation' (1977, p. 223). The character of cities and patterns of urban growth and decline are also the products of economic dynamics: the city 'is forged upon the hearth of a given mode of production' (Hill, 1977, p. 78; see also Gordon, 1976; Harvey, 1973; Smith, 1979). State policies generally are concerned with reproducing capitalist relationships, while specific urban policies are designed to benefit local economic interests. Thus Friedland (1980) argues that the distribution of urban renewal funds across American cities was a 'response to the power of the corporations headquartered' in those cities (p. 221; also Friedland, 1983). Molotch (1976, 1979) maintains that policies of central-city revitalisation in the United States are designed in concert with and serve the speculative interests of the rentiers and investors who operate the 'growth machine' (see also Fainstein *et al.*, 1983).

This book develops a theoretical perspective on the relations between state and city in advanced industrial societies which differs in two fundamental respects. First, in our view the modern democratic state has more autonomy in formulating and executing policy than it is accorded by most pluralists or neo-Marxists. The powers and resources of the national state have increased so greatly during the last fifty years, both in absolute and relative terms, that it is absurd to think of the state as subordinate in theory or practice to any class or constellation of interest groups. In fact the contemporary democratic state has more concentrated power than almost any possible coalition of private interests. Second, the purposes pursued by the modern state with respect to cities are not primarily those of private capital or social movements or other interests outside the state, nor of the 'general welfare'. Rather they are the interests of the state, which is to say the primary interests of the state in maintaining public order and authority in urban populations, in securing public revenues, and the interests of officials in the pursuit of *their* programmatic goals with respect to urban welfare. In our theoretical perspective the economic processes which reshape cities and the contending private interests which influence urban policies are limits or constraints on the state's policies, not determinants of those policies.[1]

Underlying our conception of the state's actual and potential role in shaping cities is a theoretical argument about the nature of the state in advanced industrial societies. This theory shares many of the assumptions of the new literature on the autonomous state, a literature which ranges from neo-and post-Marxist analyses of the state's relative autonomy from capitalism (see Carnoy, 1984, ch. 8; Clark and Dear, 1984) to more conventionally framed theories about the freedom of public officials in liberal democracies to act on their own preferences (Nordlinger, 1981). Our distinctive assumptions, above, parallel two common arguments in this literature: first, that state officials, or 'managers' as Fred Block (1977) calls them, hold interests which are distinct from those of groups outside the state, and second, that they have (in varying degrees) the will and means to pursue them independently. Officials may choose to align the state and its policies with one or another societal interest, but that is a matter of choice more than a response to structural necessity. The general conceptualisation of the state and its interests developed in the first part of this chapter provides the basis for the second part's historically-grounded account of the evolution of the interests of the national and local state in the viability of cities in Western societies.

We do not develop an explicit 'theory of the city' to complement our theory of the state, but do make some explicit assumptions about the character of cities. They are spatial concentrations of people engaged in highly differentiated economic and political activities, as a consequence of which they have a high density of social interactions, common political interests different from those of other spatial entities and distinctive internal divisions and conflicts. Historically some cities were relatively autonomous centres of economic innovation and productivity (see Elliott and McCrone, 1982, chs 2 and 3; Jacobs, 1984); in the modern world all are linked to an interdependent world system of urban-centred economic activity (see Chase-Dunn, 1984). Some cities also enjoyed political autonomy, but in contemporary Western societies all are 'limited' in Peterson's sense (1981) because institutionally subordinated in various ways to national governments and influenced by the currents and divisions of national politics. European and North American cities are far from being homogenous, however. Of particular importance for our analysis, they differ widely in their degrees of economic vitality, dependence on larger economic forces and relative autonomy of political action. The central issues of the study concern the ways in which the interplay of political and economic forces are reshaping the cities of the United States and Great Britain.

The potentially autonomous state

The basis for our theory of the state is a more general conception of social organisation which is, briefly, that material production, political power and ritualised knowledge are alternative bases of social control which exist in all societies, whether simple or complex. Each makes its own distinctive kinds of claim for support and compliance, claims which are effective because each potentially satisfies a set of substantive human needs: for physical well-being (food, clothing, shelter), for protection (to secure people's lives against unpredictable coercion from within the group or outside it) and for knowledge (to interpret and manipulate the natural and social environment). Each has taken distinctive institutional forms during different historical periods. Once-common modes of material production in simple societies – hunting and gathering, herding and subsistence agriculture – have been superseded by feudal, commercial and capitalist forms of economic organisation. The institutions which have embodied ritualised knowledge are religious (in which know-ledge is based on revelation and applied ceremonially by priests) and scientific (in which knowledge is based on observation and applied by technically trained adepts). Historically-common forms of political organisation such as the chieftaincy, kingdom, empire and autonomous city-state have been almost entirely replaced by or subordinated to nation-states, just as capitalism has become the dominant mode of production in the modern world and science and technology the primary sources of knowledge.[2]

Each of these spheres of human activity potentially provides the basis on which an elite can establish its dominance over people within its scope of cultural influence and administrative control. Whether or not each sphere of activity has its own distinctive elite is historically variable. Similarly, the elite or coalition of elites which constitutes the dominant or 'ruling class' depends on the concrete historical situation. In pre-colonial African societies the authority of ruling lineages of most chieftaincies rested on their command of religious ritual and the right to adjudicate disputes, and only secondarily on military prowess. The lords and monarchs of feudal Europe ruled by virtue of their control of the means of agricultural production and of military power, but had to share political authority with the religiously-based authority exercised by the non-territorial Roman Catholic Church. In the states of medieval and early modern Europe the political and economic spheres were not necessarily distinct in an institutional sense: Lane (1966, ch. 24) has shown that during Europe's early colonial expansion into Asia and the New World the 'force-us-ing' and 'profit-seeking' enterprises were carried out by the same people and organisations, and that differentiated instruments of rule (or force) in colonial territories emerged only gradually. By the time of the Industrial Revolution there was a clear differentiation in most of Europe between the institutions of the state and of commerce and capital, but interpenetration of their respective elites persisted: many high officials continued to be recruited from the upper bourgeoisie and they sometimes used their political positions to advance private economic interests rather than those of the state (see Elliott and McCrone, 1982, ch. 3).

Our general proposition is that, once differentiated institutions of political rule are established, their elites acquire interests which are increasingly distinct from those of other groups. In the pursuit of these interests they come recurringly into conflict with other elites and in the course of such conflicts their sense of their own distinctive interests is reinforced. These political elites are by definition specialised in the use of power and the authoritative co-ordination of society. Such skills give them considerable capacity to attain dominances over other elites and spheres of social activity, using coercion, the symbols of authority and the distribution of privilege to subordinate potentially autonomous economic elites (landowners and traders), priests and scholars to the state's control (see Eckstein, 1982). The state is the institutionalised manifestation of their power; its pattern of recruitment, decision-making and participation embody the terms of the political elite's domination over other groups. In historical origins the elites controlling the state may have achieved hegemony on the basis of their control of material resources or religious ritual as well as their skills in the exercise of coercion. Once a differentiated state apparatus is established, with its own emergent class of officials, it acquires momentum and interests of its own which tend to supersede other interests which may have been instrumental in its establishment.

To summarise, the argument is that political, material and religious or scientific interests, and the elites which seek hegemony based on their command of power, wealth or knowledge are distinct and recurringly in competition with one another. There are no *a priori* answers to the question of which set of interests and elites is dominant, only historically-specific ones. There has been, however, a global tendency in the twentieth century toward the ascendency of political interests and elites, exercising power through the apparatus of the modern state. In contrast to the common Marxist view, we think that rulers and officials in all politically-organised societies have always had a degree of autonomy in the pursuit of state interests, that when in conflict with other interests they seek to act on and expand that autonomy, and that they have had recurring, though not always enduring, successes in establishing their primacy over other elites.[3]

The structure and interests of the modern state

'The state' as a concept in contemporary analysis carries a great deal of historical and ideological baggage.[4] Most conventional definitions incorporate the legal doctrine of sovereignty and the Weberian claim that the modern state is characterised by legitimacy and a monopoly of the means of coercion. Such conceptions confuse the contemporary global ideology of the state, widely used by rulers to justify their claims to authority (see Meyer, 1980) with the objective nature of the state. The observable reality of the state, past and present, is a bureaucratically-institutionalised pattern of authority whose rulers claim to exercise ultimate control over the inhabitants of a territory, and who demonstrate a capacity to secure acceptance of that claim most of the time over most of that territory.[5] In Weber's terms (1947, p. 156) it is 'a compulsory association with a territorial base'. Poggi, (1978, p. 1) offers a similar, more detailed definition:

> The modern state is … a complex set of institutional arrangements for rule operating through the continuous and regulated activities of individuals acting as occupants of offices. The state, as the sum total of such offices, reserves to itself the business of rule over a territorially bounded society; it monopolises, in law and as far as possible in fact, all faculties and facilities pertaining to that business.

States are directed by rulers and higher officials, a group or class of people who occupy hereditary, elective or appointive positions in which they are vested by law or tradition with authority to make decisions which are binding on other members of society. Whether those decisions are, in fact, accepted as legitimate by members of society is variable, therefore rulers' effective authority is limited. What is crucial, both in definition and practice, is that rulers can secure compliance (most of the time from most people) by invoking their right to be obeyed, irrespective of other considerations. In modern states the official class includes legislators, chief executives and higher-ranked administrators of national, regional and local governments; plus the commissioners and policy-making bureaucrats of the multitude of quasi-public authorities which have proliferated on the margins of the modern democratic state.[6] Collectively we refer to them as 'officials', distinguishing between those who are elected to office and administrators (bureaucrats) who hold appointive or senior civil service positions.

We do not assume that the officials of the modern state necessarily pursue a single hierarchically co-ordinated set of interests. They may appear to do so in extraordinary circumstances, for example in wartime or when caught up in the ideological fervour which animates post-revolutionary regimes. But ordinarily we would expect to find substantial differences in the interests of officials depending on their personal preferences and ambitions, ideological views and social commitments, and their positions within the state apparatus.[7] Underlying this diversity, however, we think that the vast majority of officials share some central, common interests in the perpetuation of the state's institutions and authority. That common interest can be assumed to be based simultaneously on officials' material interests in their status and position, and on their acceptance of the legitimacy of the state's authority (see Weber, 1947, pp. 324–41).

A key assumption of our view of state–society relations is that officials tend to hold and pursue interests distinct in degree from those of groups outside the state. They can be characterised as a class, with some of the self-serving interests or traits ascribed to the 'new class' of party officials, bureaucrats and intellectuals in the socialist states (see Djilas, 1957 and Konrad and Szelenyi, 1979) and to the 'new class' of officials and professional clients of American big government (see Kristol, 1979). To a variable but always significant extent the interests of state officials reflect their places in the state structure and are shaped by the institutional forms and norms of state agencies and offices. Thus one can refer, as Nordlinger does (1981, ch. 1), to state interests or 'preferences' as a shorthand term for the resource-weighted preferences of officials interested in a given policy area. At the micro-level this approach rests upon rational-choice arguments which assume that officials are rational, interest-maximising and usually egoistic actors. A principal application of public-choice theorising about the state concerns the political business cycle, according to which elected officials pursue economic policies which enhance their appeal to voters (see, for example, Tufte, 1978 and Golden and Poterba, 1980). Administrative behaviour also can be analysed from this perspective: administrators are assumed to seek to maximise their status and powers by maximising their bureaux' budgets.[8]

While rational-choice assumptions underlie our theory of the state, there are two serious shortcomings of a narrow self-interest approach to specifying state interests. First, few higher officials in Western democracies are so short-sighted and predatory that they are concerned only with maximising their own incumbency and resources.[9] Most have what we call 'programmatic commitments' to social and political objectives. That is, they seek to accomplish purposes in the larger society, or within the structure of the state, or in the relationship between state and society, which transcend their personal interests. These purposes range from the broadly ideological (redistribution of wealth, promotion of commerce, establishing political control over peripheral regions, for example) to the narrowly technical (building flood-control works, improving health-care services for the elderly, planning appropriate military assistance for client states, and so on). Re-election and maximisation of bureau budgets may be means to these ends but they are not the only or necessarily the most important means. A fundamental requisite for pursuing many new programmes is legislative authorisation. If the programmatic activity is a regulatory one, the political and legal extension of state power may be more significant than the budgetary allocation needed to implement it. Equally important is the development of technical and administrative expertise to establish and extend programmes. And since most programmes involve regular interactions between the state and groups outside it (clients, contractors, interest groups, those who are regulated, for example), officials seek to establish patterns of co-operative, sometimes co-optive interaction between public and private groups. In short, the pursuit of programmatic objectives requires officials to seek and use a variety of tangible and intangible resources, only one of which is money.

Second, even if it were possible to force officials' programmatic commitments into the Procrustean bed of rational-choice theorising (officials seek to maximise their egoistic objectives by promoting programmes which benefit or regulate other actors), this micro-approach ignores the constraining effects of institutional momentum. The offices and agencies comprising the state have their own legal and normative orders which shape officials' preferences and actions. In Krasner's (1984) phrase, 'Actors in the political system, whether individuals or groups, are bound within these structures, which limit, even determine, their conceptions of their own interest and their political resources' (p. 225). Their commitment to an organisation's programmes determines both their career prospects and the satisfaction they derive from daily work. At the institutional level, most higher officials are concerned also with the perpetuation of their own offices, departments and state institutions, not only or mainly for reasons of narrow self-interest but because they are socialised into a normative commitment to them. To adopt a Marxist phrase, officials seek to reproduce the authority relationships and institutions of their own agencies and of the state itself.

In summary, officials can be assumed to pursue both egoistic and programmatic interests, and to seek the reproduction of the state and its authority relations. It is analytically useful to relate these distinctions to another distinction, between officials' *short-run interests* and their *long-run interests*.[10] Higher officials' principal short-run interests are those identified in the rational-choice literature, namely to maximise tenure of office and the material and non-material resources of their institution or agency. In the short run the positions and resources thus gained are both consummatory (they gratify officials' egoistic desires for power, income and status) and instrumental (they make it possible to pursue programmatic objectives). The means to the attainment of short-run interests for elected officials are different from those of bureaucrats. The short-run objectives of elected officials are usually renewal in office and advancement within their party, which means that they must be concerned with satisfying the party organisations which slate them and the constituencies who elect them. Higher-level administrators are more concerned in the short run about persuading cabinets, the central state's budget office and key legislators about the justifiability of their requests for legislation and funding. Lower-level public employees have somewhat different interests: they share consummatory concerns about job security and income which may not be consonant with the objectives of higher officials. Both politically-dictated retrenchment and programmatic shifts can lead to conflict in which public employees use the tactics of organised labour to resist threatening change.

While the short-run interests of officials are a mix of consummatory and instrumental ones, it is plausible to assume that their long-run interests are mainly the pursuit of programmes and the maintenance of patterns of power and authority. Elected officials seek over the long run to improve their party's position by working for its programmes and principles. Senior administrators have comparable commitments to the perpetuation of their departments and implementation of their missions. Of course, there is some egoistic self-interest in these objectives, since officials' own status will be influenced by the outcomes. Our assumption is that most officials' egoistic gratifications are contingent, over the long run, on progress toward such programmatic and institutional objectives. We would expect this to be probabilistically true both in their own perceptions and in the ultimate satisfactions they derive from their careers.

The means to the attainment of officials' long-run, programmatic interests depend on their position. Elected officials are concerned with maintaining representative institutions' continued control of the direction of policy and its implementation: if they do not control the state apparatus, the programmes of party and Government cannot be pursued effectively. For administrative officials the central concerns are to establish

and expand the formal and effective powers of their departments
or agencies: usually this means strengthening its capacity to
regulate, direct or otherwise influence some sphere of social
activity outside the state. There are also *common* means to the
attainment of these kinds of objectives: progress toward realisa-
tion of party goals and bureaucratic missions both depend in the
long run on the existence of durable, legitimate and well-financed public institutions. Elected and administrative officials
thus share a common long-run interest in the perpetuation of
state institutions and their authority.

This argument applies even in those exceptional cases in
which new elites come to power committed to changing the
state's structure in fundamental ways. Neither revolutionaries
nor Ronald Reagan seek to eliminate the state; rather they want
to alter its commitments. The effective pursuit of any new
programmatic objective, including realignment of the state's
relations with private groups and changes in it's scope of
activity, requires the continued existence of durable, legitimate
institutions of state authority. Nordlinger, in a more recent
paper (1986), takes a different approach to this problem by
arguing that the common denominator of officials' preferences is
'maximising state autonomy and/or active societal support'.
But this is an abstract analytic interest, not readily observed,
and, in fact, seems contradicted by the efforts of reactionaries,
reformers and revolutionaries from time to time to realign state
interests more closely with one or another particular societal
interest at the expense of others. In our view the more apposite
assumption for a state-centred theory is that all officials have a
common long-term interest in the perpetuation of state authority and institutions. And the currency of long-term state interest
in most contemporary states is not just current revenues nor raw
power but legitimate, institutionalised power, that is, authority.

The foregoing arguments about the interests of state officials
are summarised in Figure 1.1. The short-term interests of
elected officials and their means to those ends are distinct from
those of administrative officials. And whereas their long-term
programmatic interests and some of the means to these ends are
also different, both categories of officials are likely to be in
agreement on the perpetuation of the institutions and authority
of the state.

	ELECTED OFFICIALS	ADMINISTRATIVE OFFICIALS
SHORT-TERM		
Interests	Retention of office	Maximising agency resources, positions, regulatory powers
Means	Satisfying party and constituencies	Negotiations with elected officials, other agencies
LONG-TERM		
Interests	Realisation of party goals	Realisation of agency mission
Common means	Maintaining the state's authority Maintaining the state's sources of revenue	

FIGURE 1.1 *General interests of state officials and their means*

It should be evident that we do not assume that the state is monolithic in its interests, any more than private capitalism is monolithic. There is much contention about the allocation of power and resources within the state and debate about alternative programmatic objectives. Some of this contention takes place between elected representatives of political parties who seek to use some of the state's power to advance particular or general interests outside the state. Contention also takes place among senior officials seeking to advance the programmes of one agency over those of others. There are also differences, sometimes sharp ones, between the interests and objectives of 'street-level' administrators, concerned with clients and implementation and resentful of retrenchment and reorganisation, and higher administrators who are responding to larger policy issues and institutional imperatives.

Particularly important for this analysis is the contention between local and national authorities which characterises both federal and centralised political systems. The distinction developed in Chapter 2 between the national and the local state only makes sense if it can be plausibly assumed that local authorities have interests significantly different from those of national authorities, and have the institutional and political resources to pursue those interests with some degree of relative autonomy. In federal systems such as the United States the problem is further complicated by the existence of three levels of government. It is evident that both the American states and city governments do have a measure of autonomy in both senses (see, for example, Gelfand, 1980), though constrained by their subordination to higher authorities. Studies of municipal government in the centralised British and French states suggest that their municipal authorities also are significantly autonomous in interest and action in some spheres (see Pahl, 1975; Cockburn, 1977; Webman, 1982; Wolman, 1982 and Boddy, 1983).

Despite the cross-cutting currents of contending interest within the state, we repeat our assumption that virtually all higher officials in societies where the state apparatus is well established, East and West, share a common commitment to the perpetuation of the institutions and authority of their national states. While self-interest provides one basis for such commitments, their ideological basis is decisive because it binds officials to the state even when acceptance of its authority is personally costly. The immediate sources of this ideological commitment include the socialisation of officials to acceptance of institutional norms (which bind them to the state apparatus) and the patterned interactions among elected officials and civil servants, higher and lower officials (which contributes to their acceptance of mutual interdependence among the elements of the state apparatus). There is also a powerful historical force to the states of most of the advanced industrial societies: they are capable of inspiring loyalty among their officials and acceptance from their citizens by virtue of their sheer size, persistence and accomplishments. This argument is speculative but subject to empirical test. It implies, for example, that commitments to the institutions and policies of the national state are likely to be weaker among new officials (freshmen legislators and newly-recruited bureaucrats for example) than among careerists; relatively weak among bureaucrats whose positions are insulated from frequent interaction with officials outside their departments (officials in military and security agencies, quasi-autonomous public bodies); and more tenuous among the officials of newly-established and personalistically-ruled states than of more durable and institutionalised states.[11]

Sources and limits of state autonomy in advanced capitalist societies

Although the idea of 'the relative autonomy of the state' has come to be associated with neo-Marxist analysis, the crucial assumption that officials in advanced industrial societies have the will and means to pursue state interests is independent of Marxist analysis and consistent with a variety of conceptions of the nature of political and social order. Those who share this state-centred perspective also recognise the potentially powerful constraints which private interests impose upon state activities, especially those of private capital, but attribute greater potential autonomy to the state in its relationship with society than does neo-Marxism. And, in sharp contrast with liberal and social-democratic theories, state-centred theories assign a secondary role to the general welfare and private sectoral interests as determinants of public policy in advanced capitalist societies.

States in capitalist societies vary in their degrees of autonomy. Some of the explanations are historically specific and have to do with the social bases and purposes of their political elites. European social democrats in power generally have sought to expand the scope and autonomy of the state, most conservatives to restrain the state's scope if not necessarily its autonomy. The powers and relative autonomy of democratic states have also tended to increase during crises such as the global depression of the 1930s and the exigencies of wartime emergency (see Skowronek, 1982, ch. 1). More abstractly, the relative autonomy of contemporary democratic states can be interpreted in terms of the constraints that limit political elites in the pursuit of their preferences.

Five general types of constraint on state autonomy can be identified. Some are essentially *technical*: for example, the limitations of available knowledge and technology, which make it very difficult to reduce 'acid rain' and its effects, or to anticipate and prevent attacks by lone terrorists, or to develop a perfect defence against nuclear missiles. A second category of constraints is *institutional*: limitations on the capacities of complex organisations to get fallible people to act in exactly the way that state managers want them to act. There are irreducible limits to how much co-operation and compliance political elites can achieve with respect to such diverse problems as rivalries among intelligence services, waste and fraud in procurement, and compliance with tax laws. Most of these constraints are of no great interest for our kind of analysis because they tend to affect all states in advanced industrial societies more or less equally: technical and organisational innovations tend to diffuse rapidly among modern societies. Of greater interest are the constraints which arise from the resistance or active intervention of interests outside the state in the public domain. Such constraints are of two types, *political* and *economic*.

Political constraints arise from two types of sources. Some are legal: restrictions on the exercise of state power *vis-à-vis* private interests, specification of powers reserved to different branches and tiers of government (see Chapter 2). The fully autonomous state could alter such restrictions at will. There are two underlying factors which restrain democratic states from doing so: their legitimacy depends in part on abiding by the restrictions, and attempts to circumvent them are likely to generate resistance both within the state and outside it. More diverse and unpredictable in their effects are organised political interests outside the state: opposition parties, interest groups, national social movements, community action groups, for example. The activities of such groups are the stuff of democratic politics in Western societies, and constitute a sticky web of restraints on the unbridled exercise of state powers.

The 'bad' constraints on the autonomy of the state for most analysts are economic ones. Revenues are often insufficient for the achievement of state purposes because of tax resistance from businesses and well-to-do individuals, and organised economic interests, especially those representing private capital, seek to turn state power and policies to their own purposes. Our intention here is to classify these sources of constraint, not to evaluate their relative importance. To state the obvious, the relations between state and private capital have attracted the greatest critical attention in discussions of state autonomy.[12] Block (1981a) offers a particularly interesting revision of the neo-Marxist view of the limits on the state's autonomy when he suggests that 'the growth of the state's role in the economy can reach a tipping point past which capitalists lose their capacity to resist further state intervention, leading ultimately to the Leviathan state' (p. 40). His point of reference is Nazi Germany. In our view such a 'Leviathan state' is unlikely in contemporary industrial democracies because of the political influence of countervailing private forces. It is our expectation, however, that in most circumstances the states of advanced industrial societies will continue to act in their own interests even when these are contrary to the interests of private capital. The state may seek to avoid overt conflict but not to the point that it consistently subordinates its preferences to those of private economic interests. Mollenkopf (1983) makes a similar point with specific reference to urban development policies in the United States: 'forces arising within the political system itself, not those imposed from outside, governed public intervention into the urban development process ... Public actors, not private actors, generally possessed the critical initiative, and the results of their actions shaped private interests just as much as private interests shaped public action' (pp. 7, 9).

The fifth kind of constraint on state autonomy in advanced industrial societies is paradoxically a consequence of the expansion of state powers and functions into what was once private domain. *Incoherence* is Sharkansky's (1979) label for the extraordinary problems of administrative complexity, lack of effective political oversight and economic inefficiencies which have afflicted the over-extended liberal democratic state (ch. 1). Another facet of the problem is the emergence of political resistance to further state expansion, for example the 'tax-welfare backlash' of the 1970s (Wilensky, 1976). In effect, continued state expansion is likely to tighten the other bonds of constraint. Publicly-owned enterprises in mixed economies illustrate the full range of potential problems. The management of such enterprises poses problems of political and administrative control for the state's top officials. They are a constraint on state spending, directly because they usually require state capital investment and operating subsidies, indirectly because if they operated more efficiently in the private sector they would be a source of tax revenues. Politically they are often a bone of contention between the state and the private sector, and their employees, who nominally are part of the state apparatus, often use political and labour organisations outside the state to improve their positions within the state. In short, the liberal democratic state which takes on direct responsibility for material production is testing the limits of effective state autonomy.

A crucial link in our argument for state autonomy in capitalist societies is the contention that the state has substantial *capacity* to act on its interests even in the face of an array of constraints (see Evans, Reuschemeyer and Skocpol, 1985, pp. 15–18). One can distinguish three dimensions of capacity, the first two of which are discussed below: the state's control of resources, the scope of its regulatory powers and its administrative capacities. Even if such capacities are high in the aggregate, they are not likely to be uniformly distributed across all policy areas (see Krasner, 1978, p. 58). A national state may be more successful at making and executing foreign policy than domestic policy, and better able to provide transportation and communication services than to control crime or regulate the private economy. Some issue areas are less tractable than others, some generate more social and political resistance to state intervention. Capacities also vary as a function of historical levels of intervention in particular policy areas: we will see in Chapter 4 that the American federal government is able to project its authority in cities in part because of the close institutional links that developed in the 1930s between the national and local states, links which bypass the regional states.

The relative size of government and the resources it commands *vis-à-vis* the private sector is one indicator of the state's capacity to pursue its own interests. The greater the state's fiscal resources the more numerous are its agencies and officials, the greater the potential scope and impact of public regulation and the greater the impact of state spending on the private economy (see von Beyme, 1985). The conventional measure of the size of the public sector versus the market sector is total government expenditure expressed as a percentage of national product. Public sector goods and services are those 'whose distribution is organised by the government and whose production is financed out of public means' (van der Wielen,

1983, p. 62). The growth of the public sector in Western democracies since the 1950s is well documented. In 1950 the average size of the public sector in six Western democracies (Ireland, New Zealand, West Germany, Sweden, the United Kingdom and the United States) was 29 per cent of GDP, in 1978 it was 45 per cent, a proportional increase of more than half (from Gould, 1983, fig. 12.1).[13] Public-sector growth continued in the early 1980s, though at a slower rate, so that by 1982 the spending of all units of government approximated 50 per cent of national product in a number of countries: in the United Kingdom 51.1 per cent, West Germany 50.6 per cent and France 48.9 per cent. The highest levels of public spending in industrial democracies were in the Scandinavian countries, with Sweden at 69.9 per cent and some of the lowest were in North America, with the United States at 36.7 per cent.[14]

In fact, the recent expansion of the public sector to these commanding levels is a continuation of a trend that is first widely detectable in the nineteenth century. Some representative historical data on central-state expenditures in Italy, Germany, Sweden and the United Kingdom are summarised in Table 1.1. In 1875 the central state's share of national product averaged about 6 per cent, increasing to 8.5 per cent in 1900, 11 per cent in 1925 and 19 per cent in 1950.[15] The upward trend is the same in all countries despite their different experiences of war and internal political upheaval. The data are evidence of the relative growth of state power *vis-à-vis* private groups in general and the capitalist class in particular: as the public economy expanded, so did restrictions on the bourgeoisie's unrestricted pursuit and use of profits and income.

The expansion of the state's regulatory powers has been as significant as the growth of its fiscal powers. Though there are no standard indicators of the scope and detail of state regulation,[16] the volume of laws and directives has grown enormously since the nineteenth century to the point that no significant sphere of private activity remains unregulated, from family life to the market economy. In Karl Polanyi's (1944) analysis state policy was necessary to the establishment of 'free markets' (pp. 140–1). Much of the state's intervention in the market economy during the last 150 years was a response to the

TABLE 1.1   *The growth of the state: central state expenditure as a percentage of national product, 1850–1982*

	1850	1875	1900	1925	1950	1982[a]
Great Britain	10.3	5.5	9.4	15.9	25.6	44.3 (51.1)
Italy	nd	10.7	11.1	12.2	20.6	51.8 (nd)
Germany[b]	nd	3.5	6.8	8.4	11.9	32.0 (50.6)
Sweden[c]	nd	5.7	6.7	8.1	17.3	48.3 (69.9)
Averages		**6.4**	**8.5**	**11.2**	**18.9**	**44.1 (57.2)**

NOTES
(a)   The figures in parentheses are general government expenditure (including local and regional government expenditures) as a percentage of national product. Comparable figures are not available for earlier years.
(b)   For 1950 and 1982, West Germany only. The national product figure used before 1950 is Net National Product, for 1950 and 1982 it is Gross National Product.
(c)   The first percentage shown is for 1881. The national product figure used before 1982 is Gross Domestic Product, for 1982 it is Gross National Product.

SOURCES   Through 1950, calculations are from data on central government budgets and estimates of national product in B. R. Mitchell, *European Historical Statistics 1750–1970* (New York: Columbia University Press, 1976), tables H4 and K1. For 1982, the calculations are from data on Gross National Product in International Monetary Fund, *International Finance Statistical Yearbook*, 1983 and government finance data from International Monetary Fund, *Government Finances Statistical Yearbook*, 1984.

disruptive conditions created by the growth of industry and cities. 'The great transformation' of the nineteenth century was a double one: the unchecked growth of the market economy, and the imposition of market controls 'on the transactions of labor, land, and money in response to elementary needs of community stability and cohesion' (Dalton, 1968, p. xxv). It was the state which imposed those controls, of course, and it was the state whose relative power with respect to the private economy grew as a consequence.

The scope of state power and its command of resources in contemporary Western societies, both material and nonmaterial, provide ample means for officials to pursue their own interests even when opposed by private groups. Of course, the state's political interests are not and can never be entirely independent of the base of production. As Block (1977) observes, 'those who manage the state apparatus – regardless of their own political ideology – are dependent on the maintenance of some reasonable level of economic activity' (p.

15). But whether the requisite economic activity is carried out by private entrepreneurs who rely on the state to regulate and co-ordinate the market economy, or by public managers of state-owned enterprises, or in partnership between public and private, is in principal and historical fact an open question. During the early stages of the Industrial Revolution the states of western Europe did resemble 'a committee for managing the common affairs of the whole bourgeoisie,' as the *Communist Manifesto* put it, because the agenda of the national state was dominated by officials elected or chosen from among landowners, merchants and capitalists. This was paralleled at the local level, where public services and works were managed by boards dominated by businessmen for the benefit of other businessmen (see Elliott and McCrone, 1982, chs 3 and 4). The expansion of the state apparatus and its professional bureaucracy altered the balance of influence within the state between elected and appointed officials; the emergence of professional politicians beholden to political parties further diluted the direct influence of businessmen on government.[17] The net long-run result was the development of a distinctive set of state interests, formulated and pursued by an official class which dealt with other elites from a position of relative independence. The growth of the state and its autonomy in the industrial democracies has been checked by the constraints discussed above, and during the last decade has been challenged in the United States, Great Britain and elsewhere by the political (re)mobilisation of corporate interests, but the most they are likely to accomplish is a modest realignment of state policy. The state apparatus itself and its primary interests will persist because of the ethos of the official class *and* the very substantial political support on the centre and left for an activist state.

Over the longer run it has often been in the interest of officials to subordinate economic activity to state authority, directly or indirectly, first to minimise constraints on the pursuit of their personal and programmatic objectives, second to ensure an ample and reliable flow of revenue, just as it is in the narrow self-interest of entrepreneurs to maximise profits and minimise state intervention in economic activity. State officials may also have ideological commitments, as in most social democratic regimes, to extend public influence over the private economy. And, as was stated above, virtually all officials have a common interest in reproducing the state and its authority relations, if necessary at the expense of the interests of private capital. Our state-centred analysis thus converges with one line of development in the neo-Marxist analysis of states, represented in Block's (1981a) work and in Miliband's (1983, p. 65) recent argument that 'the relationship between the dominant class in advanced capitalist societies and the state is one of *partnership between two different, separate forces* ....'

The national state's primary and expedient interests in cities

Contemporary urban analysis in the United States gives little weight to public officials as autonomous actors pursuing self-interested ends in the shaping of cities. In Britain there has been considerable debate over the extent to which the managers of urban services, housing in particular, act in accord with an ideology of professionalism (see Pahl, 1975), but without much reference to how this potential manifestation of state autonomy at the local level relates to other state interests or to larger structural constraints (see Kirby, 1979). This relative neglect of the role of state power and interests in shaping cities stands in marked contrast to historical and anthropological studies in which the emergence and growth of cities and national states are closely linked. The cities of older civilisations have been analysed as 'redistribution centres' in which political elites concentrated resources – obtained through trade or by exacting labour and agricultural surplus from their subjects – and used them to construct the physical and bureaucratic infrastructure of the state. Such cities were also centres of religious activity, used by the political elite to help legitimate their rule, and of cultural activity which met elite desires for comfort, entertainment and status. Cities were the stratified and specialised concentrations of people who carried out such functions for the state and its elite.[18] In Mumford's words (1961, pp. 46 and 48), the early historical city was both 'royal control centre' and 'sacred precinct ... of a powerful god'. Sjoberg (1963) offers a more specific interpretation of the purposes which cities serve for the elites of empires. The concentration of population into small spaces facilitates protection. Urban concentration also 'serves to maximise communication and to facilitate the exchange of goods and services among the various categories of specialists' (p. 109). Most important, 'the leaders of the political, education, and religious organisations have, by residing in the city, been able to maximise communication with one another and thereby sustain the system, as well as their sense of group identity ... .' (p. 109). These urban functions help sustain political elites and states, which 'helps to explain the impact of the political structure on urban growth. The political organisation, to perpetuate itself, must provide a favourable climate for the development of cities. Conversely, cities cannot survive without the support of a stable, viable political system.' (p. 111).

One can ask why such state-centred interpretations of the nature of historical cities are not applied to the cities of contemporary industrial societies. At a minimum it would have to be acknowledged that decisions by political elites about the location, structure and functions of capital cities have affected their size and vitality both historically and at present. It is also evident that official decisions (including decisions about the location of state enterprises) shape the urban systems of socialist societies. But the prevailing perception is that cities in advanced capitalist societies are shaped mainly by private economic activity. Our intention is to present an argument and evidence in support of an alternative assumption: that rulers and officials have had enduring interests in all cities, commercial and industrial as well as capital cities, and that whereas state policies were secondary determinants of patterns of urbanisation during the early and middle stages of industrialisation, they are equally or more important than private interests in shaping the future of cities in advanced industrial societies.

In our theoretical perspective, the specific urban interests of officials in modern states can be derived directly or indirectly from officials' general, long-run interest in the perpetuation of state institutions and authority. Primary and expedient kinds of urban interest can be distinguished: *primary interests* are those which are essential to the perpetuation of state institutions and authority, *expedient interests* are those pursued because they are useful to the attainment of primary objectives – for whatever historical, structural or ideological reasons. Specifically, it is in the primary interest of officials to establish public order in cities, to secure acceptance of the state's authority among urban populations and to maintain durable and adequately-financed institutions of local governance. If these conditions are not met at some minimum level, the state's claim that it governs cities is as hollow as the historical claim of the Holy Roman Empire to sovereignty over the Germanic peoples.

In pursuing the state's primary interests officials have often found it expedient to assume responsibility for providing various special and general collective goods and services for urban populations. The state's provision of essential utilities and transport, housing and social services has become primary in contemporary Western societies, in the sense that they are now necessary means to the continued maintenance of public order and state authority. Initial decisions to assume responsibility for, say, sanitation, urban transport, public housing and urban unemployment were specific to particular historical circumstances in which officials' expedient interests in establishing order and retaining office may have figured as much as long-run interests. Once the state assumed responsibility for providing limited collective goods, however, it established the conditions for their continued expansion. Outside the state apparatus, interest groups and social movements press for more and different kinds of collective goods (see Castells, 1983). Within the state, especially its administrative agencies, institutional momentum develops to expand the provision of these goods. Thus, out of specific expedient interests in meeting immediate needs and demands emerge programmatic commitments by officials, reinforced by groups outside the state, which both influence and constrain future policies toward cities.

Public authority and order

The most essential, irreducible interests of officials are the maintenance of the state's authority and the use of authority to maintain order. Authority refers to the state's capacity to secure public compliance with officials' directives by invoking legitimacy – the state's right to obedience – rather than sanctions. Authority can be maintained at gunpoint or through bribery. Voluntary compliance based on acceptance of the state's legitimate authority is far more efficient than compliance, which must be coerced or purchased.[19] Historically, the development of means for securing the recognition of rulers' authority were at the core of the process of state-building in Western societies. Rulers' power, the durability of states, and the capacity of officials to achieve other purposes have all been dependent upon the degree to which this essential objective was achieved (see, for example, Strayer, 1970 and Giddens, 1985, especially chs 4 and 7).

The nature of public order is by no means as self-evident as it might seem: in Schott's recent (1984) systematic theory of the modern state she asserts that its 'overriding and basic function' is that it 'maintains the social and economic order' (p. 136) but nowhere does she define order, although one can infer that she means by it routine, non-conflictual relations among workers and capitalists. It could be argued that early European states were much less concerned with maintaining social and economic stability than were feudal lords and the Church. Medieval monarchs *assumed* social and economic order and sought rather to establish their right to obedience and revenues. Rebellion was a greater potential threat to those objectives than were irregularities in social and economic behaviour. Thus the core historical meaning of public order can be said to be the control of organised, violent challenges to the state's authority. In early modern Europe those were mainly rebellions; since 1789 riotous urban crowds pose a comparable threat. This does not mean that early states necessarily sought to control other kinds of violence. Interpersonal violence was rampant in medieval and early modern Britain, for example, and in the thirteenth and fourteenth centuries the Crown's interests in it were limited to homicide as judged by the Eyre Courts, less from concern with 'order' than because the Treasury benefited from the confiscation of the property of those adjudged guilty (Given, 1977). Thus there is little point in proposing a universal, denotative definition of public order because the objective behaviours which the state attempts to 'order' have varied so much over time. European states' concern with controlling common crime evolved gradually from the fifteenth to the nineteenth centuries; public attempts to control social deviance began in the mid-nineteenth century, interpersonal violence within families and institutions is a twentieth-century concern (see Gurr, 1976).

The importance to the modern state of maintaining legitimate authority and civil order in cities can scarcely be overstated. Most people in advanced industrial societies live in cities, public revenues come disproportionately from urban sources, most social and political movements have urban origins, the vast majority of public officials live and work in cities. If officials cannot restrain conflict and secure acceptance of their authority in cities, they are unlikely to be able to do so anywhere. The maintenance of urban public order is also in the interest of entrepreneurs who want a reliable labour force and wish to secure private property against theft, but it is for them a secondary or expedient value; for the contemporary state and its officials, public order is a *sine qua non*. Their authority and ultimately the survival of the state require it.

The history of policing in Western societies illustrates the emergence of the state's concern with maintaining public order in cities. Before the nineteenth century 'policing' meant simply the internal governance of a community: both 'police' and 'politics' derive from the Greek *polis*. As Marenin (1985) observes, 'the quality of policing is the quality of ruling' (p. 101). In the small cities of pre-industrial Europe there was little need for specialised and centralised police in the modern sense. The riotous urban crowds of *menu peuple* who periodically challenged officials could be handled with concessions most of the time, and otherwise with a show of force by military garrisons (see Hobsbawm, 1959, ch. 7). The need for more specialised agencies to control urban disorder first became evident to political elites in national capitals. The first separate police command in France was established in 1667 in Paris and made responsible to the monarch rather than to the municipal administration. The British tolerated endemic urban rioting and common crime for another 160 years before instituting the first centralised, uniformed police in 1829. Here as in France, the force was established first in the capital – London was then the largest city in Europe – and was under the authority of central government, not the local authorities. In both countries, professional policing of the capital proved so effective in maintaining public order that the new systems were soon extended to other cities and regions (Bayley, 1975). There is substantial evidence from European societies that both the establishment of professional urban police forces and their subsequent expansion and reform tended to occur during or after periods of collective political violence (Bayley, 1975, p. 360; Gurr, 1976, ch. 4 and Silver, 1967).

In the United States, riots and common crime were a familiar feature of the urban landscape during the nineteenth century. There were no effective public means of controlling them until the establishment of a uniformed, professional police force in New York City in 1853, based on the London model. Despite its early politicisation – in June 1857 there was a riot between the police force appointed by the new mayor and his predecessor's force – it proved effective enough that during the next forty years it was emulated in virtually all of the hundred largest American cities. A number of scholars have commented on the correspondence between episodes of disorder and public concern about crime in nineteenth-century American cities and decisions of their municipal governments to establish or reform police forces (Richardson, 1970, Lane, 1980 and Monkkonen, 1981).

Public institutions, public finance

Officials of both the national and local state have a primary interest in the establishment and maintenance of centralised, effective, well-financed and durable institutions of state authority. The history of European state-making from medieval times to the twentieth century is, in effect, the history of successes and failures in creating institutions of rulership, representation and administration with these properties.[20] No such institution-building could be accomplished or sustained without a reliable financial base. Rulers repeatedly found their 'fiscal possibilities ... strictly limited by the structure and trend of the economy' (Ardant, 1975, p. 174) and often responded by active intervention in the economy aimed at enhancing trade or productivity, hence raising state revenues (see Ardant, 1975). The contemporary manifestation of these constraints is the 'fiscal crisis of the state', which is conventionally attributed to rising demands upon the state. It is equally attributable to officials' pursuit of programmatic commitments which entail expansion of the public sector, with concurrent enhancement of the state's powers and resources. The response of contemporary conservative governments in the United Kingdom and the United States to fiscal crisis is analogous to the policies of early modern rulers faced with similar constraints: they attempt to stimulate private economic activity, while their advocacy of fiscal restraint is belied by the continued growth of the public sector.[21]

Many European cities once enjoyed a degree of political autonomy which stood in opposition to the efforts of rulers to centralise national power and gain access to urban wealth. In Europe, more than in the United States and Canada, local power has been subordinated to the nation-state in a process discussed in more detail in Chapter 2. Officials of the national state are no longer concerned with cities as possible foci of rebellion but as loci of political support and opposition as well as sources of state revenue. In the short run this means that governing national parties and coalitions are concerned to maintain sufficient electoral support among city populations so that they will not provide the basis for victory for an opposition party or coalition. The longer-run interest of the national state is a more general one: to ensure that local interests remain subordinate to national authority, so that they do not interfere with the smooth operation of the national state or the pursuit of its interests (see, for example, Saunders, 1979 and Kirby, 1982).

In contemporary industrial societies, national patterns of political authority have been effectively routinised and bureaucratised. The historical tension between the demands of expanding national states and local resistance has been transformed into complex institutionalised patterns of co-oper-ation, dependency and conflict between the national state and the local state. We observed earlier that contention over relative shares of power and resources occurs within all states.

What is distinctive about cities in the modern state is that city officials are often concerned with enhancing their shares of power and resources *vis-à-vis* the claims of other localities and the national state. And they use local political and bureaucratic resources in the pursuit of those objectives: the political influence of national legislators from urban constituencies and the connections between local administrators and their opposite numbers in national agencies.

With respect to finances, the key issue for local officials is the extent to which the regional economy provides sufficient revenues, through taxation, to support the local state. The greater the local state's dependence on local revenues versus grants from the national state, the more concerned it is likely to be about local development and the more co-operative with local commercial and entrepreneurial interests (see Chapter 2). But this is not to say that the local state thus becomes the instrument of local capital and property owners, as some scholars assume (Cockburn, 1977; and Saunders, 1979, ch. 4). From the statist perspective, local officials' interests in private economic activity are functionally (not necessarily politically) limited to what is necessary to ensure a steady and sufficient flow of tax revenues.

From the national state's perspective, cities are of varying political and economic importance, an argument which will be developed more fully in Chapter 3. Capital cities and administrative centres are likely to be more important than others because national officials seek congenial urban environments in which to work and live. An equally important determinant of a city's importance to the national state, mentioned earlier, is its political orientation to the ruling party or coalition. The economic vitality of urban systems is a third determinant of national concern because national revenues derive largely from urban-based economic activities (see Jacobs, 1984). But from the national perspective it is the economic viability of the urban system as a whole that is important, not necessarily the viability of any given city. It may be more cost-effective for the purpose of raising national revenue to promote growth in economically vital cities than in cities with obsolescent and non-competitive industries. The corrective to such differential national concern is often political: the elected representatives of cities slighted in national policy will use their influence in an attempt to redress the imbalance.

Thus, while a minimum level of public order and economic vitality is in the national state's interest in all cities, national officials can be expected to be recurrently in conflict with local officials and their elected representatives over 'how much'.

The provision of collective goods

The foregoing account has emphasised the national state's fundamental interests in the maintenance of its authority and political control as determinants of patterns of urban policy. Another facet of the changing relationship between the state and cities is the expansion of the state's responsibility for providing collective goods and promoting private economic activity. In terms of the distinction made above between primary and expedient interests, our general interpretation is that officials originally undertook limited responsibility for providing collective goods for reasons of short-term expedience. As the scope of state responsibility grew, however, expectations were established within the state and among private groups that the state would continue to increase supplies of collective goods. In consequence, the continued provision of these goods has become a primary means to the maintenance of the state's legitimacy and authority.

1.   Essential urban services. Certain collective goods are necessary to the survival of cities but cannot effectively be provided by the market place. The common services without which modern cities cannot survive include public health, water supply, streets, fire protection and refuse collection. Whatever other interests or programmatic commitments may be pursued by the state in respect of cities, some minimum level of these collective goods must be provided if cities are to exist at all. The plagues, devastating fires and high mortality rates of medieval and early modern cities are reminders of what urban life and death were like when such services were rudimentary or nonexistent.[22] In 1600 only about 5 per cent of the European population lived in towns of 30 000 or more, a figure which increased to 10 per cent by 1815. Britain was then the most urban European society, about 20 per cent of its people living in cities (McEvedy, 1972, pp. 38 and 88), and the growth of its cities impelled local governments to provide the services which made it possible for urban growth to be sustained. How well such services are provided above the minimum necessary for survival, and how evenly they are distributed across cities, districts and social classes, reflects the interplay of diverse state and private interests. But it is in the primary interest of the local state to provide the minimum degree of services necessary to protect the lives, health and free movement of city dwellers, and it is in the expedient interest of the national state to ensure that local states have the means to do so.

In addition to these minimal services, local and national states also assumed responsibility gradually for the provision of other collective goods which add to the attractiveness of urban life for most or all city dwellers: public education, free or subsidised medical care and mass transit, recreational facilities, adequate housing and so forth. The question from a state-centred perspective is whether and how the provision of these amenities contributes to the interests of the state, aside from the self-interest that the officials who administer them have in their perpetuation. In our view the primary purposes served by the provision of these collective goods are to minimise violent disorder and to enhance public acceptance of the state's authority. Most such urban-centred responsibilities were assumed by European states beginning in the mid- to late nineteenth century in expedient response to a variety of specific interests and political demands: civic pride, liberal reform, programmatic demands of working- and middle-class parties, the need of entrepreneurs for healthy and literate workers and so on.[23] Justifications for such state functions were embodied in an emerging doctrine of liberal, now social democratic, ideology according to which the state *is expected* to provide such service.

Moreover, the provision of these collective goods is no longer necessarily linked to the interests which led to their inauguration. Public education, mass transit and recreational facilities have developed vested interests among their professionals and clientele who are now autonomous forces pressing for their perpetuation and expansion. Thus the local and national offices which provide these services have programmatic commitments to them, while it is in the larger interest of the democratic state in its entirety to legitimate itself by continuing to provide them. To the extent that it fails to do so it can expect to face political challenges to its right to rule.

The Marxist alternative to our interpretation is that the state assumed responsibility for the social costs of urbanisation to legitimate not the state but the capitalist system. At the abstract level of analysis the truth or falsity of the two alternative assumptions cannot be tested. Case and comparative studies of the circumstances under which particular social policies and programmes were initiated in Western societies suggest a complex interplay of political, economic and administrative interests which are inconsistent with any simple economic or political determinism (see Heclo, 1974, and the sources listed in note 21). It is also possible to demonstrate the centrality of political factors in explaining the very substantial differences among advanced capitalist societies in levels of spending for local services, as Newton and Karran (1985) do. And it would be useful to identify the ideological, administrative and functional conditions associated with innovations in the state's provision of collective goods in cities in the USSR and the socialist states of Eastern Europe – societies in which the logic of private capital accumulation is by definition irrelevant.

2. Special social services. Social services such as unemployment compensation, family allowances and welfare and medical help for the poor may be regarded as special collective goods. They have become very expensive ones in advanced industrial societies, and their beneficiaries tend to be concentrated in cities – above all in economically stagnant and declining cities. The question is what purposes their continued provision serves for the state. In historical origin most such programmes were designed to serve short-run purposes: they enhanced officials' prospects for winning and retaining office in the face of demands that something be done about the suffering and disorderly poor. After several generations during which officials gradually expanded the reach of such programmes, the provision of these services has become primary to the long-run survival of the state because politically-significant groups within the state and outside it expect them to be provided. They are now *entitlements*. The argument parallels one made above regarding the provision of such collective goods as education and recreational facilities. It is part of the evolving ideology of the social democratic state that special collective goods are supposed to be provided to large categories of people who are either disadvantaged (unemployed, handicapped or impoverished, for example) or especially deserving of public support (the elderly, parents of large families, and so on). Labour-left regimes can remain in office only if they meet most such expectations. Centre-right regimes risk intensified political activism from the poor and near-poor, and resistance from their own bureaucracies, when such services are curtailed.

Other expedient interests also are served by the provision of special social services. They can be expanded to satisfy the immediate demands of rioters and protestors, thus contributing to the maintenance of public order.[24] And social services contribute to the workings of industrial capitalism by reducing some of the demands of labour on employers for compensatory benefits for unemployed, disabled, sick and retired workers. But from the state-centred perspective this purpose is secondary to those of legitimation. This is not a cynical argument that social services are the modern equivalent of Imperial Rome's bread and circuses, although narrow self-interest on the part of political contenders may have contributed to their origins and growth. Rather, the point is that many officials and broad segments of the working, middle and professional classes believe that the modern democratic state's right to rule, hence acceptance of its authority, is justified by the provision of such services.

3. State promotion of productive activity. Urbanisation and the dynamics of economic growth have been interdependent since the preindustrial age (see Hohenberg and Lees, 1985) and to some extent continue to be so. In modern capitalist societies the urban developmental policies pursued by officials aim mainly at promoting and facilitating entrepreneural activities – the production of goods and services, provision of private housing and so forth. In general, the promotion of economic activity is of primary concern for the state because of its needs for revenue. Whether officials choose to stimulate *private* economic activity, and how, varies with the prevailing ideological commitments of the state and the social interests with which it is aligned: the continuum of possibilities ranges from state direction to almost complete reliance on private entrepreneurial initiative. From this perspective, policies of development which rely mainly on the private sector are a matter of political expediency. National urban policies in the United States from the New Deal through the 1970s were characterised by active government intervention on behalf of pro-growth coalitions (see Mollenkopf 1983). The Reagan Administration's urban policy, on the other hand, 'seeks merely to channel investment toward those areas the private sector has already determined to be the most productive and profitable' (Levine, 1983, p. 5).

For the national state it is not necessary that developmental policies be pursued in any particular city or region, only that gross economic activity is enough to provide revenues that can be reallocated across the social landscape. At the local level, however, the need to promote development may be more constraining, depending on the mix of local and national/regional revenues upon which cities depend.[25] For officials of local states which are heavily dependent on locally-derived revenues, the most important purpose of development is to maintain and strengthen the municipal economy whose resources they need to pursue public purposes and whose viability helps reinforce the legitimacy of their positions. This puts them in competition with other cities, first to attract new investment, second to increase their share of extra-local revenues. In principle and in the aggregate, local and national interests in promoting urban economic development coincide. In practice, some cities are more needful of support from the national state than others, while the national state, with other urban (and non-urban) priorities, may be much less concerned than managers of the local state with the promotion of development in any given city. In general, we expect that the greater the differentials in growth/decline rates among cities in a society, the greater the structural conflict of interests between the local and national states.

Policies for the promotion of private economic development serve a second expedient interest for the state as well. By enhancing the local economy they simultaneously tend to reduce the demand for special social services upon the state, locally and nationally. To the extent that local development falters, as it did in many older industrial cities during the 1970s, the result is fiscal stress and increased demands by the local state for extra-local revenues (see Chapter 4). More generally, fiscal stress is the product of long-term structural demographic and economic trends over which the state has imperfect control in advanced capitalist societies. For the local state it is an indicator of a painful dilemma: lowered municipal revenues, increased needs for social services, deteriorating infrastructure, a rising potential for crime and collective action, and potentially a loss of legitimacy for the local state. And national officials, in the pursuit of their primary interests in cities – the maintenance of public order and authority in the cities of greatest political salience to the national state – may choose to follow policies of benign neglect toward less-consequential cities.

	NATIONAL STATE		LOCAL STATE
Primary	_____	Maintenance of urban public order	_____
↑	Maintenance of the national state's authority in cities		Maintenance of the local state's authority in the city
			Essential urban services
	Economic prosperity in the national urban network		Metropolitan economic prosperity
	Essential urban services		
Expedient	_____	Special social services to distinctive groups	_____

FIGURE 1.2   *Interests of the national and local states in cities*

The interests we have attributed to the state and its officials are summarised in Figure 1.2, with emphasis on the points of divergence between the national and the local state. Both sets of officials have a common, primary interest in the maintenance of public order and the state's authority in cities. It follows from the spatial and political location of local officials, however, that they are more concerned with the maintenance of essential urban services and the economic wellbeing of *their* city than are national officials, who are interested more in the aggregate wellbeing of the urban system than of individual cities. The distinction between 'primary' and 'expedient' interests cannot be a sharp one, as the discussion has made clear, because responsibilities once assumed for reasons of political and economic expediency have now become essential underpinnings of the state's authority. None the less some 'essential' interests have proved more expendable than others. Nowhere has this been seen more clearly than in the responses of the national and local state to urban fiscal stress in Britain and the United States: while the core of common services is maintained, there is a general tendency to reduce public employment and services in agencies dealing with the poor and disadvantaged.

Chapter 2

The Autonomy of the Local State in a Period of Fiscal Crisis

This chapter explores the nature of local state autonomy in advanced industrial societies.[1] By 'local state' we refer principally to municipalities although most of the arguments are applicable to all local jurisdictions such as suburbs and metropolitan counties (in Great Britain) as well as to relations between regional and local states in the United States (Clark, 1984). However the propositions developed in this study about state autonomy and state–city relations are focused specifically on cities rather than on other local jurisdictions. Cities in advanced industrial societies share a sufficiently common set of features to minimise concern about generalising across them (see Kirby, 1982, on the diversity of local authorities). This is not to deny that the concept of the 'local state' is itself problematic (an issue which will be treated in detail below). From a traditional perspective it can be argued that municipalities are so sharply circumscribed by central authorities that they constitute little more than agencies of the national state. Cockburn, whose 1977 study of the Lambeth Borough council of London introduced the term 'local state' into current social science discourse, writes from an Althusserian-informed neo-Marxist perspective according to which both the national and local state act primarily to facilitate capital accumulation. In her conceptualisation the local state is made distinctive by its detailed management of families and local organisations, not its interests – which are, derivatively, those of the capitalist class. We disagree with both the traditional and neo-Marxist perspectives, arguing in this chapter that the local states of Western cities have significant, though variable, autonomy both from the central state and from private economic

43

interests. Although we differ from Cockburn's analysis of the form and policy concerns of the local state, we do consider the term 'local state' itself useful: it identifies the distinctive municipal administrative realm, which in contemporary Western societies is a part of the overall state structure but which also has a significant local impetus toward autonomy.

Our concern with the local state and municipal autonomy is twofold. First, a logical element of any theory of state–city relations is a specification of the nature and form of local autonomy: to what extent can the local state be autonomous, given our assumptions about central state interests, and how does this autonomy manifest itself? Second, it seems to us that a weakness of current writings on municipalities and their activities is the lack of a systematic theoretical analysis of their autonomy which could be the basis for understanding the impact of economic and social forces upon them (see Clark, 1984; and Clark and Dear, 1984, however). For example, in a recent paper, Wirth (1985) attempts to establish the degree to which cities have become 'dependent' on external influences and considers the effects of three such factors – external governments, concentrated economic interests and professional urban executives. While Wirth offers a judicious and interesting account of the impact of these factors, his analysis would be considerably strengthened if underpinned by some systematically stated assumptions about the nature of (and capacity for) local state autonomy. Similarly, Smith and Judd (in Smith, 1984) fail to consider local state autonomy and its limitations in their evaluation of President Carter's and President Reagan's urban policies other than to observe that 'cities are restrained by the intergovernmental system and by structural economic conditions' (p. 186).

This chapter attempts to fill this gap by analysing the constraints on the local state's autonomy in the context of our general theoretical arguments about state–city relations. We begin with a brief historical overview of state–city relations in Western societies which provides the basis for a discussion of the term 'local state' and its epistemological status. The term is then defined. This is followed by a discussion of the two fundamental dimensions of local state autonomy in advanced industrial societies: its autonomy from local social and economic forces, and from other segments of the state. The chapter concludes by examining the implications of shifting regional and global economic patterns for local autonomy, a discussion which is a prelude to a fuller treatment in Chapter 3 of the long-term consequences of urban decline and de-industrialisation for municipalities in advanced industrial societies. While our analysis parallels those of some other scholars, it is also distinct in a number of respects. In particular, our approach is differentiated from neo-Marxist arguments, exemplified by Cockburn's (1977) study, and neo-Weberian arguments such as the 'urban managerialist' thesis developed by Pahl (1975). We also distinguish our approach from Saunders' 'dual politics' thesis (1981).

The local state in advanced industrial societies

The analysis of the national state's interests in urban processes and in municipalities has been stimulated, in part, by the neglect of this central issue in the urban political economy literature of the 1970s (Zukin, 1980). Since much of this literature has utilised a neo-Marxist framework, and is particularly influenced by Castells' (1977) application of Althusserian Marxist structuralism to processes of urbanisation, its primary emphasis has been on documenting the impact of economic dynamics on those processes (see, however, Feagin, 1984; Clark and Dear, 1984, ch. 7 and Mollenkopf, 1983). Urban political economy has been criticised for neglecting the national state (see Harloe, 1981 and Elliott and McCrone, 1982) and also for emphasising economic factors to the neglect of political ones as determinants of urban forms and forces. Gottdiener (1985) argues that this is now changing and 'through the study of the urban crisis Marxian theory has itself been transformed, and the way has been cleared for the independent study of the role of the state in modern society from conventional as well as critical perspectives' (p. 423). Within the urban political economy literature some attention has been paid to the development of a theory of the local state (see, for example, Broadbent, 1977; Cockburn, 1977; Clark, 1984; Dear and Clark, 1978; Kirby, 1982 and 1985 and

Saunders, 1979). It is not entirely unfair to conclude that, aside from these works, this literature does little more than ascribe some specific functions to local state managers deriving from their linkage with the national state (Boddy, 1983).

State and economy in the growth of Western cities

Relations between state and city and the patterns of constraint within which local officials operate are not frozen in time like a fly in amber. Present patterns are the consequence of historical processes in which the significance of Western cities to rulers has undergone a succession of transformations. Whereas conventional accounts of urbanisation in Western societies emphasise the demographic and economic dimensions of change, we need an historically-grounded understanding of how the changing relations between the bases of accumulation, the demands of the national state and the impetus to municipal autonomy have contributed to the transformation of urban life. What follows is a sketch, not a complete account.

From the national state's perspective, the historical growth of European cities and their concentration of wealth, whether based on commerce, factory production or service industries, has posed a succession of challenges and opportunities. The challenges have followed from the state's primary interests in the establishment and maintenance of public order and authority (see Chapter 1). The expanding commercial cities of pre-industrial Europe were dominated by a new burgher class (see Weber, 1958; Elliott and McCrone, 1982) who sought autonomy from the authority and exactions of the feudal state. Centuries later the new bourgeoisie of the Industrial Revolution, and especially the urban petite bourgeoisie, similarly sought political privileges and local autonomy from the impositions of nineteenth-century monarchies. Each constituted a challenge by the local elites to the primacy of the national state, each poses a test of arguments about rulers' will and ability to extend state authority against the interests of powerful urban-based economic classes.

A parallel set of challenges from below arose from the concentration in cities of workers and artisans whose chronic discontents led them repeatedly to make riotous and, after

1789, revolutionary claims on local representatives of national authority. The maintenance of public order among the urban poor was a powerful stimulus to the institutionalisation of state power in growing cities. We noted in Chapter 1 that the modern police forces in Europe were first established in national capitals, and that a principal spur to their establishment was the control of collective disorder.

The opportunities for the national state were inherent in the urban concentration of new, liquid forms of wealth. The long-run interest of the state to establish centralised, well-financed institutions of authority, identified in Chapter 1, was complemented by the short-run, predatory interest of rulers in sequestering a share of private weath for personal use. To assure a reliable flow of revenues for both purposes it was vital that the centralising state subordinate cities to national authority. And as bases of accumulation changed, rulers and officials responded by developing instrumentalities of state power which could be used to expand their share of that wealth. Weber's (1958) essay on the city summarises the process of pre-industrial Europe as one in which the city was subordinated to the patrimonial state.

The capacity of national states to respond to these urban challenges and opportunities has been historically variable. In the long run and in the main, the history of European state-making has been one of consolidation and expansion of state power. But in medieval Europe national states were weak or nonexistent, and remained so in Germanic Europe and Italy until the nineteenth century, providing ample opportunities for city-states, based on mercantile capitalism and dominated by local landholders and burghers, to maintain themselves independently of the growing power of the national states.

In effect, the history of state–city relations in western Europe can be conceived as a recurring conflict between the drive of national states to enhance their control over subjects and resources (both increasingly concentrated in cities), and the quest of local elites to maintain their political and fiscal autonomy from the demands of national rulers. The patterns of these relations were cyclical, though with appreciable variations among regions. Early medieval towns were dominated by secular and ecclesiastical authority. But with the expansion of commerce from the twelfth to the fourteenth centuries towns grew, led by an emerging burgher class whose struggles against feudal rule led to the establishment of urban autonomy. By the sixteenth century, however, most independent cities had been subordinated to the growing political authority of the secular states. Economic as well as political objectives were at issue. As Norton Long (1971) notes, 'the historic function of the modern nation-state [was] to batter down the city's walls and open it to the free play of the forces of the national market' (p. 22). From the sixteenth to eighteenth centuries European cities tended to be dominated by oligarchies of merchants and aristocrats who had a symbiotic relationship with rulers who promoted and depended upon commerce as the basis of state power and revenues. With the advent of the Industrial Revolution, however, economic power shifted to the hands of the new industrial bourgeoisie and the power to shape cities, and to determine their policies, fell increasingly into their hands during the nineteenth century. Only in the national capitals like London, Paris and Berlin could one say that the national state maintained its dominance over the city.

This constitutes the historical background to analysis of the contemporary local state: a precarious tradition of autonomy, realised at certain times, but threatened by the constraints imposed by national states. This historical experience informs modern conceptions of the scope and appositeness of local autonomy: Chirot (1985) has recently argued that it was the very extent of city or town sovereignty in western Europe which prevented the formation of a united European empire and facilitated the emergence of nation-states. Particularly in northern continental Europe where 'closed' towns were common in the pre-industrial period, a tradition of municipal autonomy or independence was forged. In Italy the persistence of city-states into the 1860s obviously made the tradition of local autonomy even more pronounced. The principal west European exception to this pattern was England, where the institutions of the centralised monarchy founded by the Norman conquerers checked the impetus to autonomy among the small market towns and ports (see Strayer, 1970). In effect, the early establishment of centralised control in England preceded and forestalled the development of autonomous cities, with the partial exception of London. None the less the basis for limited autonomy was inherent in the national state's delegation of some responsibilities to cities. For example, 'the burghers in English cities were given sole rights to collect taxes, and out of this function they developed in time autonomy of fiscal administration' (Elliott and McCrone, 1981, p. 44).

In France state-formation and the growth of cities occurred more or less concomitantly but was accompanied by the persistence of strong sentiments of localism, centred on regional cities and often at odds with the nationalising political forces emanating from Paris. In the United States, the historical backdrop is different again: with some Eastern seabord exceptions, cities were founded and grew within the established authority of state governments. But in the American tradition of decentralised governments, municipal authorities also were legally accorded significant degrees of self-rule by the states. As American cities grew in relative size and economic importance, they used their political influence in state legislatures to defend and extend the scope of their legal authority. Inasmuch as the contemporary local state in the United States has some discretion over how it allocates federal and state funds, implements federal policy and chooses which services to provide and how, then it continues to exercise some autonomy. For the modern municipality generally, autonomy varies as a function of the nature of the political system (for example federal or unitary), the buoyancy of the local economy and the character of central–local institutional and fiscal relations. These factors are the focus of our conception of local autonomy.

The local state: epistemological status and definition

Several arguments underscore the significance of the local state to analyses of both urban political economy and state theory. If the state is important at all, then the local state has intrinsic importance because it is a key point of contact for most citizens with the apparatus of the national state structure, whether in federal or unitary political systems. Further, the local state is the point at which many public/private controversies and interactions become manifest to citizens and officials. The local state is typically responsible for the implementation of many centrally formulated programmes and hence frequently for arbitration between public and private interests. During the historical process of state formation, and especially since 1945, the expansion of the public sector has continuously relocated the boundaries between public and private (Lané, 1985). In many policy areas – for example, public schools in the United States and secondary education in Britain – administrative responsibility lies at the local level, which consequently becomes the focus of support and antagonism. Thus, private interests resistant or hostile to public interventions are likely to focus on the local state, which then must attempt to mediate in disagreements. That it sometimes suits the national state to delegate such interventions to the local state is an additional problem and is further evidence of the local state's importance (see Friedland *et al.*, 1977; Dear, 1981). For example, the 1985–86 teachers' strike in Britain, was centred for the most part upon local states which must operate within the central state's financial stipulations. Conflicts over collective consumption (such as housing and transport) also frequently have a distinctive urban dimension (Dunleavy, 1979 and 1980).

At a metatheoretical or epistemological level it is necessary to pose some fundamental questions about the local state: In what sense is it a state? Can it be demonstrated that local states have some autonomy? What are the nature and sources of this autonomy? Contemporary municipalities are clearly not states if these are defined by reference to the notion of sovereignty: local states have fairly precise constitutional, statutory and legal limitations on the extent of their independent activities. However, by the same token, it is equally clear that local states are *semi-autonomous concentrations of authority which can be used in the pursuit of a variety of interests.* They have (variable) powers of revenue raising; they have specific functions, whether nationally or locally formulated, whose performance affects their political environment; they have (variable) discretion on how they carry out these functions; they are headed by elected officials and are thus somewhat accountable to local electoral forces and to voters' interests. The way in which municipalities have historically evolved is especially relevant here: as described earlier, in significant parts of continental Europe, including northern Italy, the Lowlands, parts of Germany, and the Hanseatic League, cities were precursors of nation-states. Only after a period of semi-sovereignty, beginning as early as the twelfth century and lasting as late as the nineteenth century, were they effectively subordinated to the authority of the rulers of emerging national states.

Thus there are sound historical and contemporary reasons for attributing importance and analytical attention to the local state. In this we concur with the judgement of Duncan and Goodwin (1982, p. 77) that the semantic and conceptual problems associated with the term should not detract from its intrinsic importance and analytical value. Duncan and Goodwin observe that 'it does appear that social and political consciousness is focused around local issues and experiences just as much as – if not more than – national issues. Indeed, for most of the time national issues can only be directly experienced in a local context'. Katznelson's study (1981) on the patterning of class in the United States, lends support to the centrality of local politics. He argues that there is a fundamental division in American political traditions between the workplace and community which translates into the articulation of different types of issue in each arena which are not carried over from one to the other. Thus, class and economic issues generated by work experience and central to workplace politics are replaced by localised and community-based issues once citizens return home: the local state is accordingly a critical *political* arena for Americans and one to which they are accustomed to turning.

This is our definition of the local state. In contrast to existing general conceptions such as Johnston's (1982, p. 187) – 'the term local state applies to any non-sovereign body concerned with the government of a constituent area of a sovereign state' – we propose a definition specific to municipalities. There are four key elements in our conception of the local state (see also Dear, 1981). *First*, the local state has the primary, formally-constituted authority for the governance of the city population. In practice, responsibility for various public services is often divided among levels of government and among functionally-specialised authorities: the 'local state' is the *primary* governing and co-ordinating entity at the level of the city. *Second,* it exercises jurisdiction over all people and activities within a geographically-bounded space – which may include only central cities, as in the United States, or larger metropolitan regions. *Third,* the local state's structure consists of both bureaucratic (career, technocratic and appointive) and governmental (elective) offices, with the former substantially responsible to the latter. *Fourth,* the local state has the legal authority (whether conferred from within or without) to collect some revenues from citizens within its jurisdiction and to make allocative decisions about the use of these and other resources. The fact that these powers are always limited does not call into question the existence of the local state; the degree to which they *are* administratively constrained is one dimension of local state autonomy (see below). These defining features of the local state inform our discussion of local autonomy.

This conception of the local state can be juxtaposed to alternative views of the essence of the local state and urban politics. For example, Cawson (1982) concludes that a corporatist analysis constitutes the most adequate theoretical framework for understanding the local state's position within the national state structure. Scholars in general have neglected the local state's status as a semi-autonomous component of the state structure, frequently viewing it as no more than the 'local arm of the central state. But this conception implies a very simplistic notion of central–local relationships which fails to capture the evident complexity of the real world' (Cawson, 1982, p. 29). Evidence of the complexity of central–local relationships is found in studies by Dearlove (1979) and Webman (1982): the latter study documents the considerable independence enjoyed by the local state in Birmingham, England from the central government in its implementation of urban renewal policy from the 1930s to the 1970s.

Three other approaches to the local state are particularly important: Cockburn (1977), Pahl's (1975) work on urban managerialism and Saunders' (1981) 'dual politics' thesis. In general, our conception of the local state differs from these authors in the capacity for independence we attribute to it; this is qualified, of course, by national and local constraints but in a qualitatively distinct way. Thus, for Cockburn (1977), the local state can only be conceptualised as a component of the national state system: 'when I refer to Lambeth Borough Council as "local state" it is to say neither that it is something distinct from "national state", nor that it alone represents the state locally. It is to indicate that it is part of a whole' (p. 47). The policies pursued by the local state, similarly to those of the national state, are derived from its systemic context: that is, the capitalist mode of accumulation. The local state pursues policies distinct from those of the national state but in each case these derive from the needs of capital. For the local state this means specific responsibility for the management of welfare, especially servicing and institutionalising the family, and more generally the reproduction of labour and the relations of production. Cockburn's analysis of the local state does not necessarily preclude the characteristics we have ascribed to it; however, her definition remains firmly rooted in a Marxist framework whereby the content of the local state's activities is defined by capitalist dynamics. This clearly differs from our conception. For us, the term 'local state' refers to a distinct administrative apparatus with some power and authority (though constrained) within the overall state structure. Neither the form of the local state nor its policies are derivative of neo-Marxist assumptions.

The urban managerial approach developed from a major study of race and housing allocation in Birmingham during the 1960s (Rex and Moore, 1967) which concluded that access to a scarce commodity (housing) was a source of conflict, the resolution of which resulted in municipal inequalities: city-wide patterns of housing allocation, especially for coloured people, did not simply reflect occupational and class positions but were a distinctive source of inequality. This finding was more fully developed by Raymond Pahl (1970 and 1975) within a Weberian sociological framework. Pahl sought an explanation for these spatial patterns of inequality in the activities of the municipal officers, whom he termed urban managers or local gatekeepers. Pahl argued that these urban managers had sufficient autonomy in the allocation of scarce urban services to constitute an *independent* influence upon urban patterns of social and economic inequality. Professional officers or urban managers were thus deemed capable of pursuing policies relatively independent of both electoral constraints and economic interests. Initially greeted as an important theoretical advance, Pahl's work on urban managerialism rapidly became the subject of criticism, most of which Pahl himself acknowledged in a revised edition of *Whose City?* (1975; for critiques see Kirby, 1979, Dunleavy, 1980, Saunders, 1981). Two weaknesses in particular have been identified in urban managerial theory, both of which concern the limitations of managerial autonomy: critics have challenged the independence of urban managers, first from the national state as well as local elected officials, and second from the dynamics of capital. An additional problem is the exact identity of 'urban managers', not immediately apparent from Pahl's writings. It is the autonomy issue which is the more profound, however, and Pahl's (1975) revised theory accepts that the independence of urban managers from private investment and central state officials is considerably less than he first argued. Urban managers have the character of intervening rather than independent variables (Saunders, 1981, ch. 4). In our interpretation the Pahlian approach is appropriate but limited. First, urban managers may be assumed to be motivated not only by 'professionalism' – an aspect of what we have called programmatic commitments – but also by short-term interests in maximising their agencies' powers and resources, and long-term interests in maintaining the authority of the local state. And in our terms their pursuit of 'professionalism' and other objectives is constrained by the national state and its legal order, and by political and economic pressures from groups outside the state.

A 'dualistic' approach to the study of urban politics has been formulated by Saunders (1981; see also Cawson and Saunders, 1983). The basic premise is that there is a fundamental duality between national and urban politics derived from the distinctive functional activities of each level. The national and regional states are responsible for production policies and activities while the local or urban level administers consumption policies (O'Connor, 1973, Dunleavy, 1980). Each level also has distinctive politics: corporatism at the national level and competitive politics at the local level, reflecting the national/local division between production and consumption activities. This functional division between levels of the state ensures that overall state policy is responsive to the needs of capital since production policies (or, in O'Connor's terminology, 'social investment spending') are carried out at the national level; the local level formulates 'social consumption spending' policies responsive to 'localized popular pressures exerted on and through representative state agencies ... [S]ocial investment must necessarily take precedence over social consumpion (owing to the dependence of the state on private sector accumulation), and this is reflected in the subordination of local to central government' (Saunders, 1981, pp. 270–1). More recently, Saunders (1985) has emphasised the development of corporatist arrangements at the local level in response to pressures from producer interests. In contrast, our conception of the local state (and indeed of the national state) does not require distinctions between production and consumption spheres of state activity. We think that the primary interests of officials of the local state are to maintain public order and their own authority over urban populations; the provision of consumption services is secondary or expedient to these purposes (see Figure 1.2). The pressures which arise from production activities have local manifestations and local solutions as well as national ones, and in our framework are constraints on the local state, that is intervening variables rather than fundamental determinants of its activities.

The dual state thesis has not gone uncriticised: for example, Boddy (1983) observes that 'we might question ... the extent to which social consumption is primarily the concern of local government and social investment of national and regional levels. Empirical evidence suggests considerable blurring of this distinction' (p. 124). The 'dual politics' approach is important as a theoretical specification of local politics and the local state but its strength in drawing upon the production/ consumption distinction is also its limitation.

Dimensions of the local state's autonomy

The autonomy of the local state in advanced industrial societies derives from a mix of factors: its historical formation, constitutional status, revenue base, power relations between national and local political elites, incorporation of social groups, and so on. These sets of factors can be reduced to two dimensions: the autonomy of the local state in advanced capitalist societies at any given historical juncture is a function first of its relationship with local economic and social groups, and second of its relationship with the national or central state. The former have historically constituted the indispensable sources of revenue and political support upon which the (variable) autonomous power of the local state is based. The national state in all Western societies now has extensive legal powers over the local state, the cumulative result of the growth of the nation-state and the centrally-guided expansion of the public sector (see Chapter 1). These two dimensions also correspond to what we regard as the key constraints on the local state: the restrictions on its autonomy inherent in (a) limited economic resources and (b) political control by other elements of the state, whether vertically or horizontally located. The extant literature disagrees about the relative importance of each of these two sets of constraints on the local state and there is a general tendency to examine only one dimension to the neglect of the other. Wolman (1982), for example, compares local autonomy in Britain and the United States principally with respect to the local state's relationship with the national state (for other emphases see, for example, Broadbent, 1977; Cockburn, 1977 and Dear, 1981). The two sets of relationships provide us with a basis for specifying two crucial dimensions of local state autonomy, which we designate as Type I and Type II.

A somewhat similar dichotomy of local state powers has been formulated by Clark (1984). Working from the Benthamite legal distinction between the power of contrectation and the power of imperation, which applies to individuals, Clark adapts this schema to social institutions and specifically to local authorities distinguishing between the power of initiation and the power of immunity, defined thus: 'the power of initiation .. [refers] .. to the actions of local governments in carrying out their rightful duties .. [While] the power of immunity is essentially the power of localities to act without fear of the oversight authority of higher tiers of the state' (p.

198). Local state autonomy is consequently a function of these two dimensions, with four possible scenarios or ideal types, as Clark terms them. Clark concludes that in regard to the United States the reality for local government implies minimal or no autonomy: 'the American reality of local government autonomy seems much closer to absolutely no autonomy (Type 4). Essentially, local governments are the bureaucratic extensions of state governments' (p. 205). Our theoretical scheme of local autonomy and subsequent analysis of the United States (see Chapter 4) qualifies this conclusion, because it is evident that in some areas the local state does have significant potential for autonomous activity.

Local state autonomy Type I

The first dimension concerns the local state's autonomy from local economic and social forces.

I *The local state is autonomous to the extent that it can pursue its interests without being substantially constrained by local economic and social conditions.*

More concretely, the conditions most likely to constrain local state autonomy are of three kinds:

1. Limits on the revenues which can be extracted from the local economy;
2. resistance of dominant local interests to the policies of the local state; and
3. the activities of locally-based (or focused) political organisations and social movements which aim at reshaping the content of local public policy or at thwarting its implementation.

Whether the local state is part of a federal or unitary political system, it needs revenues from the local economy to ensure its perpetuation. The local state's revenue-raising capacities are a function of the carrying capacity of its local economy and of the statutory stipulations (whether national or regional) as to what within its jurisdiction is taxable and how much it can be taxed (for the United States see Bingham *et al.*, 1978; for Britain,

Newton and Karran, 1985). At a formal level the relationship between the local state and its local economy has traditionally been relatively uncomplicated: the local economy historically has been the principal revenue base for the local state, thereby providing the latter with a certain (fiscal, not necessarily political) autonomy. This formalistic relationship has been considerably restructured, however, by the increasing proportion of local state revenues supplied by the national (and regional) state. Broadbent (1977) contends that unlike the national economy:

> it is immediately clear that the local economy is a much more open system than the national economy, and by the same token ... the link between the local state and the local urban economy is much less direct than that between the national state and the national economy. (p. 128)

This sentence implies that there are sharp limitations on what the local state can do to maintain a locally healthy economy. None the less there are significant policy tools available to local states to initiate public–private partnerships, create enterprise zones, make rate or tax changes, offer tax incentives to new industry and so on.

Shortfalls in local revenues may be the result of relative expansion of the public economy, that is, a consequence of the state's past pursuit of its interests in programmatic expansion. Or shortfalls may be the result of local or regional economic decline. In either case, when insufficient funds are generated locally the local state is likely to seek additional resources from external sources, either from the national state or, in federal systems, from the regional government in which it is situated. The fiscal constraints on Type I local autonomy thus can be overcome, but at the cost of increased fiscal reliance on the national state. If increased national control of local policy follows from increased fiscal responsibility, as it usually does (but see Wirth, 1985 for a dissenting view), the effect is a decrease in Type II autonomy (see below). Thus there are important trade-offs between Type I and Type II autonomy.

Hill (1984, p. 321) presents some analogous arguments in his analysis of Detroit and the capacity of its municipal government to respond to the shifting local, national and global patterns of economic activity. To avoid becoming 'dependent', a city must formulate what Hill terms a 'development strategy' which assumes that it already has a 'genuine development capacity': this includes financial resources, organisational skills, land resources and the resources to retrain the labour force. The failure to mobilise the city's development capacity helps explain the severe economic difficulties of Detroit since the mid-1970s, or rather, its inability to respond to changing economic patterns as effectively as it would wish.

The other two local processes relevant to Type I local state autonomy are powerful economic interests outside the state, and social movements or political organisations concerned with influencing the content and execution of the local state's policies. The former include corporations, banks, developers and labour unions, either locally based or agents of national or – in the case of corporations – transnational organisations. Friedland (1976, 1980 and 1983) has argued from empirical analysis that War on Poverty and urban renewal funds in the United States were distributed in disproportionate ratio to the presence of corporate and union headquarters in cities. In the case of Great Britain, Kirk (1980) contends that the local state's autonomy with respect to decisions to grant or deny planning permission is considerably diminished by powerful economic interests, whether locally based or organised through the national state:

> compared with capital or national government, a local authority has only limited powers. In land-use planning matters this is exemplified by the limited control local councils have over the commercial development process and the location of firms. (p. 182)

Molotch's (1976) conception of the city as a 'growth machine' is somewhat analogous to this: the objective of growth acts as a unifying force for the local political elite and investors. Since the key growth-and-wealth generating commodity at the local level is land, over whose use the local state has some control, it becomes the focus of growth-related political activity.

The nature of urban social movements and their origins in urban social change have been the subject of considerable research during the last decade (see Fainstein and Fainstein, 1974; Katznelson, 1981; Katznelson, Gillie and Weir, 1982; Castells, 1977 and 1983). This reflects the re-emergence of urban-based conflict and political organisation during the 1960s and early 1970s. In the United States, the former decade was characterised by extensive and violent urban protest (see Chapter 4) while the spring of 1968 was a period of widespread urban protest in Paris and West German cities. There were also numerous incidents in Mediterranean Europe. In the 1980s urban disorder has become episodic in British cities with climacterics in 1981 and 1985. However, the extent to which any of these disorders were either underpinned by a social movement or gave birth to one is extremely limited. As Ceccarelli (1982) observes, 'large-scale urban social movements have faded out as rapidly as they originated ... This is so in spite of the fact that most of the problems which at the end of the 1960s had supposedly ignited urban movements are still unresolved or even aggravated' (p. 261).

The dominant intellectual force in this literature on urban social movements is Castells. In his early work (1977) Castells posited that urban social movements arise from contradictions centred around consumption processes. Consumption crises result, according to Castells, in the formation of urban movements; such crises are the outcome of the state's contradictory role of meeting both the production and consumption needs of capitalism. Where state policies shift away from collective consumption the resulting crisis contributes to the emergence of urban social movements. For Castells, urban social movements are defined in terms of their effects: if they engender structural transformation, and not simply reform, then they qualify as urban social movements (see Pickvance, 1976). The key weakness of this analysis, as Katznelson (1981) and others have noted, is its reliance upon a structural and somewhat automatic relationship between consumption crisis and the birth of urban social movements. It also imputes an objective to urban based movements which in its scope is likely to exclude many other groups which may be of intrinsic importance:

Castells's formulation makes the fashioning of urban movements too automatic, when in fact it is rather a contingent outcome. Not all structural possibilities find historical expression. There are ample reasons why individuals with grievances do not join organisations or act collectively. Furthermore, Castells's search for regularity misses important differences (which themselves must be explained) in both the frequency and the character of the development of urban movements in different national settings, even where the same structural causes exist. (Katznelson, 1981, p. 211)

It is clear that urban movements do have some common features regardless of national context (but see Ceccarelli, 1982): they are mobilised on a community basis rather than work organisation (Katznelson, 1981) and focus upon local issues such as housing, education and transport.

Castells (1983) presents a more complete theory of urban social movements. Their defining objective continues to be a radical redefinition of urban meaning but Castells differentiates among three types of social movements according to their specific goals: collective-consumption trade unionism, community movements and citizens' movements. Only movements which combine the objectives of all three have the potential to generate significant social change. These goals are: organisation of the city around use-value; asserting a clear cultural identity; and the establishment of some form of local power or decentralised control (Castells, 1983, p. 319). From his case studies Castells concludes that

the observed experience of urban movements points towards an alternative urban meaning, posting the alternative to the city emerging from the interests and values of the dominant class. The alternative city is therefore a network of cultural communities defined by time and space, and politically self-managed toward the maximization of use values for their residents; this use value is always decided and re-examined by the residents themselves. (pp. 320–2)

This reformulation of the theory of urban social movements is more satisfactory than Castells' earlier work in that it allows the existence of different types of movements with different objectives. For Castells the important issue is to identify those movements which combine all three objectives and thus have the potential for radical urban social change; in this regard he cites the Madrid Citizens Movement of the 1970s and 1980s. For analytical purposes, however, his threefold categorisation is potentially useful because the impact of the three types upon local state autonomy, Type I, is likely to vary. Trade unionists concerned with collective consumption seek to alter forces outside the direct control of the local state: the capitalist mode of production. This kind of conflict is deflected from the local state and while its local manifestations may threaten public order, they are unlikely to increase constraints on the local state. Community movements' demands for greater cultural autonomy are more likely to be within the scope of the local state but also may be amenable to symbolic resolution: the diversity of the urban environment is thereby increased, but not at great cost to the local state. Movements seeking more decentralised control, however, are the source of very substantial pressure on the local state: to accede to such demands is to divest the state of direct control of some of its functions and resources, in other words to restrict its autonomy.

Local state autonomy Type II

This dimension concerns the local state's autonomy from the national state.

II *The local state is autonomous to the extent that it can pursue its interests without substantial interference by the national state.*

Clearly there are always some national constraints on local policy, encroaching even on functional areas in which the local state has exclusive responsibility. These range from constitutionally-specified limitations to more recondite guidelines accompanying grants, to national political pressures and judicial decisions aimed at altering specific policies of particular municipal administrations. At issue generally is how much decisional latitude the local state has, legally and in practice, within each functional area of activity. Like Type I autonomy,

Type II autonomy is a composite of opportunities for and constraints on local policy options across the entire range of governmental activity.

Just as officials of the local state have recurrently sought to enhance their relative economic autonomy, they have sought autonomy in their relations with the national state. Thus Elliott and McCrone (1982, pp. 46–8) contend that despite nation-specific differences, one common characteristic of the development of nation–municipal relations in Europe was the quest for political autonomy by the local state. However, municipalities were forced by the dynamics of state centralisation and industrialisation to become jurisdictional subunits of the national state:

> by the sixteenth century, the independent city had everywhere lost ground to more powerful monarchs and princelings and the new authority of the state. Thus, Weber describes a cyclical process for the city: from subordination to feudal or territorial lords, a brief though important autonomy, the decay of that freedom and then the subordination of the city to the patrimonial state. Cities became rich sources of tax revenue for the ambitious monarchs and their courtiers and the control and manipulations of the cities and their corporations was a matter of statecraft. (Elliott and McCrone, 1982, p. 48)

With some national variations, the growth of the nation-state and the diffusion of capitalism combined with a new bourgeoisie to subordinate the city to the jurisdiction of expanding national authority.

National state constraints have traditionally taken two main forms. First are constitutional and legal constraints which are formally stated and embodied in explicit institutional arrangements (for example, in Britain the stipulation that local governments must maintain a balanced budget). Such formal constraints vary across federal and unitary systems, reflecting country-specific factors. Wolman (1982) provides the following contrast:

> the primary formal difference with respect to government's

effect on local autonomy is that in the United Kingdom local government may undertake no activity not explicitly authorised by the central government (the doctrine of *ultra vires*), whereas in the United States local government is not prevented by the federal government from undertaking any activity not contrary to the United States constitutional or federal legislation. (p. 172)

This formal constitutional difference is, of course, much modified by administrative and political practice. The range of activities which the local state can assume in the United States is not quite as wide as this formal distinction would imply, nor as narrow in the United Kingdom. Hill (1984) for example, notes that in relation to the United States the local state operates under serious constitutional constraints affecting its capacity to respond to economic activity: 'the accumulation of capital takes place in private enterprises. Governments are barred from producing and appropriating surpluses to reinvest in their own expanding enterprises ... In the absence of private accumulation and reinvestments, the city's own power to govern wanes' (p. 322). This is not the case in most of Europe, where local states have the authority to appropriate a share of profits from state-initiated enterprises.

In the United States, autonomy for municipalities is critically dependent upon the powers granted by the state to which it belongs. According to Dillon's Rule (articulated by Judge John F. Dillon in *Atkins* v. *Kansas* [1903] 191 US 182), cities 'are the creatures, mere political subdivisions, of the state for the purpose of exercising a part of its powers. They may exert only such powers as are expressly granted to them or such as may be necessarily implied from those granted' (cited in Wolman, 1982, p. 172; Dillon's Rule was upheld in *City of Trenton* v. *New Jersey* [1923] 262 US 182). This municipal status as 'creatures' of their states is modified in practice, however: many states have passed legislation which gives local governments, including municipalities, discretionary authority to initiate a diverse range of activities. As general-purpose governments, municipalities have responsibility for providing a range of services and policies as well as having some autonomy to act as initiators of policy.

The second type of national constraints upon local autonomy are those administrative constraints which emerge from the intrinsically political nature of the national–local state relationship, as Webman's (1982) comparative study of urban renewal programmes in Lyon, France and Birmingham, England demonstrates. He concludes that the extent of central intervention or control is markedly greater in Great Britain than in France: 'the British pattern of local–national relations consistently stressed rule-making in London and rule-application by local authorities ... In contrast, the French pattern stressed overlapping, shared or contested control over individual projects among a mix of central and local agencies all enjoying legal, financial and technical grounds for insisting upon details of design and implementation' (1981, p. 144). Thus municipal autonomy in Britain may be notably less than suggested by formal administrative arrangements.

Economic transformation and the local state in advanced industrial societies

The two dimensions of local state autonomy specified in this chapter are, to a certain extent, ideal types: that is, empirical analysis of municipal autonomy is likely to find that institutional and political practice is constrained in varying ways on each dimension in different historical periods. Our aim in specifying the nature and limitations of the local state's autonomy is to provide a guide to empirical analysis and to facilitate a more structured interpretation of research findings. In the remainder of this chapter the schema is considered in relation to the impact of shifting national and international economic trends. In Chapter 3 the dimensions of local state autonomy are drawn upon in an analysis of the increasing political salience of declining cities and of the implications of national fiscal crisis for the local state.

During the late 1960s and throughout the 1970s it became commonplace to refer to the 'crisis' of cities in the industrialised liberal democracies, particularly, though not only, the United States and Britain. This 'crisis' was a multifaceted phenomenon and we treat its broader contours in the next chapter:

urban decline, social malaise, fiscal crisis and economic restructuring. Here the focus is on the last of these phenomena: the shifting patterns of economic activity which have devastated some urban economies and forced others to diversify into new sectors; and the implications of these trends for the local state.

The origins of the economic difficulties prevalent amongst municipalities in the 1970s lies most fundamentally in the economic transition which has arisen from the internationalisation of industrial economies in the post-war period. This is reflected in the shift in manufacturing production away from developed countries and within the United States away from the industrial Northeast and Midwest. This has resulted in an interregional shift in manufacturing employment opportunities. The composition of international trade has changed too, with a smaller proportion of industrial goods and an increase in agricultural commodities. Translated into American urban and regional terms, Glickman (1980) records:

> the decline of sales of heavy manufacturing (in particular, transportation equipments, nonelectrical and electrical machinery and chemicals) abroad has had deleterious effects on the old Industrial Heartland of the Northeast and Midwest. A production hierarchy has evolved worldwide and within the United States in which high-technology industry and services are concentrated in the larger cities of the United States and other industrialised nations, while production processes have dispersed throughout the rest of the country and to the Third World. (p. 8)

The trend in capital mobility parallels this process: there are large outflows of capital from the United States and increasing investment by multinational corporations in the United States. These latter have played a significant role, Glickman contends, in the development of the Sunbelt region. At national, regional and urban levels the increasing mobility of capital and investment makes the formulation of effective public policy more complex and difficult. Investment tends to be uneven in spatial distribution and devastating in impact when disinvested: 'the problem relates to the relative speed of movements of capital relative to labour – workers cannot move as fast as capital and often are reluctant to relocate from areas where they have deep family and other ties. The affected communities cannot often find replacement industries' (Glickman, 1980, p. 12). Also working economic changes on urban areas are the effects of business cycles, long-term economic growth, capital concentration and the rationalisation of production.

The principal urban consequence of these trends has been a general decline in many once-prosperous cities, indexed by population loss, declining productivity and increased incidence of hardship and social stress (see Chapter 3). In terms of our analysis these economic changes constitute a decline in Type I autonomy for the local state, in two respects. Most obviously, the more seriously affected municipalities are no longer able to generate sufficient revenues from declining local economies to meet rising social costs. More fundamentally, the internationalisation of production means that the controlling nodes of urban economic change are increasingly distant from the local economy and thus are less subject to manipulation by the local state. This is one of the central points made by Hill (1984) in his study of Detroit:

> Detroit's fate has been wed to an economic base controlled by a small number of multinational corporations. Corporate stability and growth are premised upon the capacity to respond to changing national and international costs and conditions. The profit logic that once brought investment and growth to Detroit now brings disinvestment, decline, and decay ... Private corporations accumulate and reinvest capital. Detroit does not. Capital is mobile; Detroit is not. (pp. 321 and 333)

One major implication for the local state which follows from these economic shifts is that it is likely to be pushed into greater reliance on the national state. We are particularly interested in this issue since it has consequences for the autonomous status of the local state, and for the distribution of scarce national resources. With regard to the local state, there is detailed documentation of growing fiscal reliance on the national state. In most of the six countries which we examined across the

TABLE 2.1   *Local government expenditures, grants, and deficits, 1972–82*

	Total local expenditures in national currencies	Grants as percentage of total expenditures	Deficits as percentage of total expenditures
France (regions, departments, communes)			
1972	63 910	42.9	10.5
1982	284 800	40.7	12.1
Netherlands (provinces, municipalities, other local agencies)			
1974	32 390	76.4	12.4
1979	55 430	83.8	4.4
Sweden (county councils, municipalities, parishes)			
1972	46 840	27.7	2.9
1982	177 600	23.6	1.2
United Kingdom (counties, local government units)			
1972	9681	35.6	16.5
1982	37 074	44.4	3.3
United States (counties, municipalities, school districts)			
1972	100 990	38.0	[a]
1982	256 390	43.8	[a]
West Germany (municipalities, local authorities)			
1972	72 820	27.4	0
1982	151 020	28.0	1.9

(a)   US local governments show an aggregate surplus throughout this period, despite the fact that many larger municipalities resorted to deficit spending.

SOURCE   Our calculations from data in local currencies (usually in millions of units) in International Monetary Fund, *Government Finances Statistical Yearbook*, various editions.

decade 1972–82, national and regional contributions to local government expenditure increased in both absolute and relative terms, as shown in Table 2.1. In the United Kingdom, for example, grants increased from 5.37 per cent of GNP in 1972 when they made up 35.6 per cent of local expenditures, to 6.09 per cent in 1982 when they provided 44.4 per cent of local expenditures. In the United States, the Netherlands and West Germany increases followed a similar pattern. The increased flow of national funds to the local state has been interpreted as leading to a diminution of the latter's autonomy. Newton (1980), for example, concludes from his six-country study of local finance in Europe that 'since local authorities are less and less able to rely upon their own resources, they are also less and less able to determine how much money they will raise and how it will be raised' (p. 11).

We contend that two different questions need to be asked about the connection between increased national contributions to municipal budgets and the autonomy of the local state. One is the extent to which the uses of those funds are mandated by central authorities or are the subject of local discretion: unrestricted revenue-raising and block-grants imply greater Type II autonomy. The second question concerns the economic dynamics of growing national-to-local transfers of funds. If the result of shrinking local revenues, then a real decrease in Type I autonomy has occurred. If growing transfers are the result of the general expansion of local state services and activities, however, the net result may well be an *increase* in Type I autonomy; Fossett's (1983) study of federal aid to a sample of US cities provides evidence of such patterns. The expanding local state, financing its expansion by drawing upon extra-local sources of revenue, may be able to increase substantially its relative autonomy over local economic and social interests. The hypothetical relations among fiscal dependence, national restrictions on local use of funds and our two types of autonomy are shown in Figure 2.1.

Our data on local state finance in Sweden (see Table 2.1) illustrate another possible outcome, one in which the local state has the capacity (or is given authority by the national state) to finance its expansion from local sources. Local governments in

Cause of increased fiscal dependence	Restrictions imposed by the national/regional state on increased grants to localities	
	Low	High
Expanding scope of local state activities	Type I autonomy + Type II autonomy 0	Type I autonomy + Type II autonomy −
Contraction of local economy	Type I autonomy − Type II autonomy 0	Type I autonomy − Type II autonomy −

FIGURE 2.1 *Implications of growing fiscal dependence on the autonomy of the local state*

Sweden financed a substantial growth in programmes during the 1972–82 decade by increasing locally-derived revenues; both national grants and deficit spending decreased in proportional terms. This implies an increase in both Type I and Type II autonomy, with the qualification that changes in Type II autonomy should be assessed directly by examining the extent to which national directives delimit the local state's uses of new resources.

This line of analysis has implications for the local state's capacity for formulating public policies capable of controlling and ameliorating economic decline and its social stresses. The local state may be trapped between the extra-local source of many of its economic difficulties and the differential, potentially conflicting interests of the national state upon which it is fiscally dependent. Thus local attempts to control and respond to changing conditions often bring the local state into conflict with central state objectives. This point is well made by Young and Mills (1982) in their study of the conditions of declining municipal economies in Britain. They contend that there are fundamental conflicts and contradictions between the central and local states as a consequence of their different objectives: 'City governments must deploy policies against the tide, if only in the hope of reducing its rate of flow, so buying further time for adaptation. National governments, for their part, follow the tide because ultimately they will go where the market advantage leads'. This conflict may remain latent but is no less harmful for that: 'national and local responses to fiscal stress in cities are likely to remain contradictory and confusing' (p. 99).

Referring to Figure 2.1, the most benign situation, from the point of view of local officials concerned to maintain local autonomy, is that in which the expanding scope of local state activity leads (say, by statutory requirements) to an increased flow of funds from higher levels of government which carry a minimum of new restrictions. The Houstons and San Joses of the American Sunbelt may be in this enviable position. The worst situation is faced by officials attempting to maintain existing activities in declining cities who find that the price of increased aid is increased dictation of policy. This was the price paid by New York City officials for a federal and state bailout in 1975: they were forced to retrench municipal services and employment across the board (Tabb, 1982; Shefter, 1977). Under fiscally-conservative governments in both the United States and Britain retrenchment is the price exacted by the national and regional states for continued aid to local state in fiscal crises. It has recently been the source of sharp confrontations between the Labour-controlled municipal governments of Liverpool and Sheffield (and others, see Chapter 5 on Great Britain), which seek to maintain social services even if this means an unbalanced budget, and the Conservative government's determination to force a reduction in local public expenditure. In our framework, the local states in Liverpool and Sheffield have too little autonomy to deal effectively with crises: Type I autonomy is restricted by both the shrinking revenue-generating capacity of the local economy and by Labour's political commitment to constituencies which resist cuts; Type II autonomy is restricted by the national government's fiscal policies. The local state operates with both a reduced urban economic base and tighter central control. At one and the same time, the local state is increasingly dependent fiscally on the central state (see Katznelson, 1976, and Hill, 1984) because its municipal economy is declining and key economic decisions are taken outside its jurisdiction, while the formal restrictions inherent in the local state's position within the national structure limit its capacity to respond effectively to its shrinking economic base. The two dimensions of local state autonomy are thus closely related and it falls to the local state to formulate an effective set of public policies within the constraints each imposes.

Conflict between the central and local state is unlikely to diminish in the shortrun in the United States or Britain, given the ideological preferences of neo-conservative national governments in each country. Although the trend toward reduced central funding to cities in the United States and Britain began before these two governments took office, both have given increased momentum to the trend. The fall-off in federal aid to cities in the United States began in 1978 and reflects both national decisions about policy priorities and a desire to reduce the federal government's responsibilities for cities. With regard to changing policy priorities, recession of the later 1970s and growing deficits justified a slowdown in federal spending by the

Carter Administration. With regard to the latter, Hill (1983) notes that a key part of Reagan's New Federalism was the 'decentralization of federal authority and fiscal responsibility for a range of programs shifting to state and local levels of government' (p. 6). Despite the resumption of economic growth in the early 1980s the Reagan Administration was committed to the reduction of taxes *and* the expansion of defence spending, objectives that were potentially achievable only by substantial cuts in all non-defence sectors of the public economy. In the present political climate in the United States it is unlikely that taxes can be increased enough either to permit resumed growth of the non-defence public sector or to reduce the structural deficit. Thus the conditions exist for continued restraints and further retrenchment in public spending at all state levels. Similar trends can be observed in other advanced industrial countries, particularly Britain: 'if one single theme permeates recent developments, it is the search by central government for more effective instruments of control (not influence) over the expenditure of local government... The government has also sought to restrict the size of the public sector by divesting local government of some of its functions: privatisation' (Rhodes, 1984, p. 11).

These developments imply that the thirty-year trend of growth in social spending in these advanced industrial societies will be stabilised and may, as is occurring in the United States and Britain, actually be retrenched. As a corollary, the national state's grants to localities can be expected to contract. Michael Smith (1984, p. 10) interprets these developments in terms of James O'Connor's analysis (1973) of state fiscal crisis: 'in the current period of fiscal retrenchment and privatisation of previously public functions, it no longer appears inevitable that the systemic logic of the mode of production requires the direct expansion of the state in the reproduction of economy and society by rationalising accumulation, providing collective services and insuring legitimation'. A substantial restructuring of state–city relations is likely to follow as the local state is pushed into assuming greater responsibility for financing local services. The issue is analysed also in conventional scholarship on intergovernmental relations: 'the intergovernmental deci-sion-making network has become more complex in all the modern democracies because national government needs local-level decision-making more than ever before in our histories in seeking to fulfil the priorities of the welfare state' (Ashford 1980, p. 204). Of course, intrinsic to neo-conservative national governments is the intended objective of redefining welfare priorities. The extent to which they appear to be succeeding in this objective is an issue taken up in the concluding chapter.

Chapter 3

The Political Salience of Urban Decline: Why and how the State Responds to Urban Change[1]

In Chapter 2 we pointed out some implications of urban decline, fiscal stress and increased local reliance on national grants for the autonomy of the local state. This chapter is concerned with the entire range of responses to urban decline by all levels of government and what they imply about the net effects of the national, regional and local state on urban life. As we argued in Chapter 1, the vitality of cities in advanced industrial democracies is increasingly determined by the allocative decisions of national, regional and local governments. The evidence developed in this chapter shows that dependence on the public sector is particularly great in post-industrial cities, those which lost private-sector jobs, population and tax revenues because of the process of industrial relocation and disinvestment which began in parts of north-western Europe and the north-eastern United States during the 1960s. In some of these cities economic decline has been stabilised and reversed through the development of new administrative and service activities, many of them in the public sector; in other cities decline continues.

The economic dynamics underlying the process of urban decline and regeneration are well understood: because of changes in technology and in the structure of national and international capitalism, most old industrial cities in North America and northern Europe have lost their locational advantages to other regions and to Third World countries. Less closely scrutinised is the compensating role of the state and its policies in revitalising the private and public economies of these and other cities. The general tendency in Western

74

industrial societies throughout the post-war period has been a growth in the size of the public sector and the state's regulatory powers, growth which is documented in Chapter 1. The activities of the state, including its spending and the beneficiaries of its social programmes, are disproportionately concentrated in cities, and especially in post-industrial cities. The growth of cities' financial, administrative and service activities, which are increasingly important to their survival in an era of de-industrialisation, this is the aggregate result of private *and* public decisions about the location of investments and contracts, jobs and services. The scope of public-sector activities in cities is an empirical question for which there is not yet definitive evidence. Our speculation is that in some post-industrial cities the threshold has probably already been passed from primary reliance on the private economy to primary dependence on the public economy. Almost 50 per cent of the total income of the city of West Berlin is provided by the West German government (Katz and Mayer, 1985, p. 36), a reflection of the national state's political commitment to maintaining a glittering symbol of Western society in the midst of East Germany's drab uniformity. Among American cities, Boston has reached the same threshold, as we demonstrate later in this chapter, though due more to the enterprise of its public officials and congressional respresentatives than to concerted efforts of the national state.

The chapter begins with a brief overview of patterns of urban growth and decline in Western societies, then outlines an argument about the increased political salience of declining cities which follows from Chapter 1's general theory of the state's interests in cities. Increased salience is likely to lead to increased state presence in declining cities on a number of specific dimensions which are specified in the third section. Evidence on the growth of the state's material presence in thirteen American cities, assessed in the final section, demonstrates a close connection between urban decline and the size and growth of the public sector.

The extent and nature of urban decline

'Urban decline' in contemporary Western societies refers to a complex syndrome of conditions among which are a declining industrial sector, falling total productivity, decaying housing and infrastructure, growing concentrations of poverty and social stress, and shrinking population. These urban changes are usually attributed to larger processes of technological change, de-industrialisation and changing social preferences about where and how to live. Such changes are not autonomous, however, but are themselves shaped by patterns of state policy. For example, the structure of local government and national housing policy have channelled the private housing investment decisions which contributed to the decline of core-city neighbourhoods and the explosive growth of American suburbia (Downs, 1973; and Jackson, 1985). The private economic activity responsible for the sustained growth of Houston, Texas throughout the twentieth century has been nurtured by a series of interventions by the regional and national states (Feagin, 1985). And the depopulation of Britain's large conurbations was spurred in the 1950s and 1960s by deliberate policies of urban and industrial devolution (Hall, 1975; and OECD, 1983). Thus in the short run and in some cities one can regard economic and social changes as the primary causes of decline. But in the longer run and for the larger urban system the outcomes of publicly-guided urban change are more open. Some cities, new and old, prosper because of the growth of new economic activities, the planning and initiative for which can come from entrepreneurs or the state, or, most likely, both acting in concert.

For contemporary analysts, declining per capita productivity and shrinking population are the key indicators of urban decline. Approximately half the larger cities of Europe and the United States lost population during the 1970s. Urban development trends in fourteen eastern and western European countries have been examined in the Urban Europe project. The study includes 150 functional urban regions (cities and their peripheries) of which 19 per cent experienced absolute population loss in 1970–75, while these plus another 29 per cent lost population in their core cities. Three-quarters or more of the urban regions in Britain, the Netherlands, Belgium and Switzerland were in these two groupings (van den Berg *et al.*, 1982, ch. 7; see also OECD, 1983, vol. 1). In the United States the incidence of urban decline in 1970–75 was very similar: of

121 Standard Metropolitan Statistical Areas (SMSAs) 26 (21 per cent) lost population during these five years and 51 (42 per cent) of SMSAs had core cities with shrinking populations. As in Europe, declining American urban regions are concentrated in old industrial areas. In the north-eastern United States 23 out of 24 metropolitan areas had absolute or core-city decline and in the north central region 29 out of 33 (Bradbury, Downs, and Small, 1982, ch. 3). Neither study includes complete data for 1980 but there is ample evidence that the economic and demographic trends of the 1970s continued into the 1980s in both Britain and the United States, though the rate of decline may have slowed. De-industrialisation was not the only economic factor contributing to population decline in these regions and cities, but clearly it was the most important one.

Studies of the trends and correlates of urban population decline in the United States show that the reversal of a century of urban growth began in the late 1950s and gathered momentum in the 1960s and 1970s (Berry, 1973). Relocation from central cities to politically autonomous suburbs has had the most profound effects on older cities (Downs, 1973; Kasarda, 1976; Schwartz 1976 and Berry, 1977). Until late in the nineteenth century the boundaries of the political city expanded to keep pace with development on the urban periphery. In the 1860s Brookline, Massachusetts resisted incorporation with Boston and set the precedent for a trend which gathered momentum in the twentieth century. The pressures toward suburbanisation were in part social (the desire for individual housing and open space) and technological (the automobile) but also were encouraged by state policy. The standards for new housing and the neighbourhood grading system established by the Federal Housing Administration beginning in the mid-1930s encouraged private investment in homogeneous surburban housing developments and discouraged it in core cities (Jackson, 1985).

The urban landscape is also being transformed by significant movements from urban to rural, from larger to smaller cities, and regionally from the industrial north-eastern and mid-western cities to the south and west (Harvey, 1975; Gordon, 1976; Perry and Watkins, 1977; Gluck and Meister, 1979; Bluestone and Harrison, 1982). The latter two regions have enjoyed dramatic population growth since 1960, principally due to net migration from the north-east and north central regions. Per capita personal income and employment levels have tended to rise significantly faster in the south and west during the same period, the result of migration trends and decisions about capital investment that favour these areas. The economic development of the Sunbelt region has now become largely self-sustaining. Here again, state policies have shaped the process: municipal and regional governments in the south and west have kept tax rates low and minimised regulatory constraints on the private sector to attract business and capital away from other regions.

Thus the dynamics of core-city decline in the United States follow from social and structural economic changes, some of which have themselves been given shape by state policies. The conventional economic interpretation is that the natural resources and locational advantages of the north-east have declined in economic significance. The region's highly developed transportation network and financial institutions proved sufficiently flexible and responsive to short- and long-term economic changes until the 1960s (Greenberg and Valente, 1975), but with few exceptions underwent wrenching changes in the 1970s. The contraction of primary and secondary industries in major north-eastern and mid-western cities has been partly replaced by the rise of tertiary ones. As we show later in this chapter, many of these tertiary activities are in the public sector. Some of these cities are being functionally transformed from centres of industrial production and distribution to administrative, information-exchange and higher-order service centres. Boston and New York are among the cities which have thrived since the late 1970s on the expansion of the service sector (Ganz, 1985; Noyelle and Stanback, 1984). Jane Jacobs' (1984) alternative interpretation emphasises the role of cities as creators and exporters of goods and capital: declining cities are those which 'took to exporting capital out of proportion to their own continued abilities to generate jobs, industries and markets' (p. 108). Of course 'cities' do not self-consciously export capital. It is managers who export and invest, and their decisions in the aggregate determine the regional and temporal shifts in patterns of urban economic change. And managers respond not merely to economic forces but also to incentives and disincentives posed by state policies.

In parallel with the process of de-industrialisation are changes in the demographic composition of many declining urban areas, from predominantly white residents of European heritage to a predominantly black and Hispanic population leavened with substantial new immigration from Asia and Latin America. Employment opportunities and aggregate personal income levels have declined significantly for residents in these cities (Greenberg and Valente, 1975; Sternlieb and Hughes, 1975 and Kasarda, 1982). The drop in per capita income levels also reflects the suburban migration of many of the managerial and professional employees of the new tertiary and service industries. The regentrification of some urban neighbourhoods by young professionals is far from offsetting the flow of others to the suburbs. Core-city residents in old industrial cities now tend to be those in the least well paid occupations. Disproportionately large numbers of them subsist on social security and welfare payments, as will be seen from the last section of this chapter. This resident population, combined with the decline of traditional manufacturing industries, has made serious inroads on the tax base of north-eastern and mid-western cities (Gluck and Meister, 1979). However, the same factors have placed increased demands on urban services, resulting in varying degrees of municipal fiscal stress.

Recent work on growth and decline in European urban systems identifies a superficially similar pattern of declining core-city population, especially in larger cities (Hall and Hay, 1980). Great Britain offers the closest parallels with the situation in the United States: the major urban areas have experienced substantial population decline due to migration accompanied by very significant declines in industrial employment and productivity (McCallum, 1980; Hall and Hay, 1980 and Rees and Lambert, 1985). Analysis of the 1981 census shows that 'the bigger the city the bigger the loss'. In part this was due to government policies initiated during the 1950s and 1960s, some aimed at dispersing people from the most prosperous and overcrowded cities – London and Birmingham in particular – to New Towns, others designed to increase jobs in depressed regions (Hall, 1975; OECD, 1983, vol. 2, pp. 88–9). Equally or more significant was the shift of manufacturing activities from larger cities, where land for plant expansion was scarce and expensive, to smaller towns and rural areas (Fothergill and Gudgin, 1982, ch. 5). The net effect has been to give momentum to population decline in all large British cities. Simultaneously, a number of smaller cities, county towns and rural areas in areas with greater environmental and locational appeals have gained both in population and employment (Young and Mills, 1982; Fothergill and Gudgin, 1982). The unintended consequence is that the larger British urban areas have growing concentrations of unemployment, of lower socio-economic groups, of workers with both parents born outside the country. And, as in declining American industrial cities, employment in low-wage service industries has increased (McCallum, 1980 and Cameron, 1973).

In continental Europe the trend to declining core cities is also widespread, but with the exception of Belgium and some industrial regions of France and West Germany, the process during the 1970s was largely the result of the appeal of suburban living rather than declining urban economic opportunities resulting from de-industrialisation (van den Berg *et al.*, 1982; Hall and Hay, 1980). This pattern is paralleled by the distribution of urban crisis: Britain is the only industrial European state (with the anomalous exception of Italy) where the social and fiscal stresses of urban decline are comparable to the experience of the older industrial cities in the United States (Sharpe, 1981). On the other hand it is evident that the 'filtering out' of more prosperous people from inner cities to suburbs leads to increased concentrations of lower-income groups and the unemployed in core cities even where they remain economically viable in terms of employment and productivity. In West Germany, where foreign workers in 1976 were 6.5 per cent of total population, they made up 12 to 15 per cent of the population of some larger cities and over 20 per cent in some inner-city districts (Gude, Heinz and Rothammer, 1981).

The political salience of urban decline

Urban decline caused by structural economic change poses a threat to virtually all the state's primary and expedient interests in cities which we identified in Chapter 1. In advanced industrial democracies the maintenance of urban public order and essential urban services are crucial to acceptance of the national state's authority because the majority of the population in contemporary Western society lives in cities; so do almost all officials. Moreover, most of the economic activity upon which states depend for revenue is centred on cities: Jacobs (1984) describes cities as the 'milch cows of economic life' (p. 106): the sources of far more tax revenues than their rural hinterlands. Urban population also provide the basis for coalitions of political support for incumbent national officials and contenders alike. For these reasons and more, national officials have strong reasons for using the power and resources of the state to maintain the vitality of some, though not necessarily all, declining cities. Official attention and resources are not allocated among cities in strict proportion to the severity of urban problems because the salience of declining cities to the national state varies according to their political and administrative primacy, their actual and potential significance as sources of wealth and revenue, and in proportion to the current urban-based demands, disorder and political mobilisation centred on issues of urban change.

It should be noted that from the perspective of this study the conditions of the *political city* are most salient to the interests of the regional and national state. Economically-orientated analyses focus on larger functional regions or metropolitan areas because cities are conceived of as demographic and economic entities.[2] The city as a political entity comprises the core urban areas or 'central city' which is governed by the local state, an area which virtually everywhere in Western society is smaller than the demographically-defined city. The political city is crucial because of its status as a quasi-autonomous political actor *vis-à-vis* the regional and national states, because it is the locus of most metropolitan political and economic decision-making, and because the social and fiscal stresses of urban change are most acute within its boundaries.

The national and regional states in advanced industrial societies have a great many instrumentalities which can effect urban change, including their powers to spend, plan, regulate and provide incentives and disincentives. This chapter is mainly concerned with how state decisions affect the allocation of material resources among and within cities. The profile of state spending, for example, must take into account not only grants-in-aid to municipal governments but also social transfer payments, the siting of public institutions and public employment, private-sector contracts and investment in public enterprises. The local state has the same range of instruments at its disposal, but in declining cities must work within sharp budgetary constraints. The net effect of all state resources allocated through such instrumentalities potentially can stabilise and possibly even reverse the malign conditions associated with urban decline: unemployment, decaying housing and infrastructure, deteriorating municipal services, and social pathologies. This is not to minimise the role of the private sector in determining the outcomes of state intervention. From a state-centred perspective, however, the question is the extent to which the private sector follows up or complements the public initiatives upon which post-industrial cities are increasingly dependent.[3] The preceding argument can be summarised diagrammatically in this causal model of the likely consequences of urban decline:

urban decline $\longrightarrow$	increased political salience $\longrightarrow$	increased state presence $\longrightarrow$	stabilisation of decline

To the extent that the state does assume primary responsibility for economic and social well-being in de-industrialising cities, the causal sequence above is paralleled by this shift in the economic basis of urban systems:

cities dependent on private industry and services $\longrightarrow$	cities dependent on private services and public sector activities

In fact, the sequence of changes set in motion by urban decline is problematic. The political salience of urban decline varies among countries as well as within them. Americans seem to be prepared to abandon their older cities more readily than do continental Europeans, while conservative administrations on

Dimensions	Nature of effects	Of principal concern to
City political traits:		
Administrative status	Structural, persisting	Regional and national states
Local state as political actor	Processual, conditional on political alignments	
City economic traits:		
Economic centrality	Structural, persisting	National state
Fiscal stress	Processual, conditional on political alignments and intergovernmental distribution of authority	Regional and national states
Sociopolitical press-ures:		
Crime and deviance	Dynamic	Local, regional, and national states
Collective action	Dynamic	

FIGURE 3.1   *Dimensions of cities' political salience for the contemporary state*

both sides of the Atlantic, even if politically sensitive to urban decline, may be ideologically disposed against assuming primary responsibility for cities' material prosperity. Thus the arguments which are fleshed out below identify tendencies, not inevitabilities.

'Political salience' is a portmanteau concept for a set of state-centred arguments about the interests which push the national state and regional governments in contemporary Europe and North America to give more attention and resources to some cities than others. Six dimensions of political salience are identified in Figure 3.1. Two are political traits of cities: their administrative status and the political skills of their officials in dealing with higher levels of the state. A city's administrative status is a persisting structural condition, not usually subject to change in the short run. The effectiveness of the local state's participation in electoral politics and intergovernmental negotiations, however, is contingent on national-–local political alignments and the general policy orientation of higher levels of government. In other words, the effectiveness of the local state as political actor in the pursuit of local interests is variable, and some of the sources of variation are outside the local state's influence.

Two of the salience dimensions are reflections of the metropolitan economy. Economic centrality, like administrative status, is a structural condition which changes slowly. Fiscal stress is a complex consequence of the local state's attempt to meet social demands and mandated services in the face of declining local revenues. The extent to which local fiscal stress is transferred to the regional and national state depends on the legal/structural arrangements among levels of government and the issues of political and policy orientations which also influence the effectiveness of the local state as political actor.

The last two dimensions are more direct manifestations of urban problems and demands which affect the capacity of all levels of the state to maintain public order. They are *dynamic* in the sense that they originate outside the state, are subject to rapid change, and are regarded usually as matters which require prompt and substantial policy responses.

All six dimensions of salience can be expected to affect the allocation of state resources but, as the following discussion makes clear, not all of them are equally likely to be intensified by urban decline. In Chapter 4 we report results of an empirical study of the impact of several of these factors on the allocation of federal grants-in-aid among American cities.

Administrative status

The national state has a primary interest in maintaining an authoritative presence in cities and the surrounding regions administered from cities. The location of a city in the national state's administrative network therefore affects its political salience: the greater a city's administrative role for the national (and regional) state, the greater its political salience. The managers of the national state can be expected to be especially concerned about the quality of life in the national capital, not only for symbolic reasons but because, concretely, they want to live and work in a pleasant urban environment. The effects of such concern are obvious in 'government towns' like Bonn and

Washington; the case of London is more instructive. Greater London from 1951 to 1974 had the greatest proportional population loss of any British conurbation, and also the most substantial percentage loss of manufacturing employment – both conditions associated elsewhere with economic decline and fiscal stress (McCallum, 1980). But on most indicators of decline and stress during this period London fared better than other large British cities, thanks in part to the large and growing size of London's public administration sector (Cameron, 1980, pp. 64–5) and exceptionally high rates of increase in local government expenditure per capita (Kirwan, 1980, pp. 78–81).

Similar effects should be evident in regional administrative centres in both unitary and federal systems. A study of the capitals of the fifty American states, for example, shows that since the 1940s their populations and per capita income have increased more than those of comparable non-capital cities (Carroll and Meyer, 1983). The capitals' relative growth and prosperity, and their concentration of advanced service occupations, are all due to the expansion of state activities. We would expect similar patterns in cities which are major regional administrative centres in unitary political systems.

Unlike most other dimensions of political salience, 'administrative status' is usually the cumulative result of historical policies which have increased the status of a city in the state's administrative network. Thus administrative status is unlikely to be affected in the short run by urban decline; rather, cities which have significant administrative roles are less likely than others to experience decline (because of sustained public-sector growth) and are more likely to get special policy consideration when they do.

The local state as political actor

Cities in most Western countries have strong traditions of political autonomy, however much the legal and political practices of local autonomy have been constrained by the growth of the relative power of the national state (see Chapter 2). This means that local officials and national representatives of urban constituencies can be effective advocates in pressing the national and regional state for greater resources. The general proposition is that the greater the urban decline, the more intense the level of local bureaucratic and political efforts aimed at obtaining more resources from the national and regional state. In this instance 'political salience' increases because of institutionalised political action on behalf of the local state directed at higher levels of government.

The bureaucratic skills and political influence of the agents of the local state vary considerably. In the United States it is widely recognised that some municipal administrations became more adept more quickly at lobbying federal agencies for grants during the 1960s and 1970s than did others (Farkas, 1971; Hale and Palley, 1981 and Sbragia, 1983). The relative success of some congressional delegations in securing greater federal resources for their constituencies is equally well known. An account of Portland, Maine's renaissance from a condition of economic stagnation cites as relevant factors a 'united and effective Maine Congressional delegation that succeeded in squeezing an uncommon amount of urban renewal money' from the Carter and Reagan Administrations; new Navy contracts which helped revive a ship-repair industry; and the simultaneous attraction of new private investment (Coakley, 1983). In western Europe, where legal and fiscal obligations of the national state to local governments are more rule-bound, bureaucratic relationships might be expected to be more influential than political ones as determinants of the allocation of national and state resources among cities.

Many allocative decisions are based on formulas which are determined by legislatures and administrative agencies (on federal aid to cities in the United States, see Chapter 4). In these circumstances it is difficult for any one local state to gain a competitive edge when seeking outside public aid, except by changing the rules of the game. To the extent that electoral politics play a significant role, either in formulating the rules or in determining grants, a second general proposition becomes relevant: cities whose mayors (if partisan) and national representatives support the ruling party or coalition at the national level are likely to be favoured at least marginally in current allocative decisions. This should be especially evident with regard to new initiatives regarding public investment and regional growth plans.

Economic centrality

The national and regional states in advanced industrial society have large and expanding revenue requirements and the urban-based private sector provides the bulk of such revenues. Thus, as we proposed in Chapter 1, the economic prosperity of the urban system is a primary interest of the national state. Therefore, the more important any one city's role in the productive process, the greater its political salience. From a state-centred perspective this argument follows from revenue considerations, but its general implications for patterns of state policy are little different from neo-Marxist arguments that the state's urban policies aim at maintaining the dynamics of capital accumulation (Gordon, 1976; Castells, 1977 and Friedland, 1983). The empirical question is the relative weight of indicators of 'economic centrality' *vis-à-vis* other dimensions of salience as determinants of state presence.

Economic centrality can be conceptualised in alternative ways: (a) it may be regarded as a function of a city's total private-sector production of goods and services and (b) following both pluralist and political economy arguments, the economic centrality of a city depends on its concentration of centres of economic decision-making. Corporate headquarters, bank assets and union headquarters – and the concentration of economic power they represent – probably are more salient to national officials than are production statistics. Evidence in point is provided by studies of the allocation of federal funds for urban renewal and poverty programmes among American cities during the 1960s, showing that they correlate with the location of corporate and national labour union headquarters (Friedland, 1983). Economic centrality arguments certainly help explain the Ford Administration's decision in 1975 to rescue New York City from the brink of bankruptcy. Cleveland is one of a number of other declining cities with crises equally or more severe in the mid-1970s which benefited from no such federal intervention (see Bradbury, Downs and Small, 1981).

There is an implausible circularity in the argument that public monies go where private money and power are concentrated. If this was the only or primary dynamic in the allocation of the national state's resources, both urban growth and decline would be amplified by state policy. In fact, some declining cities are the objects of expensive and sometimes successful policies aimed at economic regeneration, while others are slighted. We suggest that a more complex economic logic is at work. Urban decline is a burden on the public economy, nationally as well as locally, which means that in principle it is in the interest of the national state to promote economic revival. The costs and prospects of doing so vary among cities: some afford more opportunities or leverage for public initiatives than others. Thus the national state can be expected to make choices about which declining cities will be the object of major efforts at redevelopment. And one of the factors in the calculus, in addition to the more political factors enumerated here, will be the economic *potential* of the metropolitan region.

Fiscal stress

Urban fiscal stress or 'crisis' has two main meanings (Dearborn, 1980): first, it refers to an immediate condition whereby a city cannot meet its obligations through lack of cash and credit (Tabb, 1982); second, it refers to the culmination of the long-term economic and social dynamics responsible for urban decline, whereby revenues chronically fall well short of municipal expenditure budgets (Gluck and Meister, 1979; Alcahy and Mermelstein, 1976). In the old American industrial cities, urban fiscal stress reflects the structural, demographic and economic changes of the last twenty-five years. It also reflects the enormous growth of local expenditures, particularly for social welfare and education (Pettengill and Uppal, 1974). In one of the few comparative studies of urban fiscal stress, Sharpe (1981) concludes that the fiscal condition of European local governments varies widely, with those of Britain and Italy being in greatest difficulty. The causes of stress are similar to those in the United States: insufficient revenues for municipal expenditures, exacerbated by inflationary pressures (Kirwan, 1980).

National or regional governments in advanced industrial societies have some legal and political obligations (the specifics varying among countries) to ensure the provision of minimum levels of local services, or at least to ensure the solvency of local governments. It is also in their expedient interest to ensure that collective goods and special social services are provided in urban populations because, as contended in Chapter 1, they are instrumental in the short run for maintaining political support for incumbents, and in the long run for maintaining the state's legitimacy. Therefore, the greater the local fiscal stress in a city, the greater its salience to the responsible higher level of government. There was a sharp increase in local fiscal stress during the 1970s, mainly due to the recession which followed the oil crisis. The prevailing short-run response was increased funding from national and regional governments. Our analysis of local government expenditures in five countries during the 1970s shows consistent increases in the percentage share obtained from national and regional governments (King and Gurr, 1983, Table 3). In the United States the percentage of local government expenditures provided by higher levels of government increased from 38.6 to 48.6 (1972–79), in Britain from 39.3 to 44.6 (1971–80) and in West Germany from 27.5 to 30.4 (1970–79). An extension of this analysis to the early 1980s shows a slow-down in the growth of grants to municipalities and, in Sweden and France, a shift toward greater reliance on local sources of revenue (see Chapter 2, Table 2.1). In effect, these represent a different kind of adaptation to fiscal stress: local governments have been empowered to raise more revenues locally.

National intervention does not necessarily resolve local fiscal problems, however. In some instances the national and regional state's response has been to oblige local governments to retrench as the price of bail-out, as was the case in New York City in 1975 (see Tabb, 1982 and Shefter, 1977) and in the German city of Duisburg in 1976 (the only such German case during the 1970s according to Gude, Heinz and Rothammer, 1981). Since 1980 most declining cities in the United States have had to cut back significantly on municipal services and employment, partly because of reduced federal funding of urban programmes (see Ganz, 1985; a comparative US study of retrenchment is Levine, Rubin and Wolohojian, 1981). In Great Britain, whose urban crisis is the subject of Chapter 5, the freedom of local authorities to tax and spend is being sharply curtailed by a national government committed to shrinking the public sector.

Crime and deviance

We proposed in Chapter 1 that the maintenance of public order in cities is in the primary interest to both the national and local state. High and rising rates of personal and property crime and related forms of illegal deviance (especially drug abuse) are a threat to the state in at least three senses: first, they are prima-facie evidence of the state's inability to maintain order; they may be regarded as evidence of underlying social stresses and deprivation which potentially threaten the state's capacity to exercise legitimate authority; and the fear of crime may lead some citizens to question the competence, and hence the legitimacy, of the state. Rising crime levels are of major concern to municipal officials: in a study of perceptions of local officials in ten American cities, Jacob (1984, ch. 3) found that violent crimes and crimes against property were at or near the top of the public-order agenda from the 1950s to the 1970s. It is likely that the greater the short-term increase in a city's rate of common crime, the greater the city's salience to the national and regional state, especially to those officials sensitive to law and order concerns. Evidence in point was the creation of the US Law Enforcement Assistance Administration in the late 1960s. It was established in response to increasing crime and collective violence in cities; its purpose was to improve the training, equipment and community relations programmes of municipal police forces (see Button, 1978).

Substantial empirical evidence links increasing crime to urban decline. For example Skogan (1977), examining differential rates of increase in serious offences for thirty-two US cities between 1948 and 1970, found that cities with the greatest levels and rates of suburbanisation had the greatest increases in known offences. The main reason is that suburbanisation drains off the middle class which is less prone to common crime, leaving potential criminals and their victims, most of them also poor, concentrated in the urban core. More generally, any process of urban decline which leads to the poverty of city populations is likely to be associated with rising crime. In a more recent study of crime trends in 396 US cities from 1950 to 1975, Jacob, Lineberry *et al.* (1982) find that cities with the most rapidly declining populations experienced greater increases in *violent* crimes than do others (pp. 14–17). It is plausible to suggest that the levelling-down associated with core-city decline in American cities leads both to decreased opportunities for economic crime and to increased frustrations which are expressed in increased interpersonal violence.

There are European parallels to the American connection between urban decline and rising crime. High rates of increase in personal and property crime characterised almost all advanced industrial democracies (except Japan) during the 1960s and 1970s (Gurr, 1977). The association with urban decline is illustrated by comparative historical studies of crime in London and Stockholm: both cities had substantial population declines after 1950, accompanied by crime rates which increased more rapidly than national rates (see Gurr, Grabosky and Hula, 1977). In summary, the proposition is that increases in common crime have been greatest in declining cities, and constitute one more set of reasons for the national state to increase its presence in such cities – specifically in the form of policies aimed at re-establishing social control.

Unconventional politics and collective action

Since early in the Industrial Revolution cities have been the locus of radical political movements and less structured collective violence (see Tilly, Tilly and Tilly, 1975; and Castells, 1983). Such activities not only pose a diffuse threat to the state's authority and its citizens' sense of security, they may actively and directly challenge the authority and policies of the local and national state and occasionally bring about substantial changes in the shape and exercise of power. The general proposition is that the greater the extent of unconventional political action in a city, the greater its political salience to the state, and the greater the likelihood and level of national response. The very substantial programmatic responses of the federal government to urban rioting in the 1960s have been closely studied and are reviewed briefly in Chapter 4. In Britain the urban riots of 1981 led among other things to a substantial increase in expenditures on the Urban Aid Programme (see Short, 1984, pp. 161–2). Many of the responses are much more subtle and work changes in both the status of the protagonists and the shape of urban policy.

Whereas it is very likely that both the national and local state will respond in some way to large-scale collective action, the relation between urban decline and the occurrence of various forms of political action is less than exact. Three kinds of unconventional political action should be distinguished.

1. Violent and unstructured actions like racial riots, street brawls, youth rampages and mass looting have little or no explicit political content, but they often signal potential class or segmental disaffection which is capable of mobilisation for more structured political challenges. These violent forms of collective action tend to occur among the poor and ethnic minorities, groups heavily concentrated in declining inner cities in the United States and Britain. Studies of the structural correlates of ghetto rioting in American cities during the 1960s have yielded relatively few positive results but Downes (1970, pp. 354–5) found that declining population was one of the stronger factors distinguishing between riot and non-riot cities; others were mainly indicators of the proportional size and well-being of the black population (see also Spilerman, 1976). In Britain's episodes of urban racial and youth rioting in 1981 and 1985 the correspondence between youth unemployment, poverty and rioting was unmistakable (see Scarman, 1982; Kettle and Hodges, 1982).

2. More politicised but episodic forms of collective action include strikes by organised labour, campaigns of civil disobedience, rent strikes and building occupations, and political demonstrations aimed at those holding political and economic power. Strikes tend to be a function of the status and composition of cities' workforces, both public and private. There is a general tendency in industrial

democracies for strike activity to increase in times of prosperity and decrease during hard times. An unanswered question is whether there is a correlation between the inner-urban distribution of economic malaise and strike activity. Political demonstrations generally are organised in response to specific government policies; they may be expected to concentrate in capitals, and to a lesser extent in cities undergoing major political and policy changes (including retrenchment).

3. A more enduring and potentially consequential form of urban-based political participation is the mobilisation of issue-orientated action groups which work outside conventional parties and interest associations to pressure for, or against, particular kinds of urban change. These 'urban movements' or 'struggles' as Castells (1983) calls them usually mobilise around issues of collective consumption, the group's cultural identity or its desire for political self-management (see the review of Castells' argument in Chapter 2). Urban citizens' action groups in advanced industrial societies are usually of middle-class inspiration and leadership, though there are significant exceptions, such as the participatory groups associated with the Community Action Programmes promoted by the US Office of Economic Opportunity (Greenstone and Peterson, 1973) and the organisations of squatters in such cities as London, Amsterdam and West Berlin.[4]

Studies of citizen community participation in American cities conclude that community interest groups tend to be more effective, and more widely representative, than the institutionalised modes of participation sponsored by municipal agencies (Steggart, 1975 and Dommel *et al.*, 1982). But Margit Mayer (in Hellstern, Spreer and Wollmann, 1982, vol. 2) suggests that government-sponsored neighbourhood movements have had to restrict their efforts to what officials define as 'negotiable' issues, thus defusing or deflecting more explosive conflicts. Heinz (Gude, Heinz and Rothammer, 1981) says that citizens' action groups in German cities are primarily defensive – opposing bureaucratic projects and planning – and over-represent professionals and students. Such groups in declining inner-city neighbourhoods rarely include low-income groups or foreign workers. In Great Britain, government-sponsored local Community Development teams in the 1970s sought to engage poor people in devising their own solutions to urban problems, but the government withdrew support when these teams took radical initiatives which brought them into conflict with local authorities (Kraushaar, 1981; Laurence and Hall, 1981, p. 93). Such examples suggest that the presence of citizens' groups may prove to be more a reaction to the interests and expansion of state activities in declining cities than an independent reflection of local concern about urban decline.

None of the foregoing comments is a threat to the validity of the general proposition that unconventional political action increases the salience of a city to the national and regional state. But they do suggest that the ordinary residents of the most seriously declining cities may be politically more quiescent – except for unstructured violence – than people of other cities.

Dimensions of the state's material presence in cities

The political salience of a declining city to regional and national officials is largely a function of the six types of condition outlined above, for reasons which follow from the state's urban interests identified in Chapter 1. As salience increases because of changes in one or several of those conditions, official concern is likely to be manifested in increased legislative activity, planning, implementation of new programmes, and so on. Many of these responses are intangible and their impact on cities difficult to assess except through case studies. Here we focus on those dimensions of action by the national and regional state which have tangible material consequences: they result in the increased flow of resources to the city. Some of these resources accrue directly to the local state, others flow to private individuals, firms and other organisations. Some are directed to cities specifically in response to decline, others are an incidental consequence of the pursuit of other policies.

The *material presence of the state* in a city is the aggregate of all public resources spent in the city through the exercise of public powers to plan, tax, regulate and allocate money, whether or not as a deliberate response to urban stress. While we are primarily concerned here with externally-provided resources, those which flow to a city because of national and regional decisions, the aggregate material presence of the state in a city also includes the spending of the local state.

There are five general dimensions of activity by the national and regional state which contribute directly to their material presence in cities. Some consist of programmes designed specifically to meet urban problems. Examples in the United States include general revenue sharing, anti-recession fiscal assistance, community development block grants, comprehensive employment and training programmes and grants for local public works (Cuciti, 1978; and Glickman, 1980). The theoretical argument of this chapter dictates a higher level of generalisation. A full profile of the state's material presence in any city (or other local government) needs to take account of *intergovernmental grants, social transfer payments, public employment, government procurement* and *economic redevelopment programmes.* Grants and regional redevelopment programmes almost always follow from state interests in the problems of urban areas. There is some evidence that in times of crisis increased transfer payments are targeted to categories of people who are concentrated in declining cities. While decisions about where to increase public employment and where to place government contracts may also be informed by concern about urban decline, in contemporary Britain and the United States they ordinarily are not.

Grants from national and regional governments

Intergovernmental grants make up a large and growing share of the local state's expenditures in most Western countries. In six countries we examined in the decade from 1972 to 1982, grants increased from an average of 41 per cent of total local expenditure to 44 per cent (see Table 2.1 on p. 68). While this increase may have had its immediate origin in the fiscal crisis of the 1970s, as was suggested above, in a larger perspective it is only the latest phase in a persisting historical trend. Newton and Karran (1985), using national sources, report that grants to local authorities in Britain increased from 10 per cent of local authorities' tax plus grant revenues in the 1880s to 25 per cent at the end of the First World War, to two-thirds in the 1970s (pp. 73–4).

The figures used in our cross-national comparisons include both unrestricted grants such as general revenue sharing in the United States and block grants in Britain, and grants targeted for specific programmes. Grants under some such programmes in Europe and the United States are allocated on the basis of population rather than need. Other programmes, designed to help disadvantaged people, allocate funds using spatial criteria whose effect is to benefit everyone in a 'poverty area' whether or not they are poor (see Edel, 1980). American urban programmes designed initially in response to the problems of declining cities experienced a 'spread effect', with other jurisdictions soon seeking and getting entitlements. None the less at the aggregate level there is substantial variation around the norm of proportionate distribution. Our arguments about decline and political salience are centred precisely on those deviations from proportionality. In an examination of state and federal grants to US cities, for example, we found that substantially more grants per capita go to declining than to growing cities. In both 1970 and 1980, federal and state aid per capita to the most seriously declining quartile of cities was roughly three times as great as it was to the most rapidly-growing cities (King and Gurr, 1983, Table 5; see also the last section of this chapter).

Social transfer spending

Payments made under social insurance and social assistance in 1980 contributed between 12 and 25 per cent of household income in eight Western countries, with the United States and the United Kingdom at the low end of the range and France and the Netherlands at the high end (Therborn, 1984, p. 28). Family allowances, disability payments, unemployment compensation and publicly-funded pensions are paid to 'people not places', but the people who receive these transfer payments are more often concentrated in large and declining cities than elsewhere (for the US, see Anton, Cawley and Kramer, 1980, pp. 89–91). Thus decisions by the national and regional state about which categories of people in need to help, and how much, inevitably affect the magnitude of public funds feeding into local economies. Moreover, there is substantial evidence that welfare expenditures under the federally-financed programmes of Aid to Families with Dependent Children (AFDC) increased in the 1960s in response to the riots in American cities; the greater the number and severity of riots in a city or state, the greater the subsequent local expansion of AFDC rolls and payments (Betz, 1974 and Jennings, 1979). The evidence suggests that increased political salience, arising in this instance from collective action, can significantly affect the magnitude of transfer payments flowing to cities.

The state as employer

In welfare democracies the state has become a major employer. In thirteen Western countries in 1979 public-sector employment averaged 25 per cent, including employment in public corporations. In the United States the figure was 17 per cent, the lowest of the thirteen, whereas in the United Kingdom it was 30 per cent (see Table 3.3 on p. 108 and Therborn, 1984, p. 34). Local government in the United States is the major public employer, with 7.7 million employees in 1977 compared with 2.7 million civilian federal employees (*State and Municipal Area Data Book, 1982*). The 7.7 million constituted about 8 per cent of the civilian labour force. Local authorities in Britain in 1979 employed 9 per cent of the national workforce (Byrne, 1985, p. 168), or about one third of all public employment.

The general implication of these data is that public decisions about where to locate and how to staff administrative offices and educational and cultural institutions can have a major impact on the vitality of cities and regions by taking up the slack in private employment. The empirical question is the extent to which declining cities like Newark, New Jersey and Glasgow, Scotland are favoured or disfavoured in the allocation of new public sector jobs by contrast with growing cities like Houston, Texas and Norwich, England. Some British evidence is suggestive. Employment by local authorities increased between 1961 and 1980 from 1.87 to 3.01 millions, that is, by 61 per cent (Thomson, 1982, p. 111). Comparison of 1961 with 1971 census data for the large (and declining) British

conurbations shows that total employment in public administration proportional to population increased in the conurbations by one third while in the rest of Britain it remained
proportionally constant (Cameron, 1980, p. 65). Some empirical evidence for a sample of American cities in the final section
of this chapter suggests a more complex pattern.

The state as contractor

A substantial part of public-sector spending consists of
government purchases of arms and other goods and services
from the private sector. In the United States in 1978,
procurements by the Department of Defense totalled $60.8
billion dollars, more than one-eighth of the total federal budget
and equivalent to 3 per cent of the country's GNP (Anton,
Cawley and Kramer, 1980, pp. 4 and 223). The allocation of
defence contracts has become intensely politicised because of
efforts by congressional delegations to ensure that industries in
their districts benefit. The local and regional impact can be
substantial: the vitality of metropolitan areas such as Dallas,
Seattle–Tacoma and San Jose is attributable in part to high –
some would say disproportionate – concentrations of defence
spending. Whatever effects government procurement has on
urban or regional growth and decline in the United States are
incidental rather than intended. While there is some effort to
favour small and minority-owned firms when awarding
contracts, there is no larger scheme to direct procurement
contracts to declining urban areas.

The effects of the regional distribution of government
contracts is not only an American concern. Young and Mills
(1982), in a recent analysis of urban economic decline in Great
Britain, assess 'policies against the tide' (of decline) and
comment that 'There are also areas of public decision whose
consequences for industrial cities tend to go largely unnoticed.
There is a new interest in the analysis of the spatial distribution
and the impact of public expenditure programmes, and the
1980s are likely to see proposals for more finely tuned and
impact-aware procedures in allocating resources and in the use
of government purchasing power' (p. 93). While there is
insufficient empirical work for comprehensive policy analysis

of the impact of government procurements on the spatial distribution of growth and decline, some work is beginning to emerge pertinent to this issue, especially in Britain (Ball and Leitenberg, 1983; Breheny and McQuaid, 1985). One study of domestic defence procurements in Britain concludes that these benefit disproportionately the south-west of Britain at the expense of the North (Simmie and James, 1986). And the same authors note that 'this was true even before Mrs Thatcher came to power in 1979. The difference now is that it is not counterbalanced by other aid' (p. 179). In Britain, at least, government spending on defence procurements has significant consequences for spatial patterns of growth and decline.

Programmes of economic redevelopment

This refers to a large and diverse set of state activities designed to stimulate local economies using the state's powers to tax, regulate *and* invest public monies. The essential element in such programmes is planning: officials design strategies and programmes to redirect investment and productive activities to economically-stagnant cities and regions. The prevailing approach in most capitalist democracies is to rely on 'partnerships' between public and private sectors, the state providing a favourable 'climate' in which private entrepreneurs can work profitably. This approach relies on private-sector response to public incentives, which can sometimes be increased if the state also provides some of the facilities and investment funds needed by entrepreneurs. The public-sector option is to establish state-owned and state-directed enterprises in declining regions, but apart from France most regimes in capitalist states have been unwilling to choose this option for reasons both political (private-sector resistance) and economic (public corporations tend to be less efficient and profitable). Meehan (1980, p. 282) comments on the 'almost universal belief in the superior ability of the private sector to "get things done"' which limits the state's role in American urban development programmes.

Among the almost infinite variety of urban redevelopment programmes one can distinguish macro and metropolitan approaches. The macro approach involves comprehensive national planning to minimise economic imbalances among and within regions. Such planning has long been practiced by European states but not in the United States. British national/regional policy after 1945 aimed at 'steering industrial growth from the more prosperous regions to the depressed areas ... to be accomplished not only by positive inducements to locate in these latter areas, but also by negative controls over the location of new industry ... in other areas' (Hall, 1975, p. 125). Another dimension of British policy during the 1950s and 1960s was to shift people and jobs away from the most prosperous metropolitan areas and into the depressed hinterlands. The fundamental aims of this kind of urban planning were to create employment in the targeted hinterlands and to reduce congestion and pressures on housing in the prosperous core metropolitan areas. In the 1960s these two kinds of policy tended to work at cross-purposes: according to one study, national/regional policy attracted 80 000 to 120 000 jobs to the three most depressed conurbations of Tyneside (Newcastle), Clydeside (Glasgow) and Merseyside (Liverpool) at the same time that urban dispersal policy diverted 55 000 to 140 000 jobs away from them (OECD, 1983, vol. 2, pp. 88–9).

Post-war regional planning in France and West Germany has also aimed at stimulating economic growth in peripheral and declining regions. The Rhine–Ruhr area of Germany has been adversely affected by the decline of its coal and steel industries and the Lille region of northern France by the collapse of the textile industry. The policies followed in both countries emphasise the provision of better infrastructure and financial incentives to private investors in these and other regions targeted for growth (Hall, 1975: ch. 8).

National policies of stimulating regional growth only benefit declining cities indirectly. Their complement, in principle if not in practice, are programmes aimed at redeveloping specific cities and districts within them. Some of these take place within the larger context of comprehensive municipal plans which regulate land use, the siting of productive activities, provision of transportation and other services. One specific innovation is the 'urban enterprise zone', the basic idea of which is to persuade entrepreneurs to open new businesses in blighted urban areas by easing regulations and providing them with services and tax incentives. British experiments in enterprise zones, inaugurated in 1981 after several years of intensive discussion, have spurred similar efforts in the United States (on Great Britain, see Davies, 1981; Young and Mills, 1982; on the United States, Butler, 1981b). Critics have questioned whether the incentives have been enough to attract significant new investment, and whether the investment and jobs produced will offset the public costs of the zones (Clarke, 1982). A somewhat different approach focuses not on 'zones' but on the urban poor themselves. Between 1979 and 1985 about 200 000 of the unemployed in Britain and France have taken advantage of programmes that enable them to use jobless benefits to start new businesses, most of them small, most in the service sector. Substantial state support is provided, including renovated space in derelict factories and public buildings (widely used in the British programme), training in business skills and common management services (German Marshall Fund, 1985).

National and regional programmes to promote local economic revitalisation have their parallels in the efforts of the local state to keep or attract enterprises by providing infrastructure, tax incentives, and other relative advantages. But this kind of 'inter-urban competitive struggle' has potentially negative consequences: it can intensify interregional shifts from declining to growing cities and regions, and cause local governments to incur costs, including investment in infrastructure and forgone tax revenues, which exceed returns. The general preference of European officials and experts is that state efforts to stimulate urban and regional economic growth should be nationally planned (see in particular van den Berg *et al.*, 1982: chs 11 and 12).

*   *   *   *

The effects of aggregate public-sector spending and programmes in declining cities are problematic for a variety of reasons. One is the lack of comprehensive planning which incorporates in a single framework all public programmes which have an impact on cities. Moreover, it follows from the 'political salience' arguments that, even if all urban programmes of the state were to be integrated in a comprehensive plan, not all declining cities are likely to be equally favoured. In fact, most urban policies are designed in response to particular situations and coalitions of interests, therefore 'urban policy' in the industrial democracies is a mosaic of programmes, each with its own history, rationale, advocates, clientele and bureaucratic momentum. There are also substantial differences among countries in the severity of urban problems, in the resources available to the state to deal with them, and in the political will do so. The only general conclusion we can offer is the proposition, already stated, that there are strong tendencies toward public-sector growth in declining cities. The following section presents some American evidence.

Growth of the public sector in declining American cities

The American urban landscape provides good terrain for testing our core argument that declining cities experience the greatest public sector growth, because the 121 metropolitan areas vary widely in growth patterns. The strategy used here is to compare the characteristics of a sample of thirteen cities, some growing and others declining, with particular attention to differences among them in the size of the urban public sector. The thirteen cities listed in Table 3.1 are a purposive sample rather than a fully representative one: they were chosen to represent the extremes of urban growth and decline, but to exclude smaller cities (those under 200 000 population). A serious constraint on the choice of cities was the availability of comparable data. Most statistical information on American urban regions is aggregated and reported by county and Standard Metropolitan Statistical Area (SMSA) rather than by municipality. As a result, the accounting unit for most of our variables is different from the political city which is the object of our conceptual and substantive interest. The cities selected are ones for which we can identify a 'core metropolitan county', one which encompasses the political city but relatively little of the surrounding suburban sprawl. Notes to Table 3.1 indicate the degree of correspondence between county and municipal population; in Newark, Detroit and San Jose the county is

TABLE 3.1 *Growth and decline in thirteen core metropolitan counties, 1970–80*[a]

City	Population change 1970–80 per cent	Per capita income 1979 $	Ratio of per capita income growth 1969–79[b] in the core county to income growth in: SMSA	Region
Baltimore	−13	5877	.78	.82
Philadelphia	−13	6067	.80	.80
St Louis	−27	5880	.86	.83
Newark	−09	7560	.86	.80
Means	**−16**	**6346**	**.835**	**.813**
Boston	−12	6557	.91	.87
Detroit	−12	7625	.92	.86
Indianapolis	−04	7677	.93	.86
Chicago	−04	8272	.94	.86
Means	**−08**	**7533**	**.925**	**.863**
Denver	−05	8580	.92	.99
Tucson	+51	7152	(1.00)	.97
Alberquerque	+33	7136	.99	1.04
San Jose	+22	9545	(1.00)	1.03
Houston	+38	9144	1.02	1.18
Means	**+28**	**8305**	**.990**	**1.042**

(a) The core metropolitan counties include the municipalities shown on the left. In the cases of Denver, St Louis and Philadelphia the county is coterminous with the municipal jurisdiction. In the case of Baltimore, the county of Baltimore has only .83 of the city of Baltimore's population. In all the other instances the county population is larger: Newark (Essex County, 2.58 times the city's population), Boston (Suffolk, 1.15); Detroit (Wayne, 1.94); Indianapolis (Marion, 1.09); Chicago (Cook, 1.75); Tucson (Pima, 1.61); Alberquerque (Bernalilo, 1.27); San Jose (Santa Clara, 2.06); Houston (Harris, 1.51). All data are from the *State and Metropolitan Area Data Book 1982*, US Bureau of the Census.

(b) Our calculation from data on per capita income in current dollars. SMSA is the standard metropolitan statistical area of which the core county is a part; in the cases of Tucson and San Jose the core county is the entire SMSA. 'Region' refers to the group of states in which the city is located. Ratios of less than 1.00 indicate a lower rate of growth in per capita income in the core county than in the larger area.

substantially larger. The likely consequence is to understate the growth of the municipality of San Jose, and to underestimate decline, and the size of the public sector, in the political cities of Newark and Detroit.

The cities are grouped into three categories based on changes in the population and per capita incomes of their core metropolitan counties during the 1970s. The core counties of the Baltimore, Philadelphia, St Louis and Newark metro areas all had substantial population losses during the decade, averaging 16 per cent, and growth in their per capita incomes lagged 14 to 22 per cent behind income growth in their immediate and larger regions.[5] The second group of cities experienced less pronounced decline during the 1970s: the core metropolitan counties which include Boston, Detroit, Indianapolis and Chicago averaged 8 per cent population loss and income growth which lagged 6 to 14 per cent behind their regions. Cities in the third group are all at the core of relatively prosperous and rapidly expanding urban areas. Denver's relatively low position in this group is a statistical anomaly, the result of the fact that, unlike the others, the municipal and county jurisdictions are coterminous. In all cities in this group, per capita income during the 1970s kept pace with or exceeded that of the west and south-west taken as a whole.

Our strategy for comparing the size of the public sector in these cities is to calculate mean scores for each group on ten indicators, including intergovernmental grants, social transfer benefits, public employment and total public-sector income.[6] Two of the thirteen cities have special characteristics which warrant treating them separately. Boston is regarded by city-watchers and scholars as the north-east's most successful case of urban transformation. Ganz (1985, p. 453) characterises it as one of the country's three 'preeminent services activities cities' and the 'Downtown Indicators Report 1983' ranks it fifth in economic growth and improvement among all large American cities (cited in Ganz, 1985, p. 455). Our data show that Boston also has become the quintessential public city, ranking at or near the top of all our indicators of state presence. Houston is Boston's polar opposite on the state presence indicators, a city whose vitality is due almost entirely to private-sector growth (but see Feagin, 1985 on the state's role in promoting that growth).

Intergovernmental grants and municipal expenditures

The municipal governments of the declining cities are substantially more dependent on federal and state grants than the growing cities (Table 3.2). The proportion of the municipal budget provided by state and federal grants in the four seriously declining cities is thirteen percentage points above the national average for all cities of 33 per cent, the rapid-growth cities are several points below it. Boston's fiscal dependency is still greater than that of other declining cities, while in Houston it is only 13 per cent. There is a parallel pattern in the changes since 1970: the greater the urban decline the greater the proportional increase in grants from higher levels of government. In Boston fiscal dependency increased from 23 per cent to 48 per cent during those thirteen years; in the four growing cities (other than Houston) fiscal dependency actually declined by several percentage points.

The per capita municipal expenditures and grants per capita tell much the same story. The declining cities get more grants and spend more per capita. The Boston–Houston contrast is particularly stark: Boston gets ten times as much in grants per capita and spends nearly three times as much as Houston. When the data for individual cities are examined, however, it becomes evident that there is a curvilinear relation between municipal expenditures and the extent of decline. Newark and St Louis generally rank at the bottom in studies of urban decline and hardship (see, for example, Nathan and Adams, 1976, Table 2), but get and spend substantially less than cities like Baltimore and Boston where decline is less pronounced. When the eight declining cities are regrouped in pairs, from most to least seriously declining, these are their mean per capita levels of municipal expenditures and grants:

	Expenditures ($)	Grants ($)
Newark, St Louis	856	395
Philadelphia, Baltimore	1432	733
Boston, Detroit	1456	717
Chicago, Indianapolis	685	248

TABLE 3.2 *Government finance in growing and declining American cities, 1983*[a]

	Fiscal Dependency		Level of Municipal Expenditures	
	Percentage of municipal budget in grants 1983	Absolute percentage change 1970–83	Total expenditures per capita 1983 $	Federal + state grants per capita 1983 $
Boston	*48*	*+25*	*1790*	*859*
Average for four seriously declining cities	45.9	+12.3	1146	539
Average for three gradually declining cities	41.1	+9.1	831	357
National average, all cities	*33.1*	*+4.4*		
Average for four rapidly growing cities	30.5	−2.3	852	252
Houston	*13*	*+9*	*629*	*81*

(a) All fiscal data are for municipal governments, from the US Bureau of the Census, *City Government Finances in 1970–71 and 1982–83*. The 'absolute percentage change 1970–83' in fiscal dependency refers to the difference between the 1970–71 percentage and the 1982–83 percentage of budgets met by federal and state grants. The per capita municipal expenditures data are calculated using 1980 city population data.

The cases are too few to be definitive, but the pattern implies that a relatively high level of state effort, locally and at higher levels, has helped stabilise economic decline in political cities like Baltimore and Boston. In the worst-case cities of Newark and St Louis, however, local revenues and grants are too little to make much difference. Alternatively, of course, local and extralocal authorities may be responding differentially to perceived economic opportunities: Newark and St Louis may lack the potentials for redevelopment of Boston and Baltimore. In such circumstances the local state may be concerned only to provide the minimum level of urban services (on Newark, see Guyot, 1983).

People with public-sector incomes

About 17 per cent of the total US population were employed by the government in 1980 while another 20 per cent were receiving benefits under the federal government's social security (OASI) or AFDC welfare programme (see Table 3.3). These figures provide indicators – not an exact estimate – of the proportion of the urban population which is financially dependent on the public sector. Government employment also tends to be somewhat more heavily concentrated in declining cities, as is evident from the first column of Table 3.3, but only by a few percentage points. The declining cities also experienced proportional growth in public employment during the 1970s while it remained stable or declined in the growing cities. Most of the growth must be attributed to the state and federal governments because there have been strong pressures on the governments of declining cities to reduce public employment: twenty-two of thirty large cities analysed by Ganz (1985, pp. 458–9) reduced municipal employment between 1975 and 1983, some by more than 15 per cent – including St Louis, Baltimore, Boston and Philadelphia.

The indicators of transfer-payment recipients demonstrate the human impact of urban decline much more sharply. There were proportionally twice as many OASI and AFDC recipients in 1980 in the seriously declining cities as in the rapidly growing cities. Moreover, the increases of the 1970s were far greater in the declining cities. When government employment

TABLE 3.3 *People with public-sector income in growing and declining American cities, 1980*[a]

	Government Employment (all levels)[b]		OASI and AFDC Recipients[c]		
	Percentage of total population 1980	Absolute percentage change 1970–80	Percentage of total population 1980	Absolute percentage change 1970–80	Percentage of total population with public sector income 1980[d]
Boston	*19.5*	*+2.1*	*29.8*	*+5.0*	*50.3*
Average for four seriously declining cities	19.6	+2.8	34.2	+11.3	53.8
Average for three gradually declining cities	15.1	+2.3	23.4	+ 8.4	38.5
National average[e]	*17.1*	*+1.0*	*19.7*	*+3.6*	*36.8*
Average for four rapidly growing cities	18.6	−0.8	17.4	+1.2	36.0
Houston	*10.9*	*+0.2*	*10.3*	*+0.6*	*21.2*

(a) All data are for the core metropolitan county within which the city is located. In St Louis, Philadelphia and Denver this is coterminus with the area served by municipal government. In the other cases the core metropolitan county includes the city proper plus some suburban areas.

(b) As reported in the 1970 and 1980 censuses. From *State and Metropolitan Statistical Area Data Book 1982* and the *County and City Data Book 1983*, both published by the US Bureau of the Census.

(c) Total number of individual recipients of OASI (social security) benefits plus individual recipients of AFDC (Aid to Families with Dependent Children) benefits, same sources as in (b) plus the *State and Metropolitan Statistical Area Data Book 1979*.

(d) The sum of government employment, OASI and AFDC individual recipients as a percentage of total population. The data should be regarded as an indicator, not an exact estimate, because they do not include recipients of benefits under welfare programs other than AFDC, nor recipients of veterans' benefits or government pensions. Moreover, the government employment figures do not include dependents of government employees whereas the AFDC data include children as well as parents receiving benefits. Many OASI and AFDC recipients also have private-sector income.

(e) Averages are for the total population, urban and rural.

data are added to the figures on recipients of transfer payments, the numbers indicate that more than half the population of the four most seriously declining cities are dependent on the public sector – an average of 54 per cent contrasted with 36 per cent in the growing cities. The difference between Boston and Houston again highlights the difference between the public city and the private: Houston has about half the government employment and one third the transfer-payment recipients of Boston, relative to population, and had virtually no proportional growth in those categories between 1970 and 1980.

Public sector income

Most beneficiaries of transfer payments are the poor and elderly, people whose incomes are considerably less than the incomes of those with regular employment. An alternative indicator of the state's material presence in cities is the percentage of total personal income which comes from public sources. Data for 1979 are summarised in Table 3.4, distinguishing between transfer payments and the aggregate of government salaries and procurements from private business. (The sources do not specify how much comes from each level of government.)

The Boston–Houston contrast is as sharp as in all other comparisons: fully half of the personal income generated in Boston comes from public-sector spending, compared with 13 per cent in Houston. It also is the case that transfer payments and government contributions to earned income provide larger income shares in the serious-decline cities than in the others. But beyond this point the pattern changes: transfer payments, and especially government contributions to earned income, add more to the personal income of rapidly growing cities than to gradually declining cities. In fact, the three gradually declining cities receive on average even less from public sources than the national aggregate of 25.3 per cent. The reasons lie in the distribution of public employment, which is proportionally lower in this category of cities (see Table 3.3), and in the allocation of government procurements. It would need a much more detailed analysis of the public economies of a large number of cities to determine whether the pattern is a general one, and which levels of government are mainly responsible.

TABLE 3.4 *Public-sector sources of personal income in growing and declining American cities, 1979*[a]

	Public-Sector Income Sources as Percentage of Total Personal Income		
	Government transfer payments	Government contribution to income of labour and proprietors	Total
Boston	*19.6*	*29.8*	*50.4*
Average for four seriously declining cities	18.3	18.4	36.7
Average for three gradually declining cities	12.1	11.7	24.1
National average[b]	*13.0*	*12.3*	*25.3*
Average for four rapidly growing cities	12.5	16.3	28.8
Houston	*6.0*	*7.3*	*13.3*

(a) All data are for the core metropolitan county within which the city is located. See note (a) to Table 3.3. The data source is the *State and Metropolitan Statistical Area Data Book 1982*, which reports total personal income and the amounts received from various public and private-sector sources.
(b) Distribution of total national personal income by source.

Conclusions

The evidence on the growth of the public sector in declining American cities strongly supports our contention that when the private economy weakens the state is likely to take on added responsibility for urban survival. In Boston several indicators suggest that the city at the beginning of the 1980s was equally dependent on the public and private economies, a pattern that is particularly surprising in view of the fact that in aggregate public spending the United States is well behind that of most European states. If one declining American city has become a 'public city', the same transition should have been crossed in a number of declining European cities. But Boston has not become a 'ward of the state' in the process. It thrives, relatively speaking, on public employment and contracting for the state. By comparison with worst-case cities like Newark and St Louis its citizens are less dependent on transfer payments and its economy is more healthy. No doubt there is a limit to the number of post-industrial cities whose economies can be transformed by the infusion of public funds, an issue discussed at greater length in Chapter 6. That it should happen in any cities at all runs against the grain of market-orientated ideologies that are in vogue around the Atlantic rim.

The American evidence does not speak directly to the more general argument that the public sector in declining cities expands *because* decline increases the political salience of cities officials of the national and regional state. More fine-grained studies are needed to test that proposition. The following two chapters on the evolution and impact of urban policies in the United States and Great Britain provide substantial evidence on that question. While the findings of both are consistent with a general urban crisis-expanded state presence model, the British case in particular demonstrates that single-minded commitment to other priorities can lead national officials to ignore, at least in the short run, the social and economic stresses of declining cities.

Chapter 4

The Political Salience of Urban Crisis in the United States: The Federal Response

This chapter begins with an overview of the evolution of the federal government's urban policies in the United States, with particular attention to the substantial expansion initiated in the 1960s.[1] The main purpose of this overview is to determine what fuelled the expansion of federal commitments and responsibilities at the municipal level. This treatment is followed by the presentation of empirical analyses testing the extent to which the allocation of federal aid to cities between 1960 and 1980 reflected the interests of the state in a way consistent with the theoretical propositions developed in previous chapters.

The evolution of state interests in municipalities in the United States: federalist ideology versus national state interests

This brief review of the history of federal–local relations in the United States focuses on two key periods of expansion in federal assistance to cities and analyses the sources of these initiatives, with special attention to the changing concerns of national officials (for detailed accounts of the history of intergovernmental relations in the United States, see Henig, 1985; Howitt, 1984; Jones, 1983 and Judd, 1984). These shifts occurred within the context of American federalism and the ideology informing the political culture which supports that particular system of government: Elazar (1984) writes that:

federalism is the central characteristic of the American political system, its principles animating the greater part of the nation's political process. The United States ... has a national – or general – government that functions powerfully in many areas for many purposes, but it is not a central government controlling all the lines of political communication and decision making. The states are not creatures of the federal government, but, like the latter, derive their authority directly from the people. Structurally, they are substantially immune from federal interference. (p. 2)

Such an intepretation is consistent with the traditional intergovernmental perspective. It is not one we entirely concur with. The principal difference lies in the power and intentionality we accord to the national or federal government: the latter has significant interests of its own to promote in relation to cities, we have contended, whether or not these clash with the rights and interests of the 50 American states. The latter enjoy constitutional control of cities but their recurrent failure to meet municipal needs at critical historical periods has facilitated the erosion of this right in political practice. As Florestano and Maranado (1981) observe in their study of regional state–city relations, 'even partisans of the state admit this power [that is, state power over cities] has been somewhat illusory. States have been unwilling or unable to assume their rightful role in the federal system' (p. 42). The strength of state resistance to federal action toward municipalities may be greater than these scholars suggest, but the general thrust of these remarks is accurate. As will be evident below, the inability of the American states to act during periods of municipal crisis has contributed significantly to the expansion of the national role in municipalities. It is necessary to add some caveats about the states' responses to city stress: first, states have at times been financially unable to expand their municipal commitment even when they wanted to. The fiscal constraints under which states themselves work have consequences for their capacity to assist cities. This was true of the 1930s to some extent, and still holds, but by the end of the 1970s many older cities located in the north-east and mid-west were receiving substantial state funding by comparison with Sunbelt cities: thus 'in 1978, 38.5 percent of New York City revenue came from New York State; Dallas got but 1.3 percent from Texas. Detroit received 24.2 percent of its money from Michigan, but Corpus Christi got only 1.6 percent from the state' (Jones, 1983, pp. 271–2). Those states with the most fiscally distressed cities have had greater pressure to respond than Sunbelt states. There has also always been a strong anti-urban element in many state legislatures resistant to expanding assistance to cities. A second caveat is to note that in some areas, for example education grants to cities, states have significantly expanded their level of funding. But the general point stands: states have been reluctant, whether because of fiscal constraints or ideology or both, to respond to cities in times of stress; and the major initiatives in expanding intergovernmental aid have come from the federal government.

The theoretical basis of our interpretation of expanded federal assistance to municipalities has been laid out in Chapters 1 and 2. Direct federal responsibilities for cities expanded in two step-level increases. The first occurred during the Great Depression, especially after 1932, the second during and after the Kennedy/Johnson Great Society initiative, from the early 1960s to 1968. Each of these were periods of crisis which increased substantially the salience of cities for the national government: in the 1930s the major concerns were urban social and fiscal stress and the threat of disorder, in the 1960s the problems were rising crime and collective action, and the re-establishment of political alignments which gave mayors and big-city congressmen influence in Washington that they had not enjoyed since the New Deal. The primary interests of the national state were at risk in both periods: the maintenance of public order and authority among city populations. The short-term interests of both elected officials and federal bureaucrats also were relevant to the federal response, as we will demonstrate.

What may be problematic theoretically is why the federal government was willing and able to override the interests and preferences of the American states when assuming direct responsibility for urban problems. It clearly was the case that the failure of some of the forty-eight, later fifty, states to contribute substantially and systematically to municipal problems increased the national salience of urban crisis. It also is evident that during the 1930s the Roosevelt Administration articulated a national ideology of the positive state which justified the assertion of the powers of the national state over those of the regional states. And municipal administrations, as potential beneficiaries of national intervention, gave their active political support to national administrations in the 1930s and 1960s. The relative autonomy of the national state *vis-à-vis* the regional states has increased as a consequence; the effects on the local state's autonomy have been more problematic, as we proposed in Chapter 2.

We will examine each of the two crisis periods in more detail. In the 1930s, mass unemployment was especially concentrated in urban areas because rural deprivation encouraged movement to the cities. But municipalities lacked sufficient funds to help the unemployed:

> The depression placed unprecedented responsibilities on city officials. In an attempt to provide relief and, in some cities, public works jobs, the cities quickly exhausted their resources. Cities could not expand tax revenues to keep pace with increased responsibilities. State-imposed debt limitations did not allow the cities to borrow for general government expenditure. (Judd, 1984, p. 134)

Farkas (1971) supports this account:

> In the United States ... it was not until the 1930s that remedies for their [that is, cities'] plights and blights began to be fashioned on the national, rather than exclusively on the local level. Urban problems came to be a subject of direct concern to the federal government. The occasion for this shift was a national catastrophe, namely, the Great Depression which impoverished the cities as well as large parts of the country's population. Price supports were given to farmers, and something had to be done to keep the cities from fiscal collapse as well. (p. 21)

The economic malaise of the 1930s placed 'many of the largest cities on the verge of financial collapse' (Gelfand, 1980,

p. 31; see also Monkkonen, 1985), a situation exacerbated by the inability of the American states to help the cities within their jurisdictions to avoid fiscal disaster. Judd concludes that the hardship of the 1930s was made even worse by the failure of the states to act effectively: 'State governments were more concerned with balancing budgets than with alleviating human suffering. As state tax revenues declined, wholesale reductions were made in public works and construction programs ... [which] compounded the unemployment crisis' (Judd, 1984, p. 136). This pattern was not uniform: some states, particularly New York, Pennsylvania and New Jersey, did expand their assistance to distressed cities as the Great Depression persisted, by adopting new taxes. It is also important to note that states were constrained by new fiscal laws which largely prohibited deficit-spending; as Patterson (1969, p. 30) notes, 'as tax revenues dwindled and unemployment increased, economy in government became a magic word'. This latter, combined with the necessarily subservient role of states in national monetary and fiscal policymaking, constituted important constraints upon their capacity to respond to the plight of cities. Whether the states were willing or not to respond to municipal hardship (and some evidently were not), most lacked the resources to be effective, and despite introducing new taxes still had insufficient funds to offer effective assistance: there was a 'clearly demonstrated incapacity of state legislatures to deal with the urban disasters within their jurisdictions'. Consequently, 'the cities turned to federal government to bypass the unsympathetic and often uninformed considerations of city problems in rural-dominated state legislatures' (Farkas, 1971, pp. 36 and 54).

The threat of fiscal collapse coupled with the inability of cities to respond to unemployment was a profound threat to public order. Despite the federalist ideology and political culture, which acted as a constraint on federal activism throughout the nineteenth century (in combination with several court decisions affirming state control of their local jurisdictional units: see the discussion of Dillon's Rule in Chapter 2 above), the enormity of urban problems in the 1930s and their implications for the national state's own interests forced a break with precedent and with federalist principles.

The outcome was a restructuring of 'intergovernmental relations by bringing about a direct relationship between the cities and the federal government' (Judd, 1984, p. 133). The historical and constitutional dominance of the American states over their cities was significantly weakened as the federal government assumed a central responsibility and fiscal commitment to cities. While the extent of this national financial commitment was relatively small by later standards, a critical institutional practice was established. Mollenkopf (1983) notes that 'the New Deal erected the basic framework for federal urban policy, much of which survives today ... In contrast to the 1920s, the federal government today strongly influences the patterns of urban physical development and urban political participation' (p. 49).

Another significant factor in the 1930s was the growth of national administrative capacities. For historical reasons due in part to the federal nature of the American polity, national government in the United States had no strong administrative agencies to formulate or pursue effectively the interests of the national state (see Skowronek, 1982). As a consequence, at the onset of the Great Depression 'the U.S. had (for a major industrial nation) a bureaucratically weak national government, and one in which existing administrative capacities were poorly coordinated' (Skocpol, 1980, p. 175). The Roosevelt Administration came to office committed to using the powers of the national state to promote capitalist economic recovery, but was frustrated by the government's administrative weakness. A comprehensive plan of administrative reorganisation was frustrated in Congress, but one kind of legacy remained: proponents of the federal government's new, more active social and economic role 'carved out domains of legislation and administration favourable to well-organised constituents and then did their best to defend these against bureaucratic encroachments or opposition within Congress or from the administration' (Skocpol, 1980, p. 197; see also Weir and Skocpol, 1985). The new urban programmes of the era were one such domain, supported by new links forged amongst city officials and mayors favouring a continuing federal response to urban problems: the United States Conference of Mayors (USCM) was founded in 1933. Thus the national state's newly institutionalised involvement in cities was reinforced by municipal-based lobbying:

> the New Deal programs served as catalysts for a new kind of federalism in which cities formed direct relations with federal government and intensive lateral relations with each other. The political circumstances of the 1930s nurtured an era of organized federal lobbying by cities (formed into groups) and by city interests. These lobbies emerged with an urban interest network, described as such because of similarity of purpose, division of labor, intergroup communication, and overlapping personnel. (Farkas, 1971, p. 66)

The USCM was the most powerful urban interest lobby in the 1930s but there were other important urban lobby groups including the National Association of Housing and Redevelopment Officials (NAHRO, founded in 1933), the National Housing Conference (NHC, founded in 1931) and the National League of Cities (NLC, previously the American Municipal Association). The USCM enjoyed prominence within this grouping mainly because it was politically very powerful, representing, as it did, the mayors of the largest cities in an era when they still exercised enormous local power, which was reinforced by President Roosevelt's reliance on the mayor's power in the implementation of the New Deal. Cities supported Roosevelt's New Deal initiative both institutionally and electorally. Equally important for our concerns was the development of an urban policy-making system composed of federal and city representatives: urban lobbying groups such as the USCM were critical to the establishment and maintenance of this system. Beginning in the 1930s 'a persistent pattern of relations emerged among groups and individuals inside and outside the federal government that established the agenda items and level of debate; and that provided the interlocking network without which no urban programs or urban policy can operate effectively' (Farkas, 1971, p. 43). The 1930s thus witnessed the development of sustained federal–city institutional relationships which provided enduring means for the national state to promote its interests in cities.

Federal assistance to cities continued to expand steadily, if marginally, from the late 1930s to the 1950s. Of critical importance, the practice of providing direct assistance to city governments (as well as to largely autonomous local organisations) persisted. Two major grants-in-aid programs related to urban development were initiated between 1938 and 1960: urban renewal was promoted by the 1948 Housing Act and given further impetus in 1954; and the Interstate Highway Act of 1956 provided assistance for their metropolitan segments (see Mollenkopf, 1983, pp. 50–1). Following the pattern of the 1930s these grants were categorical, that is, funds were for specific programme areas, and were allocated in project grants whose terms were negotiated between local and national administrators. These grants were important in maintaining the federal–municipal fiscal link but it was the 1960s that witnessed the real 'take-off' in federal aid to cities.

As in the 1930s, the backdrop to the dramatic expansion of the federal presence in municipalities was social unrest and urban crisis. This time, however, the source of the malaise was not absolute deprivation, because the economy as a whole was relatively prosperous; crisis derived to a greater extent from the growing concentration of social problems in central cities, the relative deprivation associated with racial and economic inequality, and the heightened awareness of these problems created by the civil rights movements during the 1950s and early 1960s. This time the threat of public disorder erupted in widespread and prolonged rioting of an unprecedented kind: between June 1963 and mid-1968 the American urban landscape was swept by some 250 riots, rebellions and interracial clashes. A quarter of a million blacks are estimated to have participated in them, 196 people were killed, and about 50 000 arrested (Gurr, 1979 and McAdam, 1984):

[W]ithout the riots in the urban ghettos, a recognition of [the] growing militancy in the national financial accounts would have been delayed. The widespread and frightening disorder created a sense of crisis not experienced since the early 1930s. It took such a crisis to forge the first links between the national and local levels in the Depression decade and such a crisis was necessary to broaden these ties in the late 1960s and early 1970s. (Gelfand, 1980, p. 45)

Most of the federal legislative response to the urban crisis of the 1960s was developed within the context of the Democrats' Great Society programmes. Whereas the previous decade's urban renewal programme 'was designed exclusively to remove unsightly slums and to subsidize "better" uses of inner city property', under Presidents Kennedy and Johnson 'a new concern emerged for the social problems of the cities – juvenile delinquency, crime, poverty, bad education, racial conflict, and joblessness' (Judd, 1984, p. 303). Legislation addressing these issues were at the core of the Great Society initiatives. New programmes were established, many of them in the new Office of Economic Opportunity (OEO) (established in 1964, thus pre-dating the Great Society by a year), and vastly increased resources were channelled through existing pro-grammes. Federal grants for urban renewal, for example, increased from $87.1 million in 1959 to $611 million a decade later (Iris, 1983, p. 348). Significantly, the aid to implement these policies went directly to city governments, deliberately bypassing the states. Thus the direct federal–municipal link was further strengthened, as Howitt (1984) observes:

> The Great Society represented a significant turning point in the development of the intergovernmental system. By moving into many new policy areas and greatly extending its involvement in others, the federal government became a more significant – and highly active – presence in the daily lives of state and local officials and in the delivery of government services to citizens. The relationship with local government, in particular, was altered significantly. As the country politically recognized an 'urban crisis', many of the new grant programs were set up to provide aid directly to municipal governments or local agencies rather than through the states as intermediaries. (p. 7)

While some of the Great Society programmes met resistance from municipal officials, particularly some of the grass-roots Community Action projects promoted by the OEO, the overall effect was to reinforce the federal–municipal connection.

Thus the events of 1963–67 further altered the shape of federalism in the United States, broadening and deepening the direct federal–city link which has now been called into question by the New Federalism proposals of the Reagan Administration. The second set of legislation emerging from this period focused on restructuring the system of intergovernmental/federal–city finance itself, culminating in the 1972 State and Local Fiscal Assistance Act that established revenue-sharing, which unlike the categorical and block grants-in-aid conferred substantial autonomy on cities to decide how federal funding should be distributed across budgetary priorities. In some cities this freedom translated into a shift in federally-derived funds away from social welfare needs. The Nixon Administration presided over this substantial expansion of federal assistance to cities which also included some major new block grants: the Comprehensive Employment and Training Act of 1973 and the Community Development Block Grant programme of 1974. Under the Carter Administration federal aid to large cities (that is, those over 200 000 in population) peaked (in 1978) and then began a decline which continued in the Reagan Administration, as is evident from Table 4.1. Quantitatively, the size of the federal financial commitment to cities grew exponentially until 1978: 'federal aid "passed through" the states to the localities increased by 73 percent between 1972 and 1977, but direct aid to local governments increased by 264 percent. By 1978, 28 percent of total federal aid went directly to localities, whereas in 1970 only 13 percent had. A direct federal–local relationship developed, and the state's control over municipalities consequently weakened' (Sbragia, 1983, p. 9).

New urban programmes were enacted early in the Carter Administration, notably the Intergovernmental Anti-Recession Fiscal Assistance programme, which was targeted specifically toward the most fiscally-distressed cities, and the Urban Development Action Grants programme, both in 1977 (Sbragia, 1983). However, by the end of the Carter Administration, federal urban policy was being reshaped by changing assumptions about national economic policy: the Presidential Commis-

TABLE 4.1   *Aggregate federal aid to cities 200 000+ in millions of constant (1967 = 1.00) and current dollars*

Year	Current $(000)	Constant $(000)	CPI[a]
1964	324.9	350.9	1.08
1965	401.7	425.8	1.06
1966	566.0	538.0	1.03
1967	697.3	697.3	1.00
1968	811.7	779.2	0.96
1969	929.9	846.2	0.91
1970	1367.0	1175.6	0.86
1971	1832.9	1503.0	0.82
1972	2778.3	2222.7	0.80
1973	4095.5	3071.6	0.75
1974	3468.5	2358.6	0.68
1975[b]	4530.5	2808.9	0.62
1976	5282.6	3116.7	0.59
1977	6058.5	3332.2	0.55
1978	6290.6	3208.2	0.51
1979	6660.8	3064.0	0.46
1980[b]	6677.8	2737.9	0.41

(a) Consumer price index measure used for calculation of constant dollars.
(b) In 1975 and 1978 Santa Ana is included in the aggregate; for the other years it is excluded and the total N is 74.

SOURCE Calculated from *City Government Finances*, 1964–80, in King, 1985a.

sion on the National Agenda for the Eighties 'emphasized that policies should promote national economic growth but should be neutral about where that growth took place' (Judd, 1984, p. 356). This translated into a shift away from targeting distressed or declining cities in urban policy. The shift was reinforced by the Carter Administration's growing concern in the late 1970s about reducing federal spending. Under the Reagan Administration the policy objective of reduced federal spending has been combined with a desire to extract the federal government from the close federal–city link that has developed since the 1930s. Nevertheless, under both the Carter and the Reagan Administrations, the federal government has continued to direct proportionally more funds toward the most distressed cities, in acknowledgement of their concentration of social problems and potential for public disorder. But the emphasis has shifted from the 1960s and 1970s: there is a preference for reliance on market forces in preference to state policy. Market forces are seen as the principal motors of reindustrialisation and a spatially sensitive urban policy runs the danger of conflicting with new patterns of economic activity. The natural unevenness (spatially and temporally) of such economic patterns is considered an acceptable price for aggregate economic growth. One consequence is that fiscal stress and relative poverty increased in a number of older industrial cities during the first half of the 1980s (Ganz, 1985).

We want to emphasise two summary points. First, it is apparent that the national state expanded its presence in cities during the 1930s and 1960s primarily in response to urban social and fiscal crises and their implications for public disorder. Second, in the context of American federalism, the result was to establish and reinforce direct national–local relations which bypassed the constitutional position of the American states. Strengthening these national initiatives were pressures from congressional representatives from affected cities, though in the 1930s legislators from urban areas were disproportionately outnumbered in Congress by those representing and favouring rural constituencies. In terms of the theoretical analysis, urban crisis increased the salience of cities to national officials because it threatened the maintenance of public order and the authority of the national state in urban populations. In the 1930s, and again in the 1960s, national Democratic administrations believed that those general interests, and their own electoral prospects, could best be enhanced by dramatically expanding federal assistance for general and special welfare purposes. One consequence of this expansion, alluded to in Chapter 2, is the degree to which cities in the United States have come to rely on federal funding in their municipal budgets (see Judd, 1984 and Fossett, 1983).

There is an additional dimension to the growth of national state interests in cities in the United States. This concerns the increasing intervention of the federal judiciary into urban affairs in a way largely supportive of federal interests, frequently reducing municipal autonomy from the national state (local autonomy Type II in our terms). An exemplar of this is the Fair Labor Standards Act (FLSA) of 1938 which prohibited local governments from making hourly wage payments at less than the rates fixed by Congress (upheld in *United States* v. *Darby* 321 US 100 [1941]). From this beginning, FLSA has been used as the basis for applying a wide range of federally formulated standards to sub-national governments. FLSA was again challenged in the courts following a 1974 congressional ruling that state governments should follow similar wage constraints to those of private employers: this extension was deemed unconstitutional in *National League of Cities* v. *Usery* 426 US 833 (1976). But more recently, and more profoundly, the congressional rights implied by FLSA have been judicially re-established in *Garcia* v. *San Antonio Metropolitan Transit Authority* 105 S. Ct. 1005, (1985): congressional guidelines regarding public employment must be adhered to by cities just as by federal authorities. One commentator concludes that the Garcia ruling *exempts* federalism from judicial review: 'in brief, if it is part of the constitutional plan that the constitutional boundaries of federalism are to be politically settled, rather than judicially maintained until altered by amendment, then the Court should, in decency, respect its assigned (non) role in such matters' (Van Alystne, 1985, p. 1724). Constitutional lawyers and experts have been deeply perturbed by the constitutional implications of the Garcia ruling: for our analysis, the key point is that it reinforces the power of federal government over states and municipalities, and thus gives some legal status to the federal–city connection. Federal judicial rulings have added to national constraints on the local state in many other areas as well: in public education (especially school desegregation), the provision and siting of public housing, and personnel decisions (especially regarding equal opportunities for women and minorities).

It is worth considering the extent to which this analysis of the evolution of federal–city relations and of federal urban policy in general converges with or differs from John Mollenkopf's (1983) major recent study of federal urban policy. The essential difference is that a state-centred analysis points to the relevance of a larger set of factors. Mollenkopf contends that 'the evolution of federal urban programs may best be understood as resulting from the competition among national political entrepreneurs to strengthen their political position by enacting new national programs which bolster their local constituencies' (p. 48). National Democratic political entrepreneurs saw and exploited a potential for urban support for their party: 'urban programs enabled Democrats to build national political power on a base of urban electoral majorities, and to sustain that influence over time through new nonparty organisational forms' (1983, p. 48). In our terms Mollenkopf's account concentrates on the short-term electoral interests of one party. He also interprets the Republican Party and Republican Administrations as adversarial forces, hostile to the urban-based constituencies on which the Democratic Party built its support. It was the successful election of Democratic administrations based on an urban electorate which accounts for the expanded federal role in municipalities: in such phases

> Democrats enacted urban programs in great surges. Particularly during the New Deal and the Great Society, but also during the Fair Deal and the Carter years, a mobilized urban electorate, a favorable congressional balance of power, local support, and, as time passed, advocacy from government agencies themselves led Democratic presidents to advocate and Congress to enact dramatic expansion of federal urban development programs. (1983, p. 49)

In our perspective greater attention should be given to factors which Mollenkopf addresses only in passing: the long-term interests of national officials in strengthening the state's authority and autonomy, the growth of a national administrative commitment to new urban programmes, the establishment of urban lobbying groups as part of an urban policy network, and the forging of close and durable links between national and local administrations, paralleled by complementary electoral ties. As federal–city relations evolved after the 1930s, bureaucratic routines and institutions were established by municipalities to process federal assistance. Particularly during the 1960s, as the range and complexity of federal grants expanded rapidly, cities were obliged to allocate personnel with specific responsibilities for this area: 'research indicates that those communities that have greater planning capacities tend to apply more often for federal grants' (Friedland and Wong, 1983, p. 220). From the experience of the 1930s and the failure of the states to provide adequate relief, city administrations began to gear themselves to lobbying in Washington for additional funding: the federal government was perceived as the most likely source of aid, rather than the state governments of which the cities were (and continue to be) constitutionally creatures. As Gelfand (1980) records, in the wake of the urban redevelopment and renewal programmes municipal leaders 'lobbied for a long shopping list of categorical aid programmes. As the epochal election of 1960 approached, local governments were demanding federal help with a forcefulness not seen since the darkest days of the Great Depression' (p. 36). And we have already noted the importance of urban lobbying groups in this context: 'the growth of direct federal involvement with urban problems stimulated a concomitant growth in the number, organizational quality, and spectrum of concern of interest groups impinging on federal urban policy', groups which provided a 'nucleus for an ever-expanding urban policy network' (Farkas, 1971, p. 34).

Institutionalisation of the federal–municipal linkage also occurred at the national level in a number of ways. The key elected officials in this process were the members of Congressional committees and subcommittees with responsibility for the various federal categorical and block grants, most of whom were committed to the maintenance and expansion of such programmes. The key national administrators were those who headed the new and expanded agencies created to administer the new federal–city connections. These included the National Housing Authority, set up in the 1930s and transformed in the mid-1960s into the Department of Housing and Urban Development (HUD); the Office of Economic Opportunity (OEO) (1964); and later the Law Enforcement Assistance Administration (LEAA) (1968). While the senior officials of agencies concerned with urban programmes are appointed by the White House and thus are likely to reflect the policy preferences of the current Administration, they and the agencies' senior career officials also have some programmatic commitments to maintaining specific federal–city links. These programmatic commitments are informed, in part, by proposals, ideas and options formulated and presented by the urban lobby: 'federal urban programs reflect well-structured consent among urban public interest lobbies and newly-formed or newly "urbanized" governmental institutions. Urban inter-governmental lobbying has entrenched the practice of the "third" level of government (cities) pressuring the "first" level (federal) and bypassing the "second" level (state)' (Farkas, 1971, pp. 234–5). Too little is known about the attitudes or policy-advocacy roles of senior officials in the federal system to substantiate this argument in detail. This lack of knowledge is arguably a consequence of the dominance of the pluralist paradigm in American political science, which traditionally views Congress and the White House as the key decision-making actors (see Krasner 1984).

The paucity of information about senior bureaucrats' policy preferences and actions is a general problem and not one specific to Mollenkopf's (1983) study. One useful source of relevant information is Button's (1978) study of federal policy responses to the riots of the 1960s: he interviewed senior federal officials in an effort to determine their perceptions of the urban turmoil of the 1960s and how those perceptions informed policy responses. Their policy preferences in response to the initial riots he characterises as a mix of 'liberal' and 'radical', and their agencies' responses were substantial. For example, the OEO's allocation of 'funds per poor family for the city of Los Angeles increased more than sixfold in the year following the Watts outburst' (Button, 1978, p. 31). This pattern of response was a general one: cities with riots in the 1962–66 period received increases in OEO funds on average 2.7 times greater than those received by non-riot cities. Under the Nixon Administration, however, this relationship reversed: cities with riots in 1967–68 received *less* new OEO funding than did non-riot cities. The interviews with officials also document the displacement of preferences for 'liberal' responses with a more 'conservative' interpretation of riot behaviour, though with equal concern for the restoration of public order: the context for all policy changes 'was the elite fear of disorder' (Button, 1978, p. 159). During and after the 1968 election Republican rhetoric decried policies of 'rewarding' riots and emphasised the maintenance of order – an objective pursued through the new LEAA, whose grants were designed to strengthen urban policing and improve community race relations. Button (1978) suggests that the Nixon rhetoric was mediated in part by senior administrators, amongst others: 'in reality Nixon officials (with pressure from Congress and liberal bureaucrats) not only maintained most of the new HUD and HEW programs, but substantially increased the funding of many of them' (p. 104). Whether national officials considered the black riots of the 1960s an effective means of achieving social change or not (there were differences across agencies in support for this view), public disorder was a stimulus for very substantial changes in state policy. Iris (1983) offers the important qualification that some of the programmatic expansions attributed to the riots had begun before the riots. Most of the literature, including Button's (1978) study, gives little attention to the impact of civil rights activities during the decade before the onset of the riots. These undoubtedly helped create a favourable national political climate for policies to ameliorate racial inequity (see, for example, Garrow, 1978). The riots served to accelerate the process of change, according to this interpretation, but the commitment to change pre-dated the 1960s. We would contend that the riots had an independent effect and that they particularly highlighted urban issues, many of which overlapped with racial ones.

To return to Mollenkopf (1983), we think that in focusing on electoral politics he has identified a critical source of the expanded federal role in cities – 'Roosevelt needed, and got, the administrative and political support of the large cities' (Farkas, 1971, p. 54) – but has neglected part of the stimulus for the initiatives taken. The Great Depression and 1960s were decades during which urban areas posed threats to the maintenance of public order and national authority in an unprecedented way. Presidential Administrations, Republican as well as Democratic, and senior administrators responded in full awareness of the threat. It is not clear that Mollenkopf's analysis takes sufficient account of this. His emphasis on the difference between Democratic and Republican policy preferences is compatible with our arguments: while all officials have common interests in the preservation of order and the state's authority, the specifics of policy toward those and other ends are shaped in conflicts among officials, elected and appointed. But what Mollenkopf does seriously underestimate, in contrast to our analysis, are the programmatic commitments of senior administrators to an expanded federal role in urban politics, as to other areas of the state's public policy. Once the direct federal–city link was established in the 1930s, the national state's interests in cities were institutionalised in a set of federal agencies with close links to municipal administrations. Paralleling them were political linkages between elected local and national officials, which also had their institutional expression in the establishment of congressional subcommittees concerned with urban issues. The existence of these institutionalised commitments to federal urban programmes provided centres of advocacy and defence within the national state against the sporadic efforts of some Presidents and conservative congressional coalitions who have sought to cut back the federal–city fiscal and policy connection.

Finally, what are the theoretical implications of our analysis of federal–city relations for the autonomy of the local state? For the most part, we have been discussing issues relevant to local state autonomy Type II: that is, the local state's autonomy from the national state. In the United States, this is obviously complicated by the presence of regional states which enjoy constitutional control of local governments. The development since of the 1930s of a direct federal–municipal link has made clear inroads into regional state influence upon cities, as we have noted above. But hand in hand with this has come greater national state influence upon municipalities through both expanded federal funding and federal (including judicial) constraints on local policy decisions. As the discussion in Chapter 2 indicated, increased federal funding does not necessarily result in a condition of fiscal dependence. However, the evidence of this chapter is that the evolution of federal–city relations has diminished local state autonomy Type II: to the extent that the national state has successfully pursued its interests in cities through its urban programmes then municipal autonomy from the federal government has been reduced. The major force offsetting this general propensity is the powerful urban lobby which has ensured that some positions and policies favourable to municipal autonomy have been incorporated into urban policy. Thus, the institutionalised federal–city relationship clearly includes elements representing both national and urban interests, which policy then reflects to some extent. But cities remain vulnerable to changes in federal policies: the federal–city connection means that changes at the national level can have profound implications for the local state. One recent example of this is the 1985 Gramm–Rudman budget amendment: in seeking substantial cuts in the federal budget, this amendment implied that local governments will have to increase their taxes to pick up the fall-off in federal funding. Thus, having reduced local state autonomy Type II (especially for those cities with weak local economies and thus little scope for local state autonomy Type I) the national state can place some municipalities in a still more vulnerable position by changing its funding policies.

The realisation of national state interests in municipalities: an empirical analysis of the determinants of federal aid to cities, 1960–80

We have interpreted the growth and institutionalisation of the federal government's commitment to cities since the 1930s as the consequence of the national state's protection of its primary interests in cities, following the arguments of Chapter 1. The evidence also illustrates the dynamics of the expansion of national presence as specified in Chapter 3: economic and distributional crises which threatened interests of the national state have twice led to ratchet-like increases in the scope of its direct responsibility for urban order and welfare. We now turn to an empirical analysis of the distribution of federal aid to some seventy large American cities between 1960 and 1980. The object is to assess hypotheses about the extent to which factors implied by the theory influenced the allocation of federal aid among cities. The essential question is whether cities whose problems should have been most salient to the national state in theory received the largest increases in federal funding in practice.

As documented above, federal aid to cities expanded enormously during the 1960s and 1970s (see Table 4.1 on p. 122). About three-quarters of all intergovernmental grants are allocated by legislative formula which take population and indicators of city needs into account (Hale and Palley, 1981, p. 79); none the less there are very substantial differences in per capita federal aid received by cities. Also, significant debate surrounds the selection of need indicators to be included in the specification of formulas. Further, formulas were much less significant in the 1960s than in the 1970s: in the former decade decisions by federal bureaucrats had a critical impact on the allocational patterns of federal aid across cities and these tended to be influenced by Democratic representatives (Friedland and Wong, 1983). Both Democratic representatives and bureaucrats shared a commitment to responding to urban crisis. Thus in the 1960s there was greater scope for elective and appointive state officials to influence directly the allocation of federal assistance to cities. In the 1970s the focus of attention shifted to the production of formulas in Congress which reduced the scope for input from appointive or bureaucratic state officials. Sbragia (1983) suggests the intensity of these congressional debates over formulas: 'because these formulas determine how much money, if any, each locality will receive the battles over which variables the formulas should incorporate continue to be among the most heated in Congress' (p. 17). She continues:

> Those formulas 'targeted' to help the most needy areas substantially more than others, rather than spreading money around the majority of congressional districts, often do not survive in Congress ... Compared to many nonformula-based programs, those based on formulas were not as focused on big declining northeastern and midwestern cities. (pp. 17 and 18)

Friedland and Wong (1983, p. 216) argue that with regard to CDBG funds the formula used 'tended to reward only those local governments that were growing rapidly ... The formula also gave much weight to poverty, a consideration that favored southern cities, which had higher levels of poverty than their

northern counterparts'. The authors give support to Mollenkopf's (1983) arguments about the importance of electoral
motivations: Johnson and Carter's grants programmes focused
on older, declining central cities while Nixon and Ford focused
on growing cities and suburbs. Each were responding to their
respective key electoral constituencies.

These are the contextual political and electoral factors
influencing the process by which decisions are taken about the
distribution of federal assistance to cities. There are clear
similarities between these contentions and Mollenkopf's
(1983) analysis reviewed earlier. However, the changing
political context of the allocation decisions, the shifting
parameters of the formulas used, the variation across different
programmes, and the short-run and long-run interests of
elective and appointive state managers collectively create a
distributional process of considerable complexity and include a
broad range of factors. Our state-centred perspective implies
that the allocation of federal aid to municipalities will be
significantly influenced by the national state's interests in cities
outlined in Chapters 1 and 2. It is now necessary to reformulate
them as testable hypotheses, and to discuss the city sample,
data sources, variables and methods used in assessing their
validity. Because this analysis is of a preliminary nature we are
unable to evaluate competing economy-centred hypotheses.
This reflects principally limitations in the availability of data
and appropriate indicators but should not diminish the
intrinsic value of the analysis reported here. After setting out
four hypotheses derived from our theoretical arguments we
report a set of bivariate correlations and multiple regressions.

*State-centred hypotheses about the distribution of central state assistance
across municipalities*

*HYPOTHESIS 1:   Central state aid is allocated across cities in order
to promote the short-run electoral prospects of national officials.*
Electoral considerations are among the short-term interests of
state managers discussed earlier. Concretely, in the American
context they are the interests of congressional representatives
and the President in optimising their own electoral prospects
and those of their national party. The existence of an 'electoral

business cycle' in which fiscal and monetary policies are used to enhance the Presidential party's electoral prospects is well documented at the national level (Tufte, 1978; Alt and Crystal, 1983; Hicks, 1984; Frey and Schneider, 1978). The universal acceptance of Keynesian deficit-spending from the mid-1950s to the mid-1970s freed the central state managers for a time from constraint by the level of revenues available. It is not unreasonable to expect that the geographic distribution of federal assistance across states and cities is affected by similar dynamics. Most of the expansion of urban aid in the 1960s and 1970s was funded by Democratically-controlled Congresses (see Mollenkopf, 1983; and Friedland and Wong, 1983), attuned to urban populations generally and increasingly to minority and organised-labour constituencies. We index these independent variables using measures of the minority percentages of each city's population; and the number of national union headquarters in each city. The latter is used as an indicator of organised labour's political salience since data on numbers of union members are not available on a city-by-city basis. We also take into account one partisan consideration not linked to any particular party: whether municipal government is directed by a manager or an elected mayor and council. The argument is that cities with mayor–council governments are likely to be more effective than managerial ones in using political connections with the national administrations to ensure that their cities are favoured in allocative formulas; and we would expect that the concomitance of Democratic city councils and Democratic congressional representation would have a positive effect on the size of central state funding.

HYPOTHESIS 2:   *Central state aid to cities is allocated in order to promote the programmatic objectives of appointive state officials.* It is an accepted fact in the literature on 'the growth of government' that higher-level bureaucrats seek to expand their resources and scope of authority (see Fiorina and Noll, 1977; and Niskanen, 1971). Something more than a narrow and short-term self-interest is at work, however: higher appointive state officials in each administrative entity usually share a strong sense of commitment to the programmes which give their unit its *raison d'être*. While these programmatic commitments vary among government agencies, we deduce from the overview of federal–city relations discussed above that there was a general consensus among federal administrators concerned with urban problems in the 1960s and 1970s that *cities should be assisted in response to their levels of economic, social and fiscal need.* We have cited evidence from Button's (1978) interviews with senior officials in the OEO and HUD in support of this argument. This objective converged with the interests of many elected officials (including Democratic Presidents) and, needless to say, with those of most municipal officials, but whereas congresspersons and mayors were particularly concerned with increasing the flow of federal funds to *their* constituencies and *their* cities, federal administrators were more likely to promote equitable solutions to the problems, as they defined and measured them, of all urban populations and municipal governments. And the predominant administrative approach, until revenue-sharing was introduced in 1972, was the project grant in which federal officials stimulated local state officials to define their needs, using federal guidelines, and then determined how much federal money to grant them (see Gelfand, 1980).

To the extent that the programmatic preferences of federal bureaucrats have prevailed, we would expect central funding to be distributed in proportion to indicators of urban need. Three basic sets of indicators of need have been identified by ' Cuciti (1978) (see also Ross and Greenfield, 1980; Nathan and Adams, 1976; and Bunce and Glickman, 1980): *social need,* which refers primarily to the needs of people in cities and is operationalised in terms of variables such as percentage unemployment, number of families below the poverty line, size of dependent population, extent of overcrowded housing, level of education and age of housing; *economic need,* composed of indicators of the health and vitality of the municipal economy such as changes in manufacturing employment, in per capita income levels and in unemployment; and *fiscal need,* which is concerned with the fiscal health of the city government or local state as revealed by measures such as long-term debt, revenues, deficits and size of property tax base. Fiscal need indicators have been particularly significant in the 1970s given the contracting revenue base of many cities. Indicators of each of these three dimensions of need – not limited to those cited by Cuciti (1978) – are used in the following analysis.

HYPOTHESIS 3: *Central state aid to cities is allocated in order to promote the common long-run interests of all state officials in the maintenance of public order and the central state's network of administrative control.* Beneath the sometimes-divergent electoral and programmatic interests of elected and appointed state officials is a common interest in the maintenance of public order and durable, effective institutions of decision-making and administration which underpin state authority. Since most people in advanced industrial societies live in cities, this means that the national state as well as municipalities will respond to increases in urban crime and collective political violence with policies designed to increase or restore social control. This is also in the interest of the regional states, but we have seen that in the 1930s many of them lacked the resources and political will to do much about it. Finally, the hypothesis implies greater national concern with the social, economic and fiscal well-being of cities which are centres of national and regional administration, not least because employees of the national state want congenial urban environments in which to work and live.

We test two different kinds of empirical implications of the argument for the distribution of federal grants to American cities. There is substantial evidence that cities with urban riots in 1964–68 received more funds and programmatic attention from the federal government than those which did not (see the discussion of Button (1978) above and the review of empirical studies in Gurr, 1980, pp. 268–80). Rising rates of serious crime also stimulated federal responses in the form of substantial grants through the Law Enforcement Assistance Administration to local police. The empirical test is whether there are significant correlations between per capita aid and increases in crime and collective disorder. Whereas these effects are likely to be transitory responses to temporary increase in disorder, we expect to find a more enduring relation between the administrative status of cities and aid. The measures used are state capital status (coded dichotomously) and employment in federal agencies as a percentage of total municipal employment.

HYPOTHESIS 4:   Central state aid to cities is allocated in order to promote economic growth to the relative neglect of municipal-level need. This hypothesis arguably owes more to neo-Marxist assumptions than to the state-centred perspective, in that the former interpret state policy as protecting capitalist interests by reflecting the objectives of dominant economic interests. Thus, Friedland's (1976, 1980 and 1983; Friedland and Wong, 1983) several studies of the distribution of urban aid across cities have emphasised the degree to which allocation is related to the presence of dominant economic interests in each city. There is, however, some support for this hypothesis within the pluralist intergovernmental relations literature: in his recent book, Peterson (1981) argues that all cities have a set of distinct interests which includes economic growth. He argues that all residents of a city share this objective. Accordingly, if Peterson's proposition is accurate, municipal government officials would lobby the central state to be responsive to potential economic growth. Within the state-centred perspective we have noted that the central state has assumed the responsibility for promoting developmental policies because, in part, it needs to ensure its supply of revenues. The alternative rationales for the central state's allocation of aid to prospering cities make interpretations of empirical patterns somewhat complicated.

We have three independent variables to test this hypothesis. These are the number of corporate headquarters in a city; the value added by manufacturing in each city per capita; and the total number of new housing permits issued in each city per capita. The last two are indicators of economic activity and growth while the first indicator represents the extent of capitalist economic interests in a city.

These are the four guiding hypotheses about the allocation of federal aid across cities in the United States. They are tested with data on the seventy-four largest US cities, excluding Washington DC. A summary list of the indicators used is given in Table 4.2. Details of the city sample, indicators, data sources and problems with those sources are provided in the Appendix on p. 209.

The distribution of central state aid to cities, bivariate analysis

The main purpose of correlational analysis is to establish the degree of association between the dependent variable of interest (federal aid per capita to cities) and the indicators of city-level independent variables specified in the hypotheses. Of course, bivariate analysis does not allow definitive conclusions about causality to be asserted but it does highlight statistically significant associations indicative of general patterns.

One potential source of bias in the analysis is the inclusion of some of the capital cities of the fifty states, fifteen of which have populations greater than 200 000. Since some categories of federal aid are recorded as received by the state capital city, even though it is later distributed to other cities within the state, this can distort the results by inflating the real amount of per capita aid received by these cities and understating the amount recorded by non-capital cities. We compared correlation and regression results from two analyses, one of which included all cities and the other excluded the state capitals. The differences were slight. Another potential source of distortion in the sample of cities is the inclusion of Washington DC, whose unique status as both national capital (and consequently home of many federal employees) and as a fiscal dependent of the federal government gives it very high values on indicators of administrative salience and federal aid. We compared results from two analyses, one of which included all cities and a second from which Washington was excluded. The results differed substantially. Accordingly, all the results reported below refer to the all-city sample which includes the state capitals but excludes the national capital. Because of missing data for some cities on some variables the n of cases in a particular bivariate correlation is sometimes less than the maximum of 74, as indicated in Tables 4.2 and 4.3.

TABLE 4.2 *Bivariate correlates of per capita federal aid to large cities in 1970 (excluding Washington DC)*

Characteristics of cities	1970	Percentage change 1960–70
Hypothesis 1: Electoral interests		
Percentage population black	.09	.14 (71)
Percentage population other minorities	−.01	.00 (71)
National union headquarters	.06	−.18[a](71)
Mayor–council form of government	−.07 (56)	—
Hypothesis 2: Programmatic objectives		
1. Social needs		
Percentage of population dependent (18, 65)	−.14	.03 (71)
Percentage of families below poverty line	−.04	.20[b]
Female headed households per capita	.24[b]	—
Percentage of housing stock pre-1940 in 1970	.34[b]	.19[a]
Percentage of population with < 5 yrs education	−.01	−.01
Percentage of population with 4 yrs + high school	−.16[a]	−.08
Percentage of population with 4 yrs college	−.17[a]	−.09 (69)
2. Economic needs		
Per capita money income	.02	−.09
Percentage of workforce unemployed	.29[b]	−.36[c](71)
Percentage employment in manufacturing	.10	−.09
Employment in manufacturing per capita	.08	−.32[b]
Percentage employment in wholesale/retail	−.20[b]	−.07
Employment in wholesale/retail per capita	−.19[a]	−.12
Total population	.02	
Total civilian employment per capita	.00	−.20[a]

3. Fiscal needs		
City long-term debt per capita	−.03	.02 (69)
City short-term debt per capita	.24[b](51)	−.08 (51)
Total city debt per capita	.11	.16[a](69)
City property taxes per capita	.27[b]	.26[b]
Total city revenues per capita	.43[c]	.51
Total city expenditures per capita	.43[c]	.36[c] (69)
City capital outlay per capita	.27[b]	—

Hypothesis 3: Public order and administrative control

Violent crime per capita	.07	.11 (69)
Property crime per capita	.13	.29[b](69)
Racial rioting 1963–69		
Arrests per capita	.17[a]	—
Days of rioting per capita	.12	—
Deaths per capita	.00	—
State capital	.16[a]	—
Federal employment per 1000	.10	—
Federal employment as a percentage of total employment	.10	—

Hypothesis 4: Economic interests

Corporate headquarters	.02	−.08 (71)
Value added by manufacturing per capita	.11	.09 (71)
Number of new housing permits issued per capita	—	—
Control for region, Sunbelt = 1	**.29[b]**	

NOTE: For 1970 the number of cities included in the analysis is 71 unless otherwise indicated; for 1960–70, $n = 70$.

(a) Significance .10
(b) Significance .05
(c) Significance .01

TABLE 4.3 *Bivariate correlates of per capita federal aid to large cities in 1980 (excluding Washington DC)*

Characteristics of cities	1980	Percentage change	
		1960–80	1970–80
Hypothesis 1: Electoral interests			
Percentage population black	.42[c]	.32[b]	.49[c](72)
Percentage population other minorities	.14	−.02	.23[b](72)
National union headquarters	.23[b]	−.15 (74)	−.09
Mayor–council form of government	.36[c]	—	—
Hypothesis 2: Programmatic objectives			
(a) Social need			
Percentage of population dependent (18, 65)	−.18[a](72)	.31[b](72)	.24[b](72)
Percentage of families below the poverty line	.24[b]	.05	.15
Female headed households per capita	.58[c]	—	.48[c]
Percentage of housing stock pre-1940 in 1970	.50[c]	—	—
Percentage of population with < 5 yrs education	−.05	−.07	−.39[c]
Percentage of population with 4 yrs high school	−.34[b]	.10 (73)	.31[b]
Percentage of population with 4 yrs college	−.15 (73)	.01 (72)	−.06 (73)
(b) Economic need			
Per capita money income	−.18[a](72)	−.20[b](71)	−.26[b](72)
Percentage of workforce unemployed	.51[c]	.45[c]	.46[c]
Percentage employment in manufacturing	.05	−.39[c]	−.41[c]
Employment in manufacturing per capita	−.06	−.44[c]	−.39[c]
Percentage employment in wholesale/retail	−.33[b]	−.21[b]	—
Employment in wholesale/retail per capita	−.36[c]	—	−.15[a]
Total population	.12	−.51[c]	.47[c]
Total civilian employment per capita	.12	.09 (72)	.08 (72)

(c) Fiscal need			
City long-term debt per capita	.06 (73)	.06 (73)	.02 (73)
City short-term debt per capita	.11 (45)	—	—
Total city debt per capita	.08 (73)	.06 (71)	−.01 (72)
City property taxes per capita	.35[c]	.34[b]	.32[b]
Total city revenues per capita	.54[c]	.56[c]	.58[c]
Total city expenditures per capita	.48[c]	.48[c]	.48[c]
City capital outlay per capita	.45[c]	—	.18[a]
Hypothesis 3: Public order and administrative control			
Violent crime per capita	.34[b](72)	.31[b](72)	.01 (73)
Property crime per capita	.07	—	−.17[a](73)
Racial rioting 1963–69			
Arrests per capita	.45[c]	—	—
Days of rioting per capita	.20[b]	—	—
Deaths per capita	.13	—	—
State capital	−.03	—	—
Federal employment per 1000	.11 (71)	—	.02 (71)
Federal employment as a percentage of civilian employment	.00	—	—
Hypothesis 4: Economic interests			
Corporate headquarters	.14	−.17[a](74)	−.18[a]
Value added by manufacturing per capita (n = 72)	.27[b]	−.26[b]	−.30[b]
Number of new housing permits issued per capita	−.52[c]	—	—
Control for region, Sunbelt = 1	**.27[b]**	—	—

NOTE: Unless otherwise indicated the sample sizes for the three periods are: 1980 = 74, 1960–80 = 73, and 1970–80 = 74.

(a) Significance .10
(b) Significance .05
(c) Significance .01

Five sets of coefficients are reported in Tables 4.2 and 4.3 for each independent variable (except for those periods where data was missing). The first column in each table reports simultaneous correlations between the city traits, 1970 values correlated with per capita federal aid in 1970 and 1980 values correlated with 1980 aid. To the extent that the coefficients are similarly strong and significant in both years, we infer that the trait in question has a persisting 'structural' relationship with the central state's political and administrative interests and fiscal decisions. The other coefficients displayed report the relationships of change in each city characteristic and the distribution of per capita federal aid: 1960–70 change with 1970 per capita federal aid in Table 4.2 and 1960–80, 1970–80 change with 1980 per capita federal aid in Table 4.3. If these coefficients are significant, we interpret them as evidence for dynamic relationships: as these traits of cities change, the central state adjusts its patterns of response. The bivariate analysis thus allows both a cross-sectional picture in 1970 and 1980 and some sense of the effect of changes in the municipal-level conditions on the distributional patterns at these two time-points.

Electoral considerations (Hypothesis 1) significantly affect the distribution of federal aid in 1980, in particular the relative size of the black population and the mayor–council form of municipal government. The central state does not appear to be responsive to the size of other minorities, who are principally Hispanics. They do not yet have effective national organisations or political clout in Washington, though the significant effects of the 1970–80 change in this variable suggests that the future may be different. Mayor–council governments, present in thirty-nine of the seventy-four cities, evidently are significantly more effective in attracting federal aid than are city–manager governments.

Most indicators of need (Hypothesis 2) are correlated in the predicted direction with federal aid per capita; a few are anomalous. Examining social need first, a key indicator at both timepoints is the total number of female-headed households per capita, which correlated 0.24[b] with aid in 1970 and 0.58[c] in 1980. That is, the greater the number of female-headed households, the more federal aid per capita a city receives. We discussed earlier the issue of distributional formulas used in federal aid allocation, many of which incorporate this indicator of social need, a practice which complicates interpretation here. In addition, the indicator of female-headed households correlates highly with the number of families below the poverty line, both of which groups are concentrated in cities: thus the 'people over places' priority (Edel in Glickman, 1980) of much central state expenditure is probably being reflected in these associations. On the other hand, female-headed households is a relatively new category in the US census (data were not collected prior to 1970) and in combination with family poverty constitutes an effective measure of urban social deprivation. The three indicators of educational attainment are all associated in the expected negative direction (the lower the average educational level the more federal aid per capita a city receives) in 1970 and 1980 while the long-term percentage changes in the population with less than five years' education is significantly related to aid at the 0.01 level. The coefficients for percentage families below the poverty level and percentage of dependent population in 1970 are negative, which is contrary to the expected direction of these relationships. However, both associations are quite weak. Moreover, when the percentage change in these variables 1960–70 is correlated with 1980 federal aid per capita, the direction of association is positive and, for poverty families, it is statistically significant at the 0.05 level. Lastly, it can be observed that there is a strong positive association between the percentage of the housing stock built before 1940 (as estimated in 1970) and the amount of federal aid received in both 1970 and 1980.

The economic need indicators (Hypothesis 2) also yield results which are plausible and internally consistent. Federal grants per capita increase when unemployment rises, when per capita income declines, and especially as total population declines. (Note that there is no structural relation between urban size *per se* and per capita aid, nor would we expect one; but population *decline* coincides with a variety of socioeconomic and fiscal stress indicators which intensify the need for federal money.) The sectoral employment variables show, not surprisingly, that less aid goes to cities with large and growing wholesale and retail sectors; and to cities with growing manufacturing employment. These are for the most part the economically-thriving Sunbelt cities. The principal unexpected finding is the lack of a statistically significant negative association between employment in manufacturing and federal aid per capita in 1970 or 1980, but the coefficients for the percentage changes in manufacturing employment for all three periods are all statistically significant and in the predicted negative direction of association. These associations are particularly strong where 1980 federal aid is the dependent variable, which implies that the long-term structural shifts in manufacturing employment are being reflected in the distributional patterns of federal urban aid.

The associations for the most common measures of fiscal need (Hypothesis 2) are generally disappointing. Thus, neither in 1970 nor 1980 do city debt, long-term debt or short-term debt (in 1980) correlate significantly with federal aid per capita received, although the direction of association of the weak correlation coefficients is generally as expected. The main exception to this is short-term debt in 1970, which is statistically significant in a positive direction. Measures of local fiscal effort, however, show strong and consistent patterns of association: high-taxing, big-spending municipal governments received the greatest aid. Where revenues are concerned the relation is in part reciprocal. In general, however, high-tax, high-revenue cities tend to be those characterised by the syndrome of economic decline, rising social need, and falling population – conditions to which the federal government responds for reinforcing political and programmatic reasons.

Some indicators of public order and administrative salience are significantly related to federal aid, but the general pattern of support for Hypothesis 3 is weaker than for the first two hypotheses. The 'public order' arguments are generally confirmed: high and rising rates of violent crime (but not property crime) lead to increased aid. There are also enduring effects of the ghetto riots and rebellions of the 1960s on the level of federal aid, effects which were considerably stronger in 1980 than a decade earlier. It seems that the scope of rioting (as measured by arrests and days of rioting) had stronger effects than its intensity (as measured by deaths). These findings also raise problems of multiple causality: the magnitudes of violent crime and rioting have tended to be higher in some northern cities which have larger black populations and high levels of need. It is entirely consistent with our theoretical analysis, and the history of the evolution of national urban policy, that the coincidences of poverty, disorder and urban decay in the 1960s sharply increased the national state's interest in and aid for declining cities. But it makes it very difficult to isolate the effects of any one analytic category of conditions in bivariate analysis.

The measures of cities' administrative salience for the central state have very weak effects on federal aid. The state capital effect disappears entirely between 1970 and 1980, probably because the 1970 data were inflated by pass-through grants which later were replaced by direct revenue-sharing to cities. The statistical effects of federal employment levels may be so small because of long-standing national policy to distribute regional federal offices widely rather than concentrate them in a few key cities. The analyses for 1970 and 1980 include a dichotomous Sunbelt–Frostbelt control variable, with Frostbelt cities coded 1. The significantly positive correlations indicate that such cities received more aid, no doubt for a variety of reasons: greater social and economic need, greater political influence in Congress, and Presidential support from Republican incumbents.

Turning to Hypothesis 4, we find virtually no evidence that the growth potential of the private economy attracts more aggregate federal aid. The presence of corporate headquarters in a city has a very slight positive association with federal aid per capita in 1970 and although the association is somewhat stronger in 1980 it is not statistically significant. With regard to changes in corporate headquarters the direction of association is negative: departures of corporate headquarters are associated with *increased* federal aid, a finding consistent with 'economic need' explanations of the distribution of federal aid but inconsistent with the 'economic growth' hypothesis. For the other two indicators the associations with 1980 aid are quite strong but not in ways that support the basic argument. In 1980 there is a significantly *negative* correlation between the number of new housing permits issued (an indicator of level of construction, a key growth measure) and federal aid per capita.

The value added by manufacturing in a city does correlate positively with aid in both 1970 and 1980, but this is due mainly to the fact that manufacturing is concentrated in the declining old industrial cities, which are high on our other dimensions of salience. This interpretation is confirmed by the fact that 1960–80 and 1970–80 percentage changes in manufacturing value added are correlated negatively with federal aid: cities where manufacturing is in decline get more aid, those where it is growing get less. Thus we have some weak supportive evidence for Friedland's (1983) argument that the concentration of corporate power attacts more federal aid, but no evidence that the allocation of federal aid favours cities with a growing private sector.

Multivariate analysis

It is apparent from Table 4.4 that a relatively small number of city-level independent variables remain significant in the

TABLE 4.4   *Composite models of the determinants of federal aid to large cities in 1970 and 1980*

Characteristics of cities	Beta	F
Dependent variable: Federal aid per capita, 1970		
Percentage of workforce unemployed	.37	3.23[c]
Control for region, Sunbelt = 1	.29	2.17[b]
Federal employment per 1000	.14	1.23[a]
Property taxes per capita	.15	1.18
Constant	**.0201**	
$R^2 = .22$ $\bar{R}^2 = .18$ $n = 74$		
Dependent variable: federal aid per capita, 1980		
Percentage taxes per capita	.31	2.96[c]
Percentage of workforce unemployed	.29	2.58[b]
Mayor–council form of government	.20	1.80[a]
Federal employment per 1000	.11	1.08
Constant	**.0487**	
$R^2 = .31$ $\bar{R}^2 = .27$ $n = 74$		

(a)   Significance .10
(b)   Significance .05
(c)   Significance .01

context of a multivariate model. While several other variables (notably violent crime per capita, corporate headquarters, state capital status and non-black minorities) were very close to being included in the final regression they did not meet the stipulated F-value criterion (see Appendix, p. 209). Several composite indicators were constructed (for example, the social need measures were combined) but these also failed to acquire the requisite *F*-value for retention in the regression equations. It is also apparent that the final equations do not explain more than a third of the variance: that is, the variables found to be relevant as predictors of the distribution of federal aid per capita across cities over 200 000 in 1970 and 1980 still account for only a comparatively small proportion of the inequalities. Statistically, this is the result of strong covariance among the independent variables; substantively, it is a reflection of the coincidence, mentioned above, of high levels of need and political and administrative salience in the same set of cities – mainly the declining old industrial cities in the north-east and mid-west.

As Table 4.4 indicates, in 1970 the most powerful predictor to urban aid allocation is percentage of the municipal workforce employed, a finding consistent with the correlational results presented earlier in the chapter. Together with the control variable for region and city property taxes per capita, these are all need-based measures deriving from Hypothesis 2 concerning the programmatic objectives of the central state. The same need-based measures of percentage of workforce unemployed and property taxes per capita remain important in 1980, though the control variable for region has dropped out.

The remaining variables in each equation represent more clearly the political and administrative ties of cities to the national state. Although federal employment had weak bivariate relations with aid in Tables 4.2 and 4.3 it proves to contribute significantly to both reduced equations. One of the variables related to the electoral considerations of national officials – mayor–council municipal governments – is retained in the equation for 1980 with a statistically significant *F*-value.

The regression estimations reported in Table 4.4 for 1970 and 1980 give qualified support to some of our state-centred arguments. While municipal-level need appears to be the most substantial determinant of federal aid allocations, other variables which reflect the electoral and power interests of the central state have significant effects on these allocational patterns. Thus the arguments developed in this study about the state's interests in cities as a determinant of aid allocation have been given modest support.

Conclusion

This chapter has reviewed qualitatively the evolution of federal–city relations in the United States since the 1930s and reports initial empirical tests of some arguments about how the national government allocated aid across municipalities during the 1960–80 period. Both exercises have demonstrated, in quite different ways, how the significant increases in aid to cities have reflected the urban interests of the national state. As such, they provide substantive referents for our theoretical propositions about state–city relations and state interests in cities developed in the first three chapters.

As Table 4.1 illustrates, federal aid to cities peaked in 1978 under the Carter Presidency: since then it has decreased each year, a trend accelerated under the Reagan Administration which, like the Thatcher Government, has sought to retrench the public sector and to maximise market relations. One important victim of these Reagan policies to date has been general revenue sharing whose share of federal outlays has fallen significantly. More generally, federal grants-in-aid to states and local governments have been cut by the Reagan Administration. Overall, the dramatic reductions in all areas of government activity anticipated under the Reagan Administration have not yet materialised, though inroads have been made into non-defence public expenditure from which the cities have not been excluded. For the future, a great deal hinges upon the Gramm–Rudman amendment. If this is held to be constitutional then whole areas of federal spending exempted from earlier cuts, such as urban aid, transportation, health spending and housing and agriculture spending, will be very vulnerable. This will reduce even further the federal assistance provided to municipalities, though elected officials of the national state will have to consider the consequences for their constituencies carefully. If Gramm–Rudman is ruled unconstitutional, we would expect congressional members with urban interests actively to oppose further substantial cuts in federal aid, though the trend initiated by Reagan toward further cuts will persist to some extent. Either way, the consequences for the fiscal health of some cities will be considerable: cuts of the Gramm–Rudman proportion will force many of the economically weaker cities to retrench public services severely (especially since many will be unable to raise additional revenues through new taxes), while those municipalities (for example, in some southern states) with buoyant economies which have accumulated large debts to finance new services may also feel fiscally strained; this latter trend can only be accentuated by the continuing decline in world oil prices. Even if the Reagan Administration's cuts are confined to a slow, steady withdrawal of federal funds to cities the cumulative effect for weaker urban economies will be serious.

Thus, the fiscal health of cities is far from certain and this has implications for the actions of the national state as we have argued in this and the preceding chapters. The historical and empirical evidence we have marshalled in this chapter suggests that if these pressures do result in urban crisis which affects the national state's interests, then the federal government will be forced to undertake another step-level increase in federal commitments to municipalities, as in the 1930s and 1960s. The local–national political links established during these two decades will also encourage such a response, as they did in the 1960s.

Chapter 5

Urban Decline and the Politicisation of Central–Local Relations in Great Britain

Introduction

The theoretical arguments developed in Chapters 1 and 2 are intended to be applicable to advanced industrial societies. Chapters 3 and 4 have considered the theoretical propositions in relation to the political consequences of urban decline and the evolution of federal–city relations in the United States. This chapter outlines the incidence and extent of urban decline in another advanced industrial society, Great Britain, as it compares with the United States; and reviews the policies pursued by the central state to alleviate the economic and social consequences associated with declining cities. This is followed by a detailed discussion of the development of municipal and local governmental structures in Britain which sets the context for an analysis of the policies toward local authorities followed by the Thatcher Government since 1979. Briefly, these policies aim at increasing centralisation in the British state by reducing local discretion over budgetary allocations and by restructuring local government. Particular attention is paid to the experience of London, where the challenges of urban change are compounded by the abolition (from 1 April 1986) of the Greater London Council (GLC), the city's key representative and administrative body.

The theoretical backdrop to the analysis in this chapter is primarily the issue of local state autonomy and what it implies about the local state's capacity to respond to the stresses of urban decline. Figure 2.1 on p. 69 outlined the general interactions between the two dimensions of municipal auton-

150

omy: autonomy from local economic and social forces, and from the central state. We noted that decline in a local state's urban economy not only reduced local autonomy Type I (by reducing the local revenue base) but also tended to reduce local autonomy from the central state (Type II) by increasing its fiscal dependence on the latter; interpretations disagree as to whether increased central funding necessarily implies local dependency. The main point is that the shifting patterns of socioeconomic activity in advanced industrial societies have a significant impact on the demand for urban services and on the availability of resources to provide them. This limits the local state's capacity to pursue its interests and brings it into potential conflict with the national state over the terms on which increased national assistance is to be provided. The local state may be forced to cut back on essential services, or to abandon programmes of special assistance (or not so special, as in the case of the Liverpool city council's housing programme) because they conflict with centrally formulated policy objectives which the national state is prepared to pursue at the expense of meeting urban needs. Increased central control is likely also to limit the range of policy options the local state can follow in efforts to revitalise the urban economy. These possibilities are not, of course, mutually exclusive. They are likely to be concomitant when both the programmatic goals and ideological preferences of central and local officials diverge as sharply as they do in parts of contemporary Britain. This translates into recurring conflicts between the central and local state in which the central state ultimately and immediately has the upper hand: it can resolve them by using its legal and fiscal powers to reduce the local state's capacity to swim against the tide of national policy. While this kind of conflict is not unique to the Thatcher Government, it has certainly intensified during this Government's tenure in office.

These theoretical and empirical issues are explored throughout this chapter. First we examine one key local condition affecting the first type of local state autonomy identified in Chapter 2: the condition of the urban economy and the local state's relationship with it. In Chapter 2 we argued that private economic interests could constrain the local state, thus limiting its autonomy, either by dominating the policy process or by restricting the resources available to the municipality. The latter is addressed in the following section: that is, we examine the shifting economic base of contemporary urban areas. This is not to assume that simply because an urban economy is relatively buoyant the local state is autonomous from it; rather, without a sound economic base the latter issue does not even arise. The second section of this chapter discusses the limits of the local state's autonomy from the central state.

Local state autonomy Type I: urban decline and the policy responses of the central state

Urban decline

Chapter 3 has documented the incidence and regional patterns of urban decline in the United States over the last three decades. Many of the same characteristics of urban malaise and economic stagnation that were common to declining urban areas in the United States have their counterparts in Great Britain. A principal difference between the two countries, however, is the central role of long-term and structural economic decline in Britain which as yet shows little sign of abating. This is much less the case for the American economy in the mid-1980s where, if there is not yet uniform national recovery, there is certainly evidence of healthy regional growth. Nevertheless, considerable similarities remain between the two countries in terms of urban economic and demographic trends. Hall (1981) notes that 'down to the mid-1970s only the United States truly compared with Britain in the range and depth of its inner city "problems"' (p. 6). And Young and Mills (1982) observe that 'inter-regional shifts in both population and employment are as marked in Britain as they are in the United States when allowance is made for a more depressed and compact space economy' (p. 82).

The extent of urban decline in Britain over the last few decades has been substantial: population has declined in all the major conurbations and in Greater London: the latter's population declined by 472 000 between 1971 and 1977 (Young and Mills, 1982). During the same period Merseyside lost

92 000 (Inner Liverpool declined from 700 000 in the 1920s to 300 000 by the end of the 1970s) and Greater Manchester lost 60 000. Offsetting the decline of large cities has been pronounced population and economic growth in smaller cities and towns located in the south and on the south-west and east coasts, such as Swindon, Oxford, Cambridge, Ipswich, Norwich and Leicester (Young and Mills, 1982, p. 83). Within the major conurbations, suburbs have gained substantially at the expense of the central cities, as in the United States. Fothergill and Gudgin (1982) summarise the general British pattern of the last few decades: 'Britain's inner cities are experiencing a rapid loss of manufacturing jobs while small towns and rural areas are quite successful in retaining and expanding their manufacturing base. As a general rule, the larger and more industrial a settlement the faster its decline' (p. 8). There are, of course, exceptions to this general pattern and there is a dominant *regional* element to these trends: broadly, toward the south of Britain away from the old industrialised north. However, the shifting nature of manufacturing production and telecommunications have rendered cities far less vital sites of industrial concentration, and this includes non-industrial urban areas. Thus, in Bristol – a frequently cited example of relative municipal economic success – unemployment is below the national average but disproportionately male: 'total employment in the decade to 1981 fell by a mere 0.8 per cent, but underlying this was a striking difference between the fall in male employment of some 16,000 and its partial offsetting through a growth in female employment of some 13,000' (ERSC, 1985, p. 15). Most of the increase in employment in Bristol has been in services (for example, insurance, banking and finance) while decline has occurred in manufacturing employment which very much mirrors national trends. Thus the factors and trends constituting urban decline in Britain are complex: while a general pattern of demographic and manufacturing decline in old industrial cities and growth in smaller cities and some rural areas can be identified, employment patterns can be deceptive. It is also the case that the shifting nature of global economic activity has profound consequences for the role and functions of cities; not surprisingly, this translates into a very unstable period of economic change, the

full consequences (in general and for cities) of which are not yet entirely clear. Thus, while urban decline in Britain has been accompanied by substantial growth in new and free-standing towns, the nature of economic activity in the 1980s and 1990s appears to be less dependent on cities as industrial centres (see Rees and Lambert, 1985, ch. 6).

While urban decline (the loss of population and manufacturing jobs) has been significant in Britain, the resulting inner city decay does not match the worst American cases (with a few exceptions such as Liverpool). There are important parallels in urban social problems between the two countries but in terms of sheer physical decay American cities seem to be exceptionally blighted, as indicated both by social science reports and as represented in fiction such as Saul Bellow's portrait of Chicago in *The Dean's December*. That said, the recent Church of England (1985) report *Faith in the City* depicts a grim picture of life in urban priority areas (UPAs), and one reminiscent of American experience

> to describe UPAs is to write of squalor and dilapidation. Grey walls, littered streets, boarded-up windows, graffiti, demolition and debris are the drearily standard features of the districts and parishes with which we are concerned ... One of the most obvious features of the UPAs is their physical dilapidation as measured by housing conditions ... The dwellings in the inner cities are older than elsewhere. Roughly one-quarter of England's houses were built before 1919, but the proportion in the inner areas ranged from 40 to 60 per cent in 1977. (p.18)

Such a characterisation is echoed by Harrison (1983): in the inner city are 'concentrated the worst housing, the highest unemployment, the greatest density of poor people [and] the highest crime rates'. (p. 21)

As a consequence of this economic, social and physical decay the inner areas of the major British cities have suffered disproportionate hardship, some of which underlay the 1981 summer riots (see below). Unemployment is disproportionately concentrated in the inner cities, as traditional manufacturing sources of work either close or relocate: 'declines [in employment] affected progressively more and more – though not all – of the major cities ... Conversely, jobs in new and expanding towns grew rapidly' (Kennett and Hall, 1981, p. 33). During the decade of the 1960s London lost '243,000 jobs, inner Manchester 84,000, inner Glasgow close to 60,000, inner Liverpool 34,000. During the 1970s this loss accelerated: London alone lost 350,000 jobs between 1971 and 1979' (Hall, 1981, p. 1). Moreover, the migration from the large cities is composed primarily of the more highly skilled workers, leaving behind a residue of unskilled or semi-skilled workers as well as minority groups and other deprived people. Although new service industries have expanded in some cities (for example, insurance, banking and finance) they have 'failed to compensate for the decline in manufacturing ones and, further, the service increase took place at the higher managerial levels, while the more routine clerical jobs have also been contracting' (Kennett and Hall, 1981, p. 34). A recent study (ESRC, 1985) provides additional information on these main trends: 'one million manufacturing jobs were lost in inner cities between 1951 and 1981 and a further one million from outer areas of conurbations and from free-standing cities' (p. 8). In inner cities there was a 36.8 per cent drop in manufacturing employment alone between 1971 and 1981 and a 32.6 per cent drop in the outer cities. Thus the last decade has seen no easing of the long-term decline in employment prospects for urban residents (see also Church of England, 1986; Fothergill and Gudgin, 1982). Table 5.1 summarises employment trends in inner cities by sector.

Quite clearly, primary and manufacturing employment has declined dramatically in inner cities while private and public service employment has expanded too little to compensate for this loss. During the 1970s inner cities were not the only areas to lose manufacturing employment but their loss was greater than was that of outer cities (−32.6), free standing cities (−28.6) and small towns and rural areas (−17.2) (ESRC, 1985); these latter also gained relatively more jobs in private and public services than accrued to inner cities.

The dynamics of urban decline in Britain thus parallel those in the United States: demographic decentralisation, a loss of manufacturing jobs and economic stagnation. While the

TABLE 5.1   *Employment decline in the inner cities by sector (1951 =*
100)

Sectors	1951	1961	1966	1971	1976
Primary	100	91	78	58	50
Manufacturing	100	92	80	68	52
Private services	100	111	108	94	88
Public services	100	101	102	103	106

The inner areas are those of London, Birmingham, Manchester,
Liverpool, Tyneside and Clydeside.

SOURCE Cambridge Economic Policy Group, *Cambridge Economic
Policy Review No. 8* (Aldershot: Gower, 1982) p. 42.

experience of each declining city is unique, certain general
factors are common to all, including the effect of market forces,
the impact of public policies and the internationalisation of
capital in the post-1945 global economy (see Chapter 2).
Young and Mills (1982) emphasise disinvestment and plant
closures: 'within the web of dimly understood urban economic
influences the rate of births and deaths in the manufacturing
sector, changing locational preferences for manufacturing
plant, and changes in corporate structure have made the most
important contribution to the "deindustrialisation" of cities'
(pp. 86–7). The locational preferences of manufacturing and
new technology industries have shifted away from the older
urban cores to the suburbs, smaller free-standing cities, and
even to rural areas. New firms, except for small ones, now
establish themselves outside the traditional inner city areas:

> industrial decision-makers are eager to invest in fringe or
> non-metropolitan locations ... Since it is the growing firm
> which first encounters the 'ceilings to growth' imposed by
> an urban location, the industrial cities have in effect
> exported their growth potential to fringe or non-urban
> locations, leading to a progressive worsening of the cities'
> own competitive position. (Young and Mills, 1982, p. 89).

Fothergill and Gudgin (1982) support this view: firms do not
expand 'because the cramped sites and premises in urban areas

do not meet the requirements of modern industry for increased floorspace' (p. 8). Thus many of the old industrial municipalities have watched their urban economy steadily erode. The local state is then caught in a vice between growing needs for compensatory services and declining locally-derived revenues; in our terms, the weakened urban economic base means that the potential for the local state to exercise autonomy from local socioeconomic forces (Type I autonomy) is reduced. A weakened or non-productive urban economy largely negates efforts by the local state to manage social and economic change.

The regional planning policies of the central state have contributed, to a certain extent, to the general trends of de-industrialisation and physical decay in old industrial cities: 'all over Britain, in prosperous and poor regions alike, the city centres went on declining. Planned "new towns" were subsidised, the unplanned – but once vital – old cities left to wither away' (*The Economist*, 1982, p. 4; see also Hall, 1976, ch. 7; and OECD, 1983, vol. 2). Insufficient finances and incentives were given to municipal authorities to modernise the old urban infrastructure until they were too far decayed: 'the Victorian multi-storey building is often unable to accommodate activities which flourish in the modern, single-storey spacious factory' (Young and Mills, 1982, p. 89; see also Fothergill and Gudgin, 1982). In addition, some local authorities in the older industrial cities believe that the central government has deliberately fostered growth in the south-east at their expense. The example of Derby, a small industrial city in the East Midlands, is illustrative: 'as seen from Derby, the central Government, based in the southeast, sees to it that the southeast gets better hospitals, better roads, better arts facilities than the Midlands. Derby's new hospital, under discussion since 1962, is only now approaching completion' (*New York Times*, 1985); this last probably reflects the post-1976 drive to equalise public expenditure on health care across England and Wales. Since the end of the 1960s the central state has pursued an urban policy of sorts and, increasingly, some metropolitan authorities have formulated and implemented locally-based policies aimed at achieving some renewed economic vigour. Short (1984) cautions, however, that the 'inner city programme is something of a misnomer. There has been no fully developed programme arising from a coherent intellectual and policy base, but rather a changing emphasis and commitment which has been perceived in varying ways at different times' (p. 158).

National urban policy

Contemporary national urban policy has its origins in the mid-1960s when inner city problems were perceived primarily in terms of the problems associated with the concentration of large numbers of Commonwealth immigrants, intensified by Enoch Powell's 1968 'rivers of blood' speech. The latter was followed by a small urban aid programme aimed at the most deprived inner city areas. Table 5.2 lists the principal urban policy initiatives from the mid-1960s on. The 1968 urban programme was considerably expanded in 1975 and in the early 1970s a number of studies were undertaken of inner cities: the Community Development Projects and Inner Area Studies. Those who undertook the former tended to adopt 'radical' interpretations of the sources of urban problems (for example, the power of capital) and to propose radical solutions, and the studies were consequently discontinued in 1977 (Kraushaar, 1981). In 1978, partnerships were established between the central and local state in conjunction with private interests to develop projects aimed at the economic revival of inner areas. After 1979 the Thatcher Government was at first reluctant to expand its commitment to urban policies, given its general goal of reducing government expenditures. However, the urban aid programme was 'swiftly reinstated in response to the [1981] riots. Spending on education, transport, housing and social services were strongly restrained at the start of 1982, as unemployment continued to rise in the cities, and the demand for local services grew' (*The Economist* 1982, p. 5). This is not the place for a detailed analysis of the success or failure of central state urban policy (see Laurence and Hall, 1981; McKay and Cox, 1979; Church of England, 1985, ESRC, 1985 for assessments), other than to note that the extent of Britain's economic decline and the disproportionate concentration of problems in central cities required a much more systematic and broader policy response than was forthcoming. Such a

TABLE 5.2 *Central state urban policy initiatives in Britain*

Legislation	Year	Objective
Local Government Act 1966, Section II	1966	Grants to local authorities with numerous Commonwealth immigrants for special services
Educational Priority Areas Programmes	1967	School policy focused on inner cities and deprived areas
Urban Programme	1968	Aid to ameliorate need concentrated in inner city areas
General Improvement Area	1969	Grants for owner rehabilitation of housing in urban areas
Community Development Projects	1969–76	Local groups attempting to end dependence of deprived groups on local bureaucracies
Comprehensive Community Programmes	1974	Analysis of inner city needs
Housing Action Areas	1974	Rehabilitation of urban housing in closely targeted areas
Inner Area Studies (Dept. of Environment)	1972–77	Analysis of city economic problems
Urban Programme (expanded)	1975	Expansion of 1968 programme
Inner Urban Area Act	1978	Economic revival of inner city areas; central/local government partnerships in large cities
Urban Development Corporations	1980	Revival of London and Liverpool docklands by UDCs rather than metropolitan authorities
Enterprise Zones	1980	Lifting of planning and other restrictions from some inner city areas to spur growth
Enterprise Allowance Scheme	1980	Support for urban unemployed to start small businesses
Inner-city Task Force Scheme	1986	£1m per area for eight areas to address employment problem

SOURCE McKay and Cox, 1979; Davies, 1980; Laurence and Hall, 1981; German Marshall Fund, 1985.

judgment was also reached by Lord Scarman in his inquiry into the Brixton disorders of April 1981:

The failure of the many attempts over the last three decades to tackle the problem of inner city decline successfully is striking. It is noticeable that large sums have been spent to little apparent effect ... [There is] a lack of an effective coordinated approach to tackling inner city problems. Looking at the examples of Brixton and Merseyside, conflicting policies and priorities – as between central and local government or between the different layers of local government – appear to have been a frequent source of confusion and reduced drive. (Scarman, 1982, pp. 158–9)

The continuing decline of inner cities, the persistently high unemployment rates and, more nebulously, the renewed incidence of public disorder in 1985, all suggest that the government's urban policy has been relatively ineffectual.

The amount of public money actually spent on the urban programmes remained comparatively modest until the late 1970s, as the current prices (column 1) in Table 5.3 demonstrate, though it had increased from its 1968 figures of £1.7 million (Short, 1984, p. 158). From 1977–78 the urban programme began to expand more substantially, reflecting the

TABLE 5.3   *Urban Programme 1974–85: Department of the Environment and other programmes*
(£ million)

Year	Amount (current)	(1974–75 = 100)
1974–75	13.2	100
1975–76	19.0	103
1976–77	23.0	103.5
1977–78	29.3	103.9
1978–79	93.4	112.4
1979–80	165.0	122.0
1980–81	202.0	126.9
1981–82	215.0	128.6
1982–83	270.0	135.9
1983–84	348.0	146.3
1984–85	413.0	154.9

SOURCE   1974–75 – 1983–84: Department of the Environment, *Report for the Financial Year 1982/83* (1983); 1984–85 Church England, *Faith in the City* (1985).

impact of the Partnership and Programme area schemes (see below), introduced after 1977 (Laurence and Hall, 1981, p. 92). In constant figures, the central state's urban programme grew by almost 50 per cent from the mid-1970s to the mid-1980s. However, this growth must be qualified by reference to the sharp cut in general central grants to local authorities from 1976 which more than offset the increase in urban aid.

This point is highlighted by the Church of England (1985) report on cities which criticises the government for reducing expenditure to Urban Priority Areas (UPAs):

the shift in the balance of policy to secure the greater involvement of the private sector in particular, has gone side-by-side with major reductions in central financial assistance to UPA local authorities despite resources for the Urban Programme nearly doubling in cash terms between 1979/80 and 1983/84. Local authorities in many UPAs have lost far more in Rate Support Grant than they have gained under the Urban Programme. There has been an overall decline in central government financial support. Although the Urban Programme – the icing – has grown in real terms, the cake – the 'bending' of main policies and programmes – has either shrunk or disappeared altogether. There is one exception: the only main central government expenditure programme to have shown a significant growth in the inner cities in real terms since 1979 is that on the police. (p. 173)

The 'partnerships' introduced in 1978 are between central and local authorities, though the Church of England report notes that 'many local authorities feel that central Government has been an unequal partner' (p. 186). In the case of Liverpool the establishment of a Merseyside Task Force in 1982 deliberately excluded involvement by the local state since the latter was perceived as responsible, in part, for urban conditions: thus there are no representatives from local authorities among the Task Force membership. The Thatcher Government has also shown a preference for policies which encourage entrepreneurial activity, such as enterprise zones, removing regulations on employment, and providing tax incentives to potential investors. It has also established Urban Development Corporations in the derelict dockland areas of East London and Merseyside: the former is called the London Docklands Development Corporation and was set up in 1981 with responsibility for developing 1000 acres of public land in London's depressed docklands. Its strategy has been to sell off this land to private housebuilders and corporate developers, though debate continues as to whether this is contrary to the interests of local residents and councils (see *New Statesman*, 1986). More recently, the recurrence of urban rioting and disorder in the summer of 1985 has renewed pressure upon the national government to expand its commitment to addressing the social and economic hardships concentrated in inner cities. In response, the Government appointed an inner-city task force which proposed in February 1986 spending £1 million per site for eight deprived inner city areas: Notting Hill and North Peckham in London, Chapeltown in Leeds, North Central Middlesbrough, Highfields in Leicester, Moss Side in Manchester, St Paul's in Bristol and Handsworth in Birmingham. Given the very high levels of unemployment (especially youth unemployment) in these areas, the primary objective of the expenditure of this money is job creation. Government critics have already noted, however, that the funds allocated under this new scheme are less than the reduction in general-purpose funding to inner cities since 1979. The Labour Party estimate is that under the Thatcher Government rate-support funding to urban areas has dropped by £1700 million.

Of the 1984–85 central state budget of £413 million for the urban programmes, the major shares went to the seven Partnership and twenty-three Programme authorities. Within these authorities 40 per cent of funding was allocated to local economic development, 40 per cent to education, social services, leisure and health, while the final 20 per cent was allocated to environmental improvement schemes. This represented a change of emphasis from 1983–84 when only 30 per cent of urban funds were allocated to economic projects and 47 per cent went to social projects (Department of the Environment, 1983). Other policies encourage large companies and local authorities to make unused inner city plant space available to new entrepreneurs: 'throughout the United Kingdom, old buildings are being reborn as business incubators. Antiquated schools and hospitals are fair game, along with redundant factories and warehouses' (German Marshall Fund, 1985, p. 5). Since unemployment is so concentrated in decayed inner cities, most of these efforts at creating jobs have been focused there.

Urban rioting

Although the 1981 and 1985 riots provoked policy responses from the Thatcher Government it is not altogether clear that the cause of these disorders can be directly or, at least exclusively, attributed to urban deprivation. Table 5.4 lists the key incidents of rioting and the urban districts in which they occurred. These areas all figure prominently in any inventory of deprived British inner cities; thus there are good grounds for assuming *some* linking between economic and social conditions and public disorder. However, there are other areas – notably parts of Glasgow – which figure equally prominently in such inventories (for example, ESRC, 1985) but which have not yet

TABLE 5.4   *Rioting in British cities, 1980–85*

Date	Location
1980	
2 April	St Paul's (Bristol)
1981	
10–12 April	Brixton (London: focus of Scarman Report, 1982)
3–6 July	Toxteth (Liverpool), Moss-side (Manchester), Southall (London)
10–12 July	Brixton
26–28 July	Toxteth
July	Incidents in Handsworth (Birmingham), Blackburn, Preston, Wolverhampton, Sheffield, Reading, Nottingham
1985	
9–10 September	Handsworth
28–29 September	Brixton
6 October	Broadwater Farm in Tottenham (London). Most serious: one police officer beaten to death

SOURCES   Kettle and Hodges, 1982; Scarman, 1982, *Observer* and *The Sunday Times*, 15 September 1985.

been sites of significant rioting. In their comprehensive study of the 1981 riots Kettle and Hodges (1982) emphasise the lack of a direct link between deprivation and riots:

> we have already pointed out that what started many of the riots was not the closure of a local factory, the failure to introduce a multi-racial curriculum or even the breakdown of liaison between local leaders, councillors and police chiefs. Instead, the major riots – certainly in Brixton and Toxteth – were started because people witnessed specific acts of street injustice which no longer seemed tolerable. Equally significant was the way that some of the riots then developed. There was obviously much indiscriminate destruction, but the rioters also showed some discrimination in their choice of targets. (p. 250)

Kettle and Hodges note that specific targets such as police vehicles were singled out for attack. In effect, there is a central racial dimension to the 1980s rioting in British cities: the areas listed in Table 5.4 not only represent areas of profound economic, physical and social disadvantage but also ones in which blacks are concentrated. Being black and living in deprived inner cities significantly compounds the degree of disadvantage and it is this which frequently finds expression in riots. Relations between the police and disadvantaged inner city blacks are also extremely fragile with a police raid on a café (St Paul's in Bristol) or a home (Brixton, 1985) capable of sparking off widespread, riotous outrage. One observer of the 1985 disorders makes a related point: 'black youths have a clearer group-consciousness than an underclass which is not ethnically distinct ... It is self-consciousness, and a sense of legitimacy arising out of injustice, which turns an underclass into a dangerous class' (Reiner, *New Society*, 25.10.85, p. 150; see also Platt, *New Society*, 11.10.85 and Harris, *New Society*, 4.10.85). Urban rioting clearly is related to deprivation but this is only part of the cause: the interaction with racial conflict is crucial.

The central state has sought to deny the deprivationist thesis: officials have downplayed the incidence of economic and social conditions as causal factors and emphasised criminality as a contributory factor. And in responding to the 1981, and especially the 1985 disorders, the central state has looked to improved police methods and strength (for example, the possible introduction of plastic bullets) as well as allocating increased urban aid to the affected cities. However, from the perspective of our theoretical arguments about the central state's interest in maintaining its authority in cities (see Chapter 1) and the increased political salience of those urban areas affected by rioting or collective disorder (see Chapter 3) it is the state's response which is critical not the underlying causes of the rioting. In other words, whether the riots are reflections of racial discrimination or economic deprivation or criminality they constitute assaults upon the state's authority to which it must respond. And the evidence for 1981 and 1985 is that the central state has indeed responded through its urban policy. That said, for the local state the problem of economic and social deprivation remains a significant one, and while rioting may attract national attention to inner city blight it hardly resolves the underlying factors. Consequently, some local authorities have sought to intervene more directly in their urban economy as a way of arresting decline.

Local state economic initiatives

Inner cities located in the old industrial conurbations suffered disproportionately from unemployment and plant closures and failed to attract sufficient new industries and investment to absorb more than a fraction of the jobless. Accordingly, by the late 1970s and early 1980s the relative ineffectiveness of central state initiatives for inner city revitalisation had led several municipal authorities to pursue their own policies. Thus in London the GLC established the Greater London Enterprise Board (GLEB) in 1983 in response to accelerating unemployment in London (400 000 by 1984, a three-fold increase over 1979 (Wheen, 1985, p. 77)). Its brief is to design policies for the revitalisation of the London urban economy and to invest in long-term jobs: 'in particular, it attempts to identify unused resources and skills, new products and services which would meet the needs of Londoners ... Projects meeting the particular employment needs of women, ethnic minorities and people with disabilities are given special consideration' (Wheen, 1985, pp. 79–80). Other agencies have developed from this GLEB initiative: for example, the London Co-operative Enterprise Board and the Greater London Training Board. The six Metropolitan County Councils (MCCs) which govern the other large conurbations have also intervened in their respective economies in an effort to revitalise and stimulate economic activity, in response to accelerating increases in unemployment and decreases in manufacturing output from the mid-1970s. The long-term decline of merseyside (Liverpool) and Tyne and Wear (Newcastle) encouraged their metropolitan county councils to set up Enterprise Boards, most of whose efforts have been directed at aiding small and medium-sized firms in financial difficulty. Their interventions have been character- ised as a 'process ... of opportunism and reaction to crisis' (Flynn, Leach and Vielba, 1985, p. 91).

Referring back to Chapter 2, such activities of the MCCs and GLC represent efforts to revitalise their local economies and therefore concern local state autonomy Type I – that is, autonomy from local economic and social constraints. If these revitalisation policies are successful then the local state will face the problem of whether it can exercise greater control or autonomy over its rejuvenated private economy. One might expect that the local state's initiating role implies greater future autonomy: that is, where policies of the local state contribute to revitalisation, its hand should be strengthened with respect to the firms and interests that have benefited. Pursuing policies aimed at economic improvement is certainly compatible with the local state's interests and general concern to maximise autonomy. In any event, the attempt has brought them into conflict with the central state, especially the activities of the GLEB in London. While the central government's critique (discussed below) emphasises the issue of efficiency, Flynn, Leach and Vielba (1985) note that:

> technical arguments about efficiency and economy mask profound ideological differences between central and local government about the proper response to a range of issues including economic decline ... It is clear that central govern- ment has become seriously concerned about the alternative

conceptions of economic policy espoused by the metropolitan counties and the GLC ... The government has clearly
also been unhappy about the attitude of all the MCCs to civil
defence. (p. 92)

Thus the conflict between the central state and municipal
authorities converges on local autonomy and the different
programmatic objectives of the central versus the local state.
Local authorities cannot afford to ignore the socioeconomic
decline of their urban base because it has adverse implications
for their continued capacity to supply the general and special
services upon which their legitimacy rests. Their efforts to
increase their revenue base by intervening in local economies
clash with central state policies which reflect an ideological
commitment to market principles and contraction of the public
sector; the advent of enterprise zones and urban development
corporations represents a success for central policy in this
regard. In addition, some metropolitan authorities use policy
strategies which are offensive to the central state. The
willingness of some local authorities to promote socialist forms
of enterprise such as workers' co-operatives obviously diverges
from the policy preferences of the Thatcher Government
(Flynn, Leach and Vielba, 1985, p. 91). Since the 1981 local
elections when all the metropolitan counties became Labour
controlled, the divergence between policy at the two levels has
increased.

This nexus of conflict is a distinct and powerful one in
central–local relations: most conflict centres on relations
between Conservative dominance at Westminister and Labour
dominance in metropolitan counties. It has introduced a
distinctive dimension into central–local relations based on
ideological differences which happen to coincide with cleav-
ages derived from economic and urban deprivation: the
Labour controlled metropolitan county councils preside over
the most severely affected urban areas in the country. The
abolition of these MCCs and the GLC in April 1986 will to a
certain extent disperse this conflict, and eliminate one local
focus of opposition. These implications are considered in more
detail in the ensuing section of this chapter.

Since 1979 the Thatcher Government has been committed,

in theory, to a free market economic strategy and does not consider state intervention to subsidise inefficient economic activities to be appropriate public policy. Thus it was disposed to continue the enterprise zones scheme (see Butler 1981a and 1981b) which removed state restrictions (such as minimum wage laws, planning controls, rent control, exemption from property taxes, and so on) on economic activity in designated areas of the depressed inner city: stimulation of private investment is preferable to increased public subsidy. More generally, the Conservative Government interprets the decline of inner cities as part of the natural working out of market forces. Only when the legitimacy of the state and urban public order were seriously threatened by the 1981 riots (and more recently in 1985) did the central state increase its fiscal commitment to cities. And the positive response after 1981 proved to be temporary, not long term. As *The Economist* (1982) observes, the larger policy framework of the central state was one of retrenchment:

> In line with government financial policy, funds available for spending by local authorities in the cities were sharply cut back. New house-building was virtually stopped. Housing renewal projects, by local authorities and by the subsidised housing associations, were severely cut. Social services were reduced. Transport subsidies, to encourage people to commute out to suburban areas where jobs were more plentiful, were limited. Local authority grants to neighbourhood voluntary organisations were restricted. Local schemes for recruiting underqualified young people as police cadets were cancelled. (p. 17)

The key programmatic objective of the Thatcher Government to retrench the public sector (which includes local authority spending, discussed below) has been modified only in response to serious rioting, which is consistent with our theoretical arguments about the salience of public disorder to the central state. But once the initial 1981 post-rioting crisis passed, the central state returned to the promotion of policies, like enterprise zones, which are more compatible with its ideological preferences. And in 1985 it was once again prompted to produce a more substantial response to rioting than was implied by free market principles (the aid for eight inner city areas discussed earlier). However, while the Government has wished to appear responsive to the 1981 and 1985 urban riots, the urban aid allocated has not been substantial at either period; further, it has sought to emphasise 'criminality' rather than 'deprivation' as causes of public disorder. Not surprisingly, municipal authorities take a different view and consider it essential that local policy should address the growing concentration of deprivation and hardship within their jurisdictions. Wheen (1985) suggests that local initiatives reveal failings in the national economic strategy. Also, 'the government doesn't like the priority which the GLC gives to groups such as women or ethnic minorities. The government may grudgingly concede that these groups are at a disadvantage when it comes to finding decent jobs; but it doesn't believe that any special effort is needed to correct this disadvantage' (Wheen, 1985, p. 83).

In summary, the efforts by some local authorities to increase their autonomy by improving the urban economy necessarily interact with local autonomy Type II, that is, their autonomy from the central state. Local authorities have interests and programmes to promote which require a sound financial base – programmes upon which their legitimacy ultimately rests. We pointed out earlier that improving the local economy does not automatically imply increased local state autonomy from economic interests, although it would appear to have this potential. Clearly, economic interests can exercise powerful constraints upon local autonomy, just as they can upon national state autonomy. Our treatment of the local state as a political institution concerned to maximise its autonomous status both from local conditions and central state constraints implies an interest in a strong urban economic base: obviously, local autonomy does not follow automatically from the latter, but economic vitality is a necessary, if not sufficient, condition for local autonomy Type I (with implications for Type II). This point can be clarified further by referring back to the discussion of constraints upon the state in Chapter 1, where we identified five different types of constraint. Two of these are relevant here: political and economic constraints. By reducing or placing restrictions on its financial assistance to local authorities, the central government imposes important political constraints upon the local state. In Chapter 2 we noted the extent to which the two dimensions of local autonomy are closely related. In the case of British local authorities in the 1970s and 1980s, this interaction has intensified because of the policy objectives and ideology of the central state. The latter has, since 1979, sought to restructure municipal administration and exercise tight control over municipal budgets, aims which have sharply constrained local states' capacity to provide those services which they deem appropriate. In addition, the erosion of the urban economy of the larger cities also reduces local states' capacity to provide services and is thus a further source of constraint. Given this, the local state's promotion of economic activity represents an attempt to increase the state's capacities by reducing economic constraints. We emphasise, again, that greater economic prosperity is not equivalent to the local state's control of the local economy. Rather the relationship between the two is an interdependent one: each needs the other.

Local state autonomy Type II: the centralisation of local government

The two main tenets of central state policy toward local authorities in Britain since the 1979 election of the Conservative Party have been central fiscal control and local government reform. Both issues imply greater centralisation of the British political system, and both have assumed a prominent position in national–local relations during the last six years. We begin with the local government system.

   In contrast to some similarities in patterns of urban decline in the United States and Britain, there is a major, systemic difference between Britain's unitary system of government and the American federal system. Chapter 4 considered the development of the direct federal–city relation in the context of a federal system and ideology resistant to such a connection; this chapter addresses the activities of municipal authorities within a highly centralised polity. As Hambleton (1978) notes, 'the principle of *ultra vires* is strictly applied so that local authorities can only undertake those activities specifically approved by Parliament' (p. 25). This principle is qualified by the scope of discretion that exists within the terms of legislation which specifies the activities of local authorities and municipalities. However, it is the issue of central state control of municipal governments which has emerged at the core of central–local relations since 1979 and the advent of the Thatcher Government. Since 1979, asserting control over local authorities has become critical to central state policy; for the metropolitan district councils and the Greater London Council (GLC), resisting the encroachment of central state control has become equally crucial, especially for councils controlled by the opposition Labour Party.

Central–local relations in Britain are dominated by the issue of how much control the central state can exercise over local policies and agendas. And because central state finances occupy a critical position in local budgetary arrangements they are at the core of the conflict. In the pursuit of macroeconomic policies (though whether this is a necessary policy element is disputed; see Newton and Karran, 1985) the central state has sought to reduce its fiscal commitment to local authorities who resist retrenchment because they are committed to offsetting the undesirable economic and social consequences of national policy. First we review central–local relations prior to 1979, then develop an interpretation of post-1979 relations by reference to the theoretical framework, paying particular attention to the experience of the GLC and the metropolitan district councils.

The structure of metropolitan government

The initial stimulus to the creation of the modern system of local government in Britain came in the nineteenth century in the wake of the economic and social consequences of the Industrial Revolution, as Jackson (1969) summarises:

An epidemic of cholera in 1831 led to the creation of local temporary boards of health, with a Central Board of Health to guide and supervise them. In 1834 the poor law organisation was taken in hand. Parishes were amalgamated into Unions for the purpose of granting poor relief; each Union had its elected Board of Guardians. Over all, central control was exercised by a body of Poor Law Commissioners. As the industrial revolution proceeded and towns developed, there came new needs – improved highways, street paving, and lighting, more efficient police, better public health, and, eventually, public education. (p. 36)

This account, though somewhat simplistically functionalist, serves to set the general context of the emergence of local authorities and specifically those responsible for municipalities. These local governmental structures were formalised in 1871 with the creation within the central state of the Local Government Board, responsible for central–local relations and supervision of local authorities. Since the end of the nineteenth century local government in Britain has passed through a series of phases under the impetus of various Commissions and reforming/reorganising legislation (see Byrne, 1985 and Dearlove, 1979). The details of these phases do not concern us here. Rather, a sketch of the structure of local government in the mid-1970s provides the basis for an analysis of the post-1979 shift in central–local relations.[1]

The Local Government Act of 1972 created six metropolitan counties (Merseyside, Greater Manchester, South Yorkshire, West Midlands, West Yorkshire and Tyne and Wear) within which were located thirty-six metropolitan district councils (and some parish countils).[2] The six metropolitan county councils were made responsible for overall planning, transport, police and fire services while the thirty-six metropolitan district councils provided education, personal social services, housing, local planning, environmental health and leisure services (see Byrne, 1985, ch. 4). London has a distinct structure: for twenty-one years it was governed by the Greater London Council, established by the London Government Act 1963 and operative from 1965, which was responsible for overall planning, transport, and some housing. Subordinate to the GLC were the thirty-two London boroughs providing housing, social services, leisure, public health and education. In addition there was the Inner London Education Authority

(ILEA), responsible for education in twelve inner London boroughs.

Central–local relations

Finance.   The contribution of central government grants to the budgets of local authorities has been steadily rising in Britain: central government grants have increased from 34 per cent of local government income in 1970 to 50 per cent in 1980 (Byrne, 1985, ch. 11). In a comparative context, however, 'local government in the United Kingdom does not stand out as a big spender among the advanced industrial nations of the West, either in relation to the national product or in relation to the size of the central government's budget' (Newton and Karran, 1985, p. 7). The resource base upon which central and local authorities must rely is none the less more limited in Britain, whose per capita productivity and growth rate are among the lowest in the European Economic Community.

Although the Thatcher Government greatly increased the pressure to control local authorities' budgets, a somewhat similar course had been pursued by the preceding Labour Government. From the mid-1970s on, when Britain's financial crisis became most pronounced, there was enormous pressure on the central state to reduce the size of the public sector and its public expenditure commitments. The Labour Government imposed 'cash limits' upon local authority's current spending (as part of its response to the pressures accompanying Britain's IMF loan), whereby central government grants were not automatically adjusted for inflation. This policy was relatively successful: from its peak in 1976 local government spending declined from 15.4 per cent of Gross Domestic Product to 12.4 per cent in 1979 (Newton and Karran, 1985, p. 11). However, the Conservative Government wanted to accelerate this trend and to gain greater control over the budgetary priorities of local authorities at the same time. Accordingly, the 1980 Local Government Planning and Land Act included legislation to accomplish this by means of a new grant system and the stipulation of penalties for authorities which exceeded centrally determined expenditure levels. In addition, the programme of privatising council houses was introduced in the 1980 Housing

Act. Collectively, these pieces of legislation worked to erode local autonomy to a not inconsiderable extent, as will be highlighted below. First, the details of the new measures.

The single most important source of a local authority's revenues is the grant it receives from central government, known as the rate support grant (RSG). Prior to the 1980 Act the RSG was distributed across local authorities in proportion to their needs, as measured by their existing expenditure patterns: while this method reinforced established spending levels without evaluating them, Newton and Karran (1985) suggest that 'it had the advantage that the basis for the distribution of grants was the spending patterns established by local authorities themselves' (p. 116). The 1980 Act abolished the RSG system and replaced it with a new block grant to each local authority; and whereas the RSG had been allocated to meet the shortfall between what each local authority raised from its rates and its predicted spending, the new system relied on central assessments (grant-related expenditure assessments) of what each authority *should* spend. Byrne (1985) provides this summary:

> Under the new scheme a 'block grant' is calculated for each local authority to cover the deficiency or gap between the cost of providing services comparable with those of similar authorities and the local rate revenue assuming it to be set at a particular level (determined by the government). In effect, the government calculates what the local authorities should spend; it then deducts what the standard (or national) rate would produce, and the difference is paid in grant. (p. 201)

A 'grant taper' penalty was built into the legislation. Local authorities which spent above the level predetermined by the central state were penalised by a reduction in the grant. Local authorities had the long-established right to raise rates to meet shortfall; the effect of the grant taper was to oblige them to raise rates still further. A supplementary 1982 Local Government Finance Act increased the penalties even more through 'grant holdback, whereby "overspending" authorities would have a proportion of their grant withheld. In addition, the right of authorities to levy a supplementary rate in mid-year was removed. This was to prevent them making good any shortfall in grant by extra rating, thus placing them at the mercy of grant taper and holdback' (Newton and Karran, 1985, p. 117). Not unsurprisingly, metropolitan authorities presiding over some of the most distressed central cities were unable to meet their designated spending levels, including Merseyside, the West Midlands, the GLC and some inner London boroughs; of course, such an outcome was a key part of the new financial arrangements. In the Government's 1983 White Paper *Streamlining the Cities* the GLC and the Inner London Education Authority were both identified as offending 'overspenders': the GLC's budget of £867 million, for example, was 53 per cent above the government's target (Forrester, Lansley and Pauley, 1985, p. 41). Conflict over central–local finances thus contributed to the subsequent decision of the central government to abolish one tier of local government. In a broad perspective, Boddy (1983) concludes that the central financial restrictions on local authorities' expenditure levels have generated profound changes:

> from a system of guidance and influence which left considerable scope for the local determination of expenditure we have thus moved towards a much firmer central control over local government expenditure. Particularly significant in the case of the Block Grant is that government has taken the power to influence not just the impact of local authority spending as a whole in keeping with macroeconomic objectives but it can influence the spending levels of individual authorities. (p. 130)

There have been many other points of fiscal contention between the local authorities and the central state since 1980, including disputes over the formula used in determining spending levels, the apparent discrepancies between the treatment of Conservative versus Labour-controlled metropolitan authorities, and especially the introduction of rate-capping by the 1984 Rates Act, designed to control local rate levels. The central government has come into intense conflict with some Labour-controlled metropolitan district councils such as Sheffield and Liverpool, and London boroughs such as

Bromley and Lambeth, which initially refused to set rates or formulate a budget within the restrictive limits of central directives; elected members of the Councils appeared to face imprisonment for failing to set a rate. This eventuality was avoided by last-minute compromises engineered by Sheffield's David Blunkett but those councillors who delayed setting a local rate subsequently faced prosecution by the Audit Commission. And this is precisely what occurred to eighty Liverpool and Lambeth (London) Labour Party councillors in March 1986: each was assessed a personal surcharge fine of between £5000 and £8000 and was barred from public office for five years following a High Court ruling which judged their delay in setting the rate to be 'without good reason' and represented a 'pinnacle of political perversity'. The legal costs involved in appealing to the House of Lords are prohibitive for these councillors, which makes this redress unlikely. Similar prosecutions are under consideration for another 200 Labour councillors. The courts have thus been brought into central––local relations on behalf of the central state.

Central–local relations are now of a salience unprecedented in recent British political history. Undoubtedly the fiscal changes form part of a larger trend toward increased centralisation in Britain (Goldsmith and Newton, 1983 and Boddy, 1983); and there is no longer much warrant for previous scholarly disagreement about the potential for central state manipulation of local budgets (see, for example, Ashford, 1974). As Goldsmith and Newton (1983) argue, 'central government has always been powerful in Britain ... but in the last few years the centre has further consolidated its powers by increasing its legal, political and financial control over local authorities. These now show clear signs of becoming little more than agents of the centre' (p. 216).

Restructuring. In addition to imposing constraints on the spending practices of local authorities the Thatcher Government has sought to restructure local government at the metropolitan level. Greenwood (1982) observes that the novelty of the 1980s 'is the introduction by central government of a new control regime to achieve its macro-economic objectives. Changing the rules of the game in central–local relations *and* simultaneously intensifying fiscal stress has provoked protest from local authorities' (p. 45). In a White Paper (Department of the Environment, Cmnd 9063, October 1983) entitled *Streamlining the Cities* the Government set out its intention to abolish the top tier of local government in 1986: that is, the six metropolitan county councils and the GLC. The White Paper proposed the redistribution of these authorities' functions across the lower levels of metropolitan government (the district councils) and, in the case of London, a series of joint boards to administer city-wide services such as fire, police and transport, as well as a host of quasi-autonomous agencies for other responsibilities (Wheen, 1985, p. 35). In 1985, implementing legislation was successfully ushered through Parliament despite fairly considerable and widely-based opposition, particularly in the House of Lords. This abolition policy will have devastating consequences for the scope of local state autonomy, especially in the case of London where the abolition of the GLC will mean that no single local municipal authority will have responsibility for the whole city.

The rationale provided by the Government for the abolition of these authorities is primarily economic: they are deemed too expensive and their abolition, in conjunction with general retrenchment of the public sector and reduced municipal budgets, will contribute to the national objective of controlling public expenditure. More specifically, the Government contends that these authorities have too few functions, constitute an unnecessary tier of administration and, particularly in the case of the GLC, spend too much public money. Previous measures to control local expenditure had not stopped some of the high-spending councils; therefore more direct central control was needed. Another objection raised by the White Paper is that the existence of the metropolitan authorities has contributed to conflict with the district councils. This is disputed by Flynn, Leach and Vielba (1985), who suggest that 'in the case of the MCCs there have been few issues over which there has been a genuine material conflict. Policies which favour inner cities have largely been central government sponsored' (p. 2). They also suggest that the MCCs have tended to promote redistributive policies, a role which will disappear with them.[3] However, some support for the

Government's contention about conflict between the different administrative tiers is provided by Parkinson and Duffy's (1984) examination of Liverpool. They suggest that conflict between Liverpool District Council and Merseyside County Council was 'peculiarly intense and damaging. The County's ambition to become the primary economic planning agency for the sub-region coloured its reactions towards urban policy initiatives and helped frustrate central government intentions to create more harmonious local government relationships' (Parkinson and Duffy 1984, p. 78). But most such conflicts in the local government system derived from the way in which boundaries were drawn in the 1974 reorganisation not from the existence of two tiers of administration *per se*. Whether such conflicts necessitated abolition, as opposed to some reorganisation, is far from self-evident.

In addition to the stated factors of efficiency, economy and national policy objectives there are important partisan and ideological factors underlying the abolition of the metropolitan authorities. Not coincidentally, these authorities have tended to be controlled by forces opposed to the central administration, personified in the figure of Ken Livingstone, the Labour leader of the GLC from 1981 to April 1986 (and in 1986 a Labour Party parliamentary candidate). Several metropolitan district councils had also become centres of opposition to the central Government, notably Sheffield, Liverpool and some London boroughs, for example, Hackney and Lambeth. The intention to abolish the MCCs and the GLC first surfaced in the 1983 election manifesto of the Conservative Party and seemed, to many observers, hastily included and motivated by antagonism to those authorities' opposition to the Government since 1981. As Flynn, Leach and Vielba (1985) note, 'although the proposals in the manifesto were decided in haste and without detailed consideration of the implication, they had their roots in a history of conflicts between the Government and the Labour-controlled MCCs and GLC' (p. 9).

We have already referred to one specific issue of contention which is both partisan and iedological: the conflict between local and central authorities over the appropriate role for locally-based economic initiatives. Not only are the metropolitan authorities hostile to the Government but they have initiated policies involving public subsidy and expenditure in direct contradiction to the central state's monetarist macroeconomic strategy. Many of the MCCs have been controlled by Labour Party members 'who believed in increasing state involvement in the private sector and disagreed fundamentally with the government's free market philosophy and its philosophy of rolling back the boundaries of the state' (Flynn, Leach and Vielba, 1985, p. 16). Some came from the new generation of local politicians who emerged in the early 1980s, committed to pursuing a decentralised, local road to socialism. Rather than a mass proletariat, they seek to form a coalition of urban groups, and by mobilising them around local issues transform popular consciousness (see Gyford, 1983 and 1985). According to Flynn, Leach and Vielba (1985) the ideological divide between the new urban left and Conservatives

> goes much deeper than the conflict over spending levels. As well as protecting services and resisting privatization, it [the New Left] has set out to exploit what it views as the socialist potential for local government. This has included developing new socialist initiatives, and attempting to win popular support and build alliances around these initiatives. (p. 43)

Such a strategy, of course, parallels the theoretical work on urban movements reviewed in Chapter 2, particularly the work of Castells (1983); he argues that the forces for social change must be mobilised at the urban level around issues of collective consumption. He also emphasises the importance of establishing coalitions between diverse groups and across classes. The new urban left certainly shares many of the socialist objectives of Castells and, although not formally organised, includes councillors, community workers, party activitists and public sector employees who 'share a common concern for the socialist potential of local government arising often from a belief in the inadequacy of traditional models of socialist politics' (Gyford, 1985, p. 17). The origins of the new urban Left lie in various community activities and struggles of the preceding decades including environmentalism, the women's movement and community development projects. Gyford (1985) says they are distinguished by these features:

a concern for issues hitherto absent from or marginal to conventional local government, such as local economic planning, monitoring the police, women's rights, and racial equality; a disdain for many of the traditional ways of conducting local authority business; a view of local govern-ment as an arena both for combating the policies of a Conservative government and for displaying by example the potential of a grass-roots socialism; and, perhaps most fundamentally, a commitment to notions of mass politics based upon strategies of decentralization and/or political mobilization at the local level. (p. 18)

The failure of Liverpool or any other municipality to avoid setting a rate has weakened the potential of the new urban Left in the short term. But in the long term, the sorts of issues motivating this grouping and the wide coalition of concerned organisations and groups suggests that the new urban Left will remain an important force in British urban politics for some considerable time.

Thus the Government's restructuring of metropolitan local government reflects several sets of factors, both economic and political. There is a firm commitment to reduce the public sector and to control public spending, especially at the local level. Combined with this is ideological resistance to the policies favoured by groups dominant in the metropolitan authorities, and partisan opposition to the groups themselves. Considered in conjunction with the restructuring of national- -local fiscal relationships already in place, the abolition of the MCCs and GLC have catapulted central–local relations and the issue of local autonomy to the centre of national politics.

Conclusion: centralisation and local autonomy

Newton and Karran (1985) pose the centralist implications of current national policy most vividly: they conclude that 'Britain stands within sight of a form of government which is more highly centralised than anything this side of East Germany' (p. 129). The statement is dramatic but the two scholars are simply stating more starkly what many other observers believe: that the combined effect of changes in central–local fiscal relations since 1980 and the restructuring of local authorities reflects a powerful trend toward centralisation in the British political system, one which denies significant autonomy to local authorities. We have already discussed in detail the consequences of urban decline for municipal autonomy; here it is necessary to review the implications of the central state's new policies.

These implications are primarily negative: the policies pursued by the central state in the area of central–local relations reduce the scope for local initiative, discretion and autonomy in most policy areas. By restricting budgetary allocations, both in the aggregate and across categories, the central state removes a vital source of local independence. The centuries-old principle that local authorities have the right to determine their own spending and revenue-raising needs has been abandoned. The sheer heterogeneity of municipal authorities and urban conditions suggests that divesting municipalities of such a key role in favour of centrally formulated levels of spending and taxing is misguided. The local state is given much less freedom to determine what its officials think the key areas of need are for its locality, which is one of the principal rationales for the existence of local authorities with elected leadership. As a result, one basis of their legitimacy is undermined: they have sharply reduced opportunities to provide the services sought by their electors. Local accountability of officials is undercut still further where a whole tier of local government is being removed, as with the GLC. The central state, by increasing its intervention in the provision of local services, for example transport and housing, has increased its relative autonomy but at potentially serious cost to *its* legitimacy. Referring back to Figure 1.2 on p. 41, it will be recalled that the national state has interests in maintaining its authority in cities, which in part requires the provision of essential urban services. However, it is also the case that national policy commitments to public sector retrenchment is manifested in reduced state services (including public housing, social services and education) at the urban level: the central state, by pursuing its objectives, creates problems for municipal authorities since it is the latter who have reduced funding for the provision of collective goods and must confront public hostility. Local state legitimacy is significantly affected by national policy; and it certainly suits the central state to transfer publicly perceived responsibility for service reductions to the local level. Thus there are fundamental linkages and tensions between central and local state interests: it is the tensions in central–local relations which have been most pronounced during the last decade. From our theoretical perspective we would expect the retrenchment of urban-level services to result in greater pressure upon the central state from both municipalities and the electorate. Given the concentration of the most severely disadvantaged in declining inner cities and their propensity to unpredictable disorder, the central state is likely to continue to respond with highly visible and symbolic but largely insubstantial policies. While rioting poses a powerful threat to the central state's authority in urban areas (and demands a response), the politically weak position of riot participants (youths, minorities, and so on) permits a marginal national response. And by playing on the larger public's fears of disorder, it can justify investing in more policing rather than in the more expensive and less certain policies of alleviating deprivation.

The abolition of the MCCs and the GLC, and the imposition of central constraints upon local spending, concurs with other centralist tendencies of the British state. An example is the greater use of quasi-elected local government organisations (QUELGOs), which are authorities with powers across different county council areas whose membership consists of local council delegates and nominated representatives of interest groups (for example, local police authorities). The council delegates are only indirectly accountable to their electorate, thus removing QUELGOs from direct popular control. The number of QUELGOs will increase with the abolition of the MCCs and the GLC: for example, the GLC's London Transport has been replaced by the London Regional Transport Board while joint boards are being created for other essential services. Similar bodies will replace MCC activities.

In all cases, these new boards, rather than the city councils, will have responsibility for allocating substantial budgets in these areas. We have concentrated upon the fiscal and institutional dimensions of central–local relations since 1979, arguing that changes here imply a much more centralised state, but these changes are complemented by other centralist tendencies.

A key consequence of abolishing the metropolitan counties is that it will make municipal authorities more exposed to the vagaries of the market.[4] Economic factors, whether local or national, will have increased influence upon urban economies without the local state necessarily being able to influence them. This obviously has serious implications for local autonomy and relates back to general issues about the relationship between private economic interests and state autonomy, at whatever level of the state. What we can conclude is that the abolition of those authorities responsible for sizeable areas (that is, conurbations and Greater London) unavoidably limits the capacity of local states with more circumscribed jurisdictions to respond effectively to market forces and private economic interests. This implies a decline in local state autonomy Type I or, in other words, greater economic influence and diminished political control in urban areas.

Since 1979 the central state in Britain has pursued a general economic strategy of reducing public expenditure, justified as the basis for renewed economic vitality nationally. The success or otherwise of this strategy is outside the brief of this study. Here we have been concerned with how the pursuit of this policy objective has affected central–local relations: it has led to increased fiscal centralisation in order to control metropolitan budgetary allocations, and it underlines a policy of restructuring one tier of local government. Both policies have contributed substantially to the centralisation of the British state. Paralleling these policies has been the sustained ideological and political conflict between politicians at both the central and local levels of the state. Here the division is fundamental in two (related) ways: with respect to ideologies (free market versus interventionist) and policy priorities. Muncipalities, we have suggested, are less able to neglect the social hardship and economic malaise within their jurisdiction than is the central state, preoccupied as it is with national policy and patterns.

This second arena of conflict is critical for understanding the intensity of central–local divisions in the 1980s and for thinking about future developments. The relative neglect of deprived inner cities by the central government creates a vacuum which local authorities must attempt to fill. When this neglect manifests itself in riotous behaviour, as it did in 1981 and 1985, the central government may be obliged to take remedial action even if contrary to its other policy objectives. But during the periods of relative calm it is the local state or municipal authority which must address local problems. This is exactly what some local authorities have been doing in Britain and their divergence from national policy has certainly contributed toward the policy to abolish them. Unfortunately, the abolition of a tier of metropolitan administration will not dispose of the real concentrations of urban decay, social hardship and economic stagnation at the heart of many of Britain's old industrial cities.

Finally, it is not intended to suggest any simple equivalence between the local state in Britain and in the United States. Rather we have contrasted the situation of the local state in the two countries in order to illuminate their individual forms. Thus this chapter has demonstrated that local states in Britain have considerably less autonomy than do their American counterparts. There are important institutional and ideological differences between the two countries underlying these contrasts. The comparative approach adopted in this book emphasises differences, rather than assuming equivalence, between Britain and the United States.

Chapter 6

Conclusion: Futures for Post-Industrial Cities

In this concluding chapter we draw together some of the principal themes and evidence of the book and consider their implications for the future of Western cities, especially but not only in the United States and Britain. These are the key themes: the capacities of the national and local state to direct and compensate for the economic changes which are reshaping the urban landscape, the mixes of public provision and private enterprise in four emerging types of cities, and the implications of neo-conservative ideologies and policies for the future of state–city relations.

Processes of urban change

Three basic processes – social, economic and political – are reshaping the cities of Western societies. The social process is one of internal migration, the aggregate of individual decisions to move in search of better places to live and work. Within metropolitan areas the aggregate flow since the 1950s has been from the central cities to suburbs, a pattern characteristic of virtually all large cities in north-western Europe and North America. This is paralleled by flows among urban regions, especially from large industrial cities to smaller cities and towns with more diverse economies. The dynamics of these shifts were reviewed in Chapter 2. We regard these demographic shifts mainly as a consequence of more basic economic factors: migration follows economic opportunities. Social and ecological considerations also figure in migration patterns. In the United States especially, but also in Britain, most of the favoured cities have more attractive environments: warmer climates in the United States, appealing rural surroundings in Britain. But few people of working age move in response to environmental appeals alone: there must be some prospect of making a living at their destination.

The economic process is the most fundamental engine of urban change thus far in the twentieth century: in this we agree with economy-centred theories about the growth and decline of cities (for example, Berry 1973; Gordon, 1976; and Jacobs, 1984). 'Economic process' is a shorthand term for a complex and interacting set of cultural, technological and organisational changes which are transforming Western societies and their cities. Technological change has fostered the growth of new kinds of industries and higher-order service activities. In the United States most high-technology industries have been sited outside the old industrial cities because of investment and managerial decisions that are guided in part by market considerations, but also by non-market considerations. Public regulation or the lack of it plays a part, as does the less tangible perception that Houston and cities like it are 'a good place for business'. Britain has fewer high-tech industries but many manufacturing firms, new and old, whose founders and managers prefer the locational advantages of small industrial and county towns, where it is cheaper to establish and expand plants than it is in the old industrial cities. In both countries entrepreneurs and managers are no less susceptible to the attraction of warm and pleasant places than are skilled workers, technicians, accountants and sales personnel who migrate in the wake of investment decisions.

A second crucial factor is the internationalisation of the control and movement of private capital. In a global market economy the locational and labour advantages once enjoyed by Western industrial cities are now found elsewhere, especially on the periphery of Asia. Decisions about large-scale investment are more likely to be made by capital managers who do not live in the affected cities and who have no particular loyalty to place, either city or country. In this they are a different breed from those nineteenth-century capitalists in Britain and North America whose profit motives were leavened with civic pride and a commitment to maintaining the prosperity of the city which was the source of their wealth.

A third economic factor reshaping cities has been the growth of the service sector relative to manufacturing. The 'service sector' is actually a multiplicity of public and private activities: public administration, health and education, transportation, wholesaling and retailing, consumer services for an affluent society, financial and administrative services in support of trade and industry, high-tech data-processing and communication systems in the service of both the public and private sectors, and so on. Decisions about siting new public services are influenced by both population movements and politics. Decisions about where to invest in private service enterprises tend to follow decisions about industrial investment, but not necessarily so. In the United States many are located in privately-developed complexes of office buildings and shopping centres with names like Irvine Spectrum and Denver Tech Center, the so-called megacentres or urban villages which flourish on the fringes of metropolitan areas (Pierce, 1985). The location of these new service activities is thus a third, semi-autonomous force reshaping the economic life of cities. All these processes – technological change, capital migration, the location of new firms and service activities – affect the productive basis of cities' vitality but relatively few can be controlled by decision-makers at the local level.

The political process shaping modern cities is equally complex. Its major feature is the century-long expansion of the resources and powers of the Western state which was documented in Chapter 1. One specific manifestation of that expansion has been the growth of state interests in, and responsibilities for, city forms and functions, an argument which we developed in Chapters 1 and 2 and documented for the US federal government in Chapter 4 and for the British central state in Chapter 5. National, regional and local states among them now have material and regulatory roles that in the aggregate can have as much impact on cities as all private economic activities. In the cross-section of thirteen American cities examined in Chapter 3 we found that, with the exception of Houston, 35 to 55 per cent of their populations had public-sector income in 1980, counting government employees and beneficiaries of major transfer-payment programmes, and that total government payments to these individuals and to government contractors provided 24 to 50 per cent of total personal income. Boston has become the archetypal post-industrial public city in the United States, with half its population and personal income directly dependent on government spending.

The urban interests and responsibilities of the local state are not necessarily the same as those of other levels of government, however, for reasons detailed in Chapter 2. Local officials are concerned above all else with their city's prosperity and with the maintenance of their own authority, conditions which are interdependent. To pursue those interests effectively local officials need some degree of autonomy from regional and national governments, whose officials may be more concerned with pursuing broader objectives than with the prosperity of particular cities and regions. The latent conflict between national and local states over the uses of state power and the allocation of public resources has been brought to a head in both the United States and Britain by a new political phenomenon – the ascendancy of neo-conservative Governments which seek to promote economic growth through greater reliance on market forces, deregulation and contraction of public-sector spending. In a larger perspective this shift in the political wind is an understandable reaction to the very rapid growth of the public sector since the Second World War. Eventually, the ideological fervour of neo-conservatism is likely to give way to beliefs and policies based on acceptance of the symbiotic relationship which exists between public and private in all advanced capitalist societies. In the short run, however, neo-conservative policies have done considerable material and political harm to cities, and especially to the declining cities whose economies were once dominated by 'smokestack industries'.

In Britain, as we demonstrated in Chapter 5, the Labour governments of the large conurbations have sharply resisted national policies of retrenchment and are paying a double price: the national Government has imposed firm limits on local spending and in April 1986 abolished the Metropolitan County Councils and the Greater London Council. In consequence, local autonomy to take remedial action in the face of continued urban decline is much diminished. In the United States, cutbacks in non-defence federal funding have hurt declining cities more than growing ones, not by design but because the declining old industrial cities have become more dependent on federal grants, whereas many other cities, especially in the south and west, benefit from the growth of defence spending. And while the local state in Britain is legally the creature of the national state, American municipal governments are the responsibility of the fifty regional states, most of them now more responsive to the needs of municipalities than is the federal government. The governments of declining American cities thus have had to accept fiscal austerity, but in theory retain substantial political autonomy to pursue their own service and development policies within those constraints. In practice, austerity everywhere decreases local officials' autonomy from the local private sector and from those who make decisions about local investment and development: the need for local redevelopment compels local officials to make greater commitments than they might previously have made – to provide services and facilities, to relax regulations, to forego revenues – as means to keep and attract private business. It also pits cities in a competitive struggle to see which can offer the most attractive package to potential investors – competition which can prove costly to winners and losers alike.

In principle, as we argued in Chapter 3 and elsewhere, the national and local state have considerable powers to guide and stimulate local economic activity. A number of European countries have mixed economies in which the state actively intervenes to promote regional and national development. The long-established techniques for doing this are based on national economic planning and entail the use of incentives such as provision of infrastructure and facilities, temporary subsidies, relocation grants and investment allowances to steer private capital to particular locales. One step beyond is state capitalism *per se*, in which the state itself invests in and manages enterprises. The most common European examples are industries which were nationalised because they were outmoded and uncompetitive under private ownership. In Britain, the state-capital sector is large and while some public industries are to be sold off, the Thatcher Government also has rationalised vigorously many state-owned enterprises 'and, in doing so, it has reconstituted capital far more effectively than the private sector has done' (Cerny, 1985, p. 218). French governments have followed a *dirigiste* industrial policy since 1946, which has meant not only channelling private investment but in addition substantial industrial investment by state agencies. The cumulative effects of state planning and state capitalism on urban and regional development are potentially enormous, great enough to reverse many of the localised effects of de-industrialisation. If that potential has not been fully realised in either Britain or France it is not because the state has lacked in power or resources but because national officials have been as much or more concerned with achieving *national* economic goals than with redressing regional or inter-urban imbalances.

In sum, it is not plausible to regard the decline of some of our cities and the growth of others as the irreversible result of economic processes. It is demonstrably possible for democratic states to use state powers and incentives to channel private investment towards declining regions, to expand the public sector in declining cities and to promote and invest in policies of industrial regeneration. There are limits to the extent and effectiveness of state intervention in capitalist economies but they are more flexible and conditional than advocates of supply-side economics would have us believe. *The continued decline of most of the old industrial cities of Britain and the United States is the result of public decisions to allow the economic fate of those cities to be determined in the private sector*. The public decisions are those of the national state, not the local state, most of whose officials would support a more interventionist role. Their own capacities to pursue remedial and developmental policies for the city are limited first by their subordination to the national state, and second by the fact that private-sector decisions affecting local economies are increasingly made by managers of national and multinational corporations who cannot be controlled or effectively influenced by the local state.

There are constraints on *how much* the national state can do to reverse urban decline. In Britain's stagnant economy, where per capita productivity is among the lowest in western Europe, there is less private capital and public spending to redirect to declining cities than in the United States. In a society where the percentage of unemployed is projected to double between 1980 and 1990 (Fothergill and Gudgin, 1982, p. 176) one might, for example, expect a socially-sensitive urban policy to aim at keeping the present disproportionate concentration of jobless people in the large cities from growing still further. But one could not as reasonably expect the state to duplicate in declining Newcastle, England the publicly-sponsored renaissance of Boston, Massachusetts because in present circumstances the price would be to reduce employment opportunities and public spending elsewhere in Britain. The unenviable task of the welfare state in a declining economy is the equitable allocation of privation. The positive strategies open to the state in the face of this fundamental economic constraint are to stimulate productivity and trade. Whether it should do so by relying on private enterprise or through state planning and investment is another matter, one determined by political ideology, will and administrative capacity.

One can also ask whether there are limits to what the American national and local states might achieve in efforts to ease urban decline. We have attributed central Boston's regained prosperity mainly to political entrepreneurship on behalf of a strategically-situated city. Few other declining cities enjoy the regional status and national political connections which favoured Boston. Built into the federal system is inherent resistance to policies which might favour declining cities in one region at the expense of prospering regions elsewhere. Moreover, the United States lacks any experience of national urban or regional planning and is governed by an Administration which opposes in principle any extension of federal responsibility for urban problems. In brief, the immediate constraints on more active state policy toward declining American cities are political rather than economic ones.

Alternative futures for Western cities

State and capital are reshaping Western cities and urban systems, sometimes in ways that have no historical precedent.

We can generalise about those changes by thinking in terms of four modal types of cities, each of them shaped by distinctive combinations of public and private activity. In all of them the state has a primary interest in maintaining public order and providing essential services. Beyond that minimum, though, the responsibilities assumed by the state differ substantially across cities and countries. The first two types are the viable industrial cities, old and new. None of the old cities which are primarily dependent on heavy industry are thriving but some have been stabilised by active state intervention in the form of planning, subsidy and direct public investment and ownership. The national and local states' role in the new industrial cities is usually more passive or indirect, limited mainly to providing incentives and maintaining infrastructure. The third type is the administrative and service city whose vitality depends on a synergistic mix of public and private sector activity. The fourth category is the welfare city in which there are no significant growth sectors, public or private, its residents subsisting mainly on transfer payments, public employment and secondary service industries.

There are other, more detailed classifications of cities based on finer distinctions among their economic functions, for example by Gordon (1976) and Donnison and Soto (1980). A seven-fold categorisation by Castells (1977, ch. 1) includes national and regional metropolises, sub-metropolitan regional capitals, diversified industrial centres with (a) substantial or (b) weak metropolitan functions, specialised industrial centres and a residual category. Our classification highlights our theoretical interest in the ways that state policies interact with economic forces to reshape the cities of advanced industrial societies. The distinctive patterns of public and private activities which characterise each of the four types of cities are shown in Figure 6.1. The following discussion of each category and the illustrative evidence on British and American cities should make it clear that the four types are abstractions from a more complex reality. In particular, the patterns of state policy in the new industrial cities and administrative and service cities are too varied to be captured adequately in a dichotomous distinction between 'active' and 'passive' state policy. And the patterns of urban economic activity are equally diverse: most

Market economy

		Stagnant	Prosperous
State **power**	Passive	welfare cities	new industrial cities
and **policy**	Active	old industrial cities	administrative and service cities

FIGURE 6.1 *Patterns of state and market activity in four types of city*

cities have a mix of old and new industry and service activities. The questions from our perspective are: which are the leading sectors in any given city, which if any is growing, and what part does the state play in promoting that growth?

Old industrial cities

A relative handful of old industrial cities are emerging from the transitions of the post-industrial revolution with modernised industries that will continue to produce basic capital and consumer goods. Detroit and the satellite industrial cities of Paris will continue to produce automobiles, and Essen and Pittsburgh to make and fabricate steel, though at less than historical levels of productivity and profits. In the United States the survival of these basic industries, and the cities whose livelihoods depend upon them, is largely a matter of Darwinian competition among national firms and their foreign competitors. But not entirely: automobile and steel import quotas have been used by the Reagan Administration to protect these American industries. In Europe, national states have taken a more direct role, including nationalisation and public investment in modernisation: the automobile and steel industries in Britain and France are largely state-owned, for example.

The revival of old industrial cities thus occurs within the framework of policy decisions by the national state, either to intervene actively in the form of state capitalism and support for modernisation, or to protect basic industries from foreign competition. Derby is illustrative, a small, old industrial city in the Midlands of England whose modern prosperity is based on the aerospace industry and British Rail's engineering works. Whether the industrial base of such cities is in the public or the private economy is immaterial to their classification: they remain *industrial* cities with industrial labour forces, whose products must compete in national and international markets.

The survival and revival of these cities is largely outside the influence of the local state. The elected representatives of old industrial cities may have some marginal effects on the shape of national policies for regional development and re-industrialisation, but considerations of the national political economy are primary. If national planners decide that the mines and mills upon which a city depends for employment are redundant and not worth modernising, local officials have little more recourse than they do when private corporations make similar disinvestment decisions. The local state does have some potential influence on redevelopment decisions by private capital through its regulatory and tax policies, and especially through public capital investment in the transportation facilities and other basic infrastructure required by industry. But these are costly investments for which fiscally-stressed municipal governments have great difficulty raising funds. In principle, public investment by the local state in old industrial cities can lead private reinvestment. In practice the essential decisions are made by capital managers over whom the local state has no controlling influence.

New industrial cities

The economies of new industrial cities are based on both the relocation and growth of old industries and on the commercial development of new technologies. In the United States, many of these cities are based on the electronics, aerospace and communications industries, but this is only a partial account. Much of the industrial growth in the United States, whether based on new technologies or old, is occurring in towns and smaller cities because it is cheaper to establish and expand plants in smaller cities than in larger ones (see Allaman and

Birch, 1975). In Britain the growth of new industrial towns and cities is more the consequence of lack of space for plant expansion in large cities than the establishment of new high-tech industries (Fothergill and Gudgin, 1982, ch. 5). Norwich is one example, a small city whose growth is based upon its role as a service centre for an agricultural region. The growth of nearby Cambridge is mainly due to high-tech industries attracted or stimulated by the presence of a major research university. And both cities have the advantage of small size.

In both countries, the costs to entrepreneurs of building new plants and offices in smaller and newer cities which are attractive to management and workers are usually much less than the costs of expanding or converting old industrial sites in the grimy cores of declining cities. The social costs for the larger and older cities are substantial but the burden of those costs does not fall on the corporations making investment decisions. Thus the national state is likely to be more concerned than private capital with the social implications of the location of new industries and branch plants and may attempt to steer private and public investment toward poorer cities and regions, as governments have done in the United Kingdom and France. In Britain, the incentives and subsidies used to implement national planning have spurred growth in some declining regions, but mainly to the benefit of their peripheries rather than their large cities.

Once a new industrial base is established in a city in any of these countries it poses fewer problems for the national or local state than do the old industrial cities. Growing economies produce ample local revenues and enough jobs to reduce the proportion of population dependent upon government transfer payments. The expanding American cities examined in Chapter 3 had proportionally about half the number of beneficiaries of social security and welfare programmes as did the seriously declining ones, for example. Public capital investment in new facilities in growing smaller cities is not the high-risk proposition it is in old industrial cities, because it is very likely to pay off in further economic expansion and tax revenues. The principal developmental objectives of the local state in such cities are to minimise the obstacles to continued growth, and to use local political resources to secure the support of the national and regional states for developmental projects.

The state actively intervenes in these new industrial cities, but in the United States it does so in ways designed to facilitate private-sector growth, not to steer or control it. Houston, a self-proclaimed free-enterprise city, provides a vivid example of a long-term, private-dominated partnership between capital and state in the promotion of economic growth. In Houston, the crucial interventions began early in the twentieth century, when local entrepreneurs and politicians successfully pressured the Texas legislature and the US Congress to provide then-unprecedented governmental funds and public financing for port development. During the Depression era the local growth coalition successfully lobbied for a substantial share of reconstruction funds. During the Second World War massive federal funds were invested in oil-related enterprises in the Houston area, and in the 1960s a major National Aeronautics and Space Administration complex was sited in Houston. From the 1930s onward the large Houston-based oil companies have benefited from federal regulation designed to protect their competitive position. Throughout this period, local officials, congressional representatives and business groups used their influence in Washington to maximise federal capital grants and regulatory protection for business in Houston (Feagin, 1985). What they did *not* do was to promote the expansion of the public sector on any of the other dimensions we examined empirically in Chapter 3. Federal and state grants per capita to Houston's municipal government in 1983 were by far the lowest among the thirteen cities examined, though they began to increase in the 1970s (Feagin, 1985, p. 1218). Public employment is low and public-sector payments benefit smaller percentages of people and contribute less to total personal income than in any other growing or declining city. The inference is that Houston's direct dependence on the public sector is small precisely because the national state's contributions to the growth of private capital have been so great.

Administrative and service cities

The economies of these and the following category of 'welfare cities' are more substantially and directly dependent upon the public sector than the economies of most old and new industrial cities. The public–private partnerships of Houston and other new-technology cities in the United States are dominated by the private sector; in the administrative and service cities the partnership is usually, but not necessarily dominated by the state.

The administrative city is distinguished by its concentration of higher-order administrative, service and financial activities. National and regional capitals are public administrative cities whose essential character predates the Industrial Revolution. In early modern Europe one could distinguish only two general types of city: the trading cities of the Lowlands, the Hanseatic League, and northern Italy; and the capitals of secular and religious authorities with their concentrations of administrative offices and craftsmen producing for the courts, officials and their dependents.

Washington, DC and Bonn epitomise the public administrative cities of the contemporary world. London and Paris have more diverse economies but fall into the same general category: in addition to being the national state's administrative headquarters they house the head offices of most of their countries' major corporations, banks and investment firms, as well as being national centres of higher education, cultural activities, mass communication and entertainment. For example, the United Kingdom's four major commercial banks are headquartered in the City of London, as are most of its merchant banks. More than half of the country's 5000 barristers have offices in London's Inns of Court. And almost all national newspapers are published from London (from Sampson, 1984, chs 9, 18 and 27). London has an industrial sector also, but it has lost a larger portion of its manufacturing employment than has any other conurbation: 38 per cent between 1959 and 1975 alone. It also has the largest concentration of Britain's electronics firms, but even this is a declining industry, substantially dependent on defence spending (James Simmie, personal communiction). New York and Hamburg typify a third group of administrative and service cities, ones whose livelihood is provided by international trade, corporate offices, financial institutions and communication services. They are administrative and service centres, but mainly for private capital, only secondarily for the state.

Administrative and service cities, whether predominantly public or private, are likely to be more salient to the national state and to have larger public sectors than have most industrial cities. Their salience follows from their role as control centres both of state authority and of private economic activity. National governments' cumulative investments in their capitals' monuments, thoroughfares and public buildings are one visible legacy of that interest. The national salience of a city such as New York can be attributed to its symbolic role as America's first city and, more tangibly, to the influence of its economic interest groups and political representatives on the federal government. New York was one of a number of declining cities whose municipal administrations faced fiscal crises in the 1970s; the federal Treasury took a leading role in arranging and financing a solution, a response not extended to old industrial cities in similar circumstances. The case of Boston was discussed in Chapter 3, an old and once-decaying city whose renaissance is attributable in significant part to an outpouring of funds from state and federal governments for public works and buildings, public-sector jobs, research and development, and defence procurements. Boston's Washington political connections have been close and effective, from the Kennedy Administration in the early 1960s to Tip O'Neil's leadership of the US House of Representatives in the 1980s.

We can offer few firm generalisations about the role of the local state in administrative cities. In the American examples cited above the municipal governments of mixed public–private administrative cities have made good use of political influence in Washington, but in New York's case it could be argued that influence worked because of the city's economic centrality, whereas Massachusetts' political clout helped make Boston a regional growth centre. National capitals should in principle be well-financed and their municipal services of high quality because of national officials' personal and public interests in the quality of life in their home cities. By the same token we would expect the municipal officials of capitals to have little autonomy to pursue policies at odds with those of national officials. London's experience is generally consistent with these expectations. Despite its enormous loss of manufacturing jobs it has gained slightly in service employment and has had higher average earnings and lower unemployment than the other conurbations. None the less, inner London has substantial concentrations of deprivation and blight, and rates of serious crime that have risen without interruption since the late 1950s (Fothergill and Gudgin, 1982; Cameron, 1980; Gurr, Grabosky and Hula, 1977). Greater London is so large that some of its problems may be beyond the ken of national officials, but the crux of the matter is one of political commitment. In fact, local states – the Greater London Council and a number of borough governments – have been thwarted in their efforts to take corrective actions by a national Government committed to the overriding political objective of shrinking the public sector.

Welfare cities

These are the old industrial cities which have not benefited significantly from any of the transformations outlined above. Most of the industries around which they grew in the nineteenth and early twentieth centuries have been shut down, have cut back production, or have moved elsewhere. Few new enterprises have been attracted in their place and those which remain employ fewer people, mainly in low-skill occupations, and generate less wealth and tax revenues. Nor have these cities acquired substantial new administrative or service functions for either the private or public economies.

Which cities fall into this category? In the United States and Britain they are the cities which rank lowest on measures of per capita income and highest on indicators of hardship. The worst-case American cities during the 1970s included Newark and St Louis, and old steel towns such as Gary, Indiana and Youngstown, Ohio (Nathan and Adams, 1976, p. 55). Their British counterparts are Newcastle-on-Tyne, Liverpool and Glasgow, which on most indicators have fared somewhat worse than Manchester, Birmingham and London. To call them 'welfare cities' may seem perjorative because all of them have some small private growth sectors, some evidence of public-sector activity, some neighbourhoods that remain free of blight.

In the aggregate, however, they have proportionally large and inexorably growing numbers of the poor and unemployed, and as a consequence relatively large numbers of their people subsist on government transfer payments. For example, more than a third of the populations of the four seriously declining American cities examined in Chapter 3 received social security or federal welfare payments – double the proportion in four rapidly-growing cities. The municipal governments of declining American cities place heavy tax burdens on the businesses and homeowners who remain *and* are heavily dependent on grants from the regional and national state (see Chapter 4). In both countries, such cities generate little wealth in the private sector: wage rates and per capita productivity are lower than those of the other types of city and they export little in the way of goods or capital. They are, in short, the economic backwaters of the advanced capitalist societies, largely abandoned by private capital, passed over in plans for regional redevelopment, and heavily dependent on government spending to maintain individual and collective existence at a subsistence level.

The main contribution of the national state to these cities is money, not for capital investment or regional development, but as payments to the unemployed, to redundant workers retired early, to welfare mothers and to other categories of beneficiaries who happen to be concentrated there. And money to cover the deficits of the local state, which is obliged to provide basic municipal services without enough local revenue to pay for them. Providing basic services in these cities can be expensive: they tend to have large budgets for capital maintenance and social services. The municipal finances of the four declining and four growing American cities help to make the point: the governments of the declining cities in 1983 spent one-third more per capita, and received more than twice as much in state and federal grants per capita.

The national state *can* provide even more funds for these cities, as the federal government has for Boston. Given the right mix of public and private funds and initiatives, the process of local economic decline is reversible in a prosperous economy. In a stagnant economy the constraints are more formidable, as we suggested in the previous section. If the economic and demographic trends of the 1950s and 1960s had continued in Boston, it probably would now be among the 'welfare cities' rather than a relatively prosperous regional administrative city. Substantial public and private efforts are underway to arrest and reverse the decline of two other eastern port and industrial cities, Baltimore and Philadelphia. But we do not know what the 'right mix' of conditions is which makes redevelopment a reality in Boston, a possibility in Baltimore, yet highly improbable in Newark and St Louis. Boston and Massachusetts' political influence on the federal government has been a major factor but far from a sufficient explanation. The research and development complex centred on two major universities is relevant also; so is the willingness of some private capital to invest in electronics and defence industries in the greater Boston area rather than in the Sunbelt. It might be argued that Boston's redevelopment has resulted from a unique combination of circumstances. We think it is more promising to look for parallels and contrasts among the redevelopment efforts of a number of old industrial cities and to attempt to identify the strategies and conditions which differentiate between the more and the less successful. Such an inquiry must recognise from the outset that there are three major partners to all such redevelopment efforts in the United States: the national state, the local state and private investors.

The analysis of redevelopment strategies for old industrial cities should be transnational. The traditions of planning and state capitalism in European societies, and the larger size of their public sectors by comparison with the United States, give the state potentially greater leverage on urban change. In Britain, however, the only European country we have examined in detail, prospects for urban redevelopment are if anything more dim than in the United States. Of the seven largest metropolitan areas of England and Scotland three probably should be categorised, on present evidence, as welfare cities. Britain has regions of economic growth but they are far removed from the large old industrial cities. The larger constraint on British public policy is relatively low national productivity, but 'poor Britain' is not a sufficient answer. We would put as much emphasis on the rigidity of national policies since 1979, which in effect deny the national state a positive role in reshaping cities. British urban policy is also rigid in another way: the local states of Britain's cities lack the political autonomy that enables municipal governments in the American federal system to horse-trade with private investors and cut political deals for more resources from regional and national agencies. If private-sector competition and innovation are supposed to regenerate the national economy, then local states also should be free to play quasi-independent roles in pursuing strategies of urban redevelopment.

State power, state interests and urban decline

The argument of Chapter 1 is that states have certain irreducible interests in the maintenance of public order and authority in cities. Public authorities also have gradually taken on additional responsibilities for providing various special and general collective goods and services for urban populations. They did so at first in response to particular exigencies – to meet critical needs for water supply and transportation facilities, to satisfy political demands to provide funds for education, to assist the unemployed and indigent, to improve housing and recreational facilities, and so on. To ensure an ample supply of revenues for these purposes the national and local state took increasingly active roles in promoting urban economic development. Responsibilities once assumed for reasons of short-term expedience are now much more compelling, and administrative and elected officials have vested, programmatic interests in continuing them. Urban populations expect them to be provided, and are likely to vote out of office the governments which fail to provide them. In a functional sense the survival of modern cities is dependent on continued public regulation, services and spending. That is, there is some lower threshold of public provision below which people will no longer be willing or able to live in cities. There is no way of saying where that threshold is in the abstract: it has already been passed for many of the hundreds of thousands of people who have migrated away from the centres of old industrial cities. There is no contemporary precedent, nor any fully documented historical ones, to tell us what is likely to happen after all those who can leave have done so, leaving such cities populated only by a dependent underclass. The triumph of market forces will be complete when the last emigrants from Toxteth and the East Bronx pause on their way out, not to turn out the lights, but to strip the crumbling buildings of light fixtures and wiring for sale as scrap.

The economic and political developments reviewed in this chapter have substantial implications for the state's present and future interests in cities. It has been demonstrated that two of our four categories of city have become substantially and directly dependent on the national state. We also suggested that the redeveloped old industrial cities and the new industrial cities are indirectly, but no less significantly, influenced by public policies and spending. What, then, are the implications of neo-conservative national policies in Britain and the United States? The contemporary political and ideological climate in both countries is hostile to state intervention in the economy in general and opposed to an active national role in urban redevelopment in particular. While these ideological and policy shifts are associated with the elections of Ronald Reagan in the United States and Margaret Thatcher in the United Kingdom, it is important to note that cutbacks in national urban programmes had been initiated by preceding administrations in each country (Levine, 1982; Tabb, 1984; Newton and Karran, 1985). The two conservative administrations have accelerated a retreat from the cities that was already underway. Urban policy in the Reagan administration is dominated by the Administration's intention of stimulating long-term, non-inflationary economic growth, a policy that in Levine's (1982) words has 'little room for the targeting of investment to the nation's relatively high cost, less productive, declining areas' (p. 1). British urban policy in the Thatcher Government can be characterised in much the same way, as reported in Chapter 5. An intellectual basis for such a policy course is provided by Jane Jacobs' (1984) recent book, which argues *inter alia* that state subsidy will never substitute effectively for market processes in the generation of economic growth. Cities are the locus of economic growth, but uneven urbanisation is the norm. The decline of cities which have exhausted their wealth-generating potential is inevitable and should be accepted as such by both policymakers and residents.

The evidence of this book contradicts the economic determinism which underlies contemporary urban policy in the United States and Britain. The dynamism of cities as diverse as Oxford, Houston and Boston owes a great deal to the national and local states' developmental policies and to public-sector spending. But as the national state retreats from its active role in urban redevelopment the assumption of economic determinism becomes self-fulfilling. If the state gives up the attempt to channel and restructure economic activities then the fate of urban economies will, in fact, be determined by private economic decisions, without reference to spatial unevenness or social inequities and hardship. The national state's disengagement from urban responsibilities coincides with the increased internationalisation of production and of capital mobility, which have contributed to the increased disparities between growing and declining urban regions. A recent study of urban policy in the United States, Britain and Australia concludes that

> the disengagement of the state from the urban arena represents a retreat backwards and an abrogation of the analysis that gave rise to urban policy in the first place. The declaration of an 'open season' for the private sector will generate greater social costs and add to the hardship caused by restructuring. The problems of and in the declining cities of advanced capitalist societies, if nothing else, will get worse. (Badcock, 1984, p. 310)

The national state's short-run retreat from responsibility for the welfare of cities is self-evidently contrary to the interests of some kinds of cities, in particular the old industrial cities. They now have fewer prospects for the restructuring necessary either to build new industrial sectors or to make the transition to administrative and service centres. More cities are likely to become or remain welfare cities, and the conditions of life in those cities will deteriorate further. The lack of national policies to stem the tide of urban decline makes it all the more urgent that local states attempt to do so, because *their* officials' authority and political survival depend upon the provision of essential urban services. But they usually lack the capacity to raise revenues to do so, and in Britain are now prohibited from doing so as a matter of national policy. In addition fiscal stress makes it more difficult for the local state in declining cities to provide the facilities and incentives that might stimulate private redevelopment.

The general implications for the local state of national withdrawal and continued urban decline are unpleasant. It follows from our analysis of state interests that larger proportions of shinking public resources will be devoted to the primary objectives of maintaining public order and officials' own positions and perquisites. In American cities there is likely to be a return to an older style of clientele-orientated machine politics in which limited resources are used to pay off or buy up a minimum coalition of supporters necessary to keep elected city officials in office. More important for the people who cannot escape declining cities, the result will be retrenchment in all but the most essential public services and reduction in locally-financed social services wherever politically expedient. Among municipal bureaucrats the results can be expected to be equally malign: a growing concern with protecting positions and perquisites, intensified competition for resources, the erosion of commitment to programmatic goals and technocratic standards of professional service, and increased politicisation of the administrative process.

In the longer run policies of benign neglect toward declining cities are also inimical to the national state's interests – summarised graphically in Figures 1.1 and 1.2 (see pages 19 and 41). National officials have short- and long-term interests in maintaining their authority against political challenges: elected officials seek to minimise electoral support for opposition parties and all officials share a common, primary interest in maintaining public order in cities and forestalling collective political action. But as we have pointed out, the legitimacy of governments in contemporary democratic states rests substantially upon the maintenance of prosperity and the provision of a high level of common and special social services. Those conditions are singularly lacking in declining old cities, which means that their inhabitants are potential sources of resistance to national policy. The greater the inter-urban disparities in prosperity and the greater the unleavened concentrations of poor and unemployed people in declining cities, the greater the potential challenges. High levels of anomic violence – murder and assault, gang activity – have contributed to the blight of inner cities in Britain and the United States since the 1960s. Rioting has been more episodic and perhaps because of that has stimulated new, ameliorative public policies in both countries – in the United States in 1964–68 and in Britain in 1981–86. But these policies have not been enough to arrest continued decline.

It is clear that neo-conservative national administrations in Britain and the United States have little partisan support among the populations of old industrial cities. Virtually all the municipal councils of these cities in both countries are controlled by Labour and Democratic governments who actively oppose national policies. A case can also be made that some of these people – ordinary people *and* local officials – no longer accept the legitimacy of the national political systems which have handed over responsibility for their future to the market place and the trickle-down effects of private-sector growth. It is difficult in the late twentieth century to imagine cities in open rebellion against the national state, but there is no question that metropolitan and borough councils in Britain have sought to evade or subvert national policies when they were harmful to local interests. Resistance by the local states of declining cities is paralleled by the potential of ordinary citizens for political activism. If and when they are mobilised by opposition political parties or political movements, they will provide the basis for electoral opposition that is likely to overturn national governments that are blind to urban problems. Mass urban protest and political violence are ominous alternatives or complements to electoral politics. In one way or the other, the Reagan and Thatcher governments are laying the groundwork for major urban-centred political challenges to their rule and to the authority of the states they manage.

There are two twentieth-century precedents in the United States which suggest the potential consequences of such challenges. We showed in Chapter 4 that in both the 1930s and the 1960s urban crisis led to step-level increases in the federal commitment to cities. In both historical episodes there was a distinctive conjuncture of circumstances: the concentration of social stress and disorder in the central cities, a lack of municipal resources to deal with them, and the ascendency of national Democrats who made political capital of responding positively to urban problems. The necessary conditions for a replay of history are largely in place; the sufficient condition, a national Democratic administration, may or may not be realised in this decade.

There are alternatives to risky and potentially self-defeating urban policies within the conservative framework as well as the liberal and social democratic ones. What the declining cities and regions of both countries need is large-scale economic restructuring and redevelopment. The social democratic approach is to rely mainly on public investment and expansion of the public sector to accomplish that purpose. The failure of the market-orientated conservative approach is not its reliance on the regenerative capacity of the private economy *per se*: that policy has had substantial aggregate pay-offs in the United States, if not yet in Britain. The failure has been the reluctance of neo-conservative administrations to use enough of the state's powers and resources to ensure that entrepreneurial innovation and investment are channelled to stagnant and declining areas. Enterprise zones are not enough; the neo-conservative state would have to act in the context of a comprehensive plan using all its regulatory and fiscal powers to maximise the potential for profitable private redevelopment in target areas. There might be some aggregate inefficiencies in such a policy of state-guided private enterprise, but they are less than the short-run social costs and the long-run political costs of abandoning old cities.

It is not our intent to recommend a detailed set of policies for reviving cities. There is not nearly enough reliable comparative information about the political and economic circumstances in which particular kinds of policies of redevelopment are likely to work. The point of this final analysis is to assert again that the national state in industrial democracies has some irreducible interests in the material and political welfare of cities. The logic of our argument and evidence is that state and city have become so interdependent that national officials who try to extricate government from responsibility for cities do so at great cost to the cities and great political risk to the state and their own administrations.

Appendix to Chapter 4

This appendix provides a detailed account of the city sample, data sources (and associated problems) and regression methods used for the statistical analysis reported in the text.

City sample

The units of analysis for this study are all central cities in the United States with populations equal to or greater than 200 000 in 1960, 1970 or 1980; this yields a maximum sample size of seventy-five. Populations of 200 000 or more were selected as the most appropriate threshold level because these cities have experienced the most radical changes in metropolitan population over the last thirty years, because the salience of large cities to the national state is presumably greater than the salience of smaller cities, and because it yields a manageable sample size. Central cities (as designated within SMSAs [standard metropolitan statistical areas]) have been focused on for the theoretical arguments outlined in Chapters 1 and 2.

Data and sources

There are serious difficulties confronting any attempt to collect exact and accurate data on the flow of federal aid to cities in the United States. As the authors of the definitive appraisal of federal data sources observe, 'the federal government knows less about its fiscal interactions with cities than about its interaction with virtually any other level of American government. An apparently simple number such as total federal spending is now impossible to obtain for a single city in a single year, let alone many cities for a period of years' (Anton, Cawley and Kramer, 1980, p. 81; see also Stein, 1981).

There are two principal governmental statistical sources of United States federal aid to cities: the figures, recorded since 1964, for each municipality in *City Government Finances*, published annually by the Bureau of the Census (which also publishes every five years the *Census of the Governments: Finances of Municipalities and Township Governments*); and the figures recorded in the *Federal Outlays* (annual 1968–77, entitled thereafter *Geographic Distribution of Federal Funds*), published by the Community Service Administration. The census data include only grants-in-aid, ignoring other types of federal funding for loans, salaries, direct expenditures and procurements. This source also excludes federal funds which are passed through the 50 states to recipient

209

cities – though this is more a problem for the study of all substate governmental units than for an examination of funds allocated to general purpose municipal governments (Stein, 1981, p. 342). With regard to the outlays data Anton (1980, p. 148) argues that they 'remain fragmentary at the city level either because outlays are reported only to counties or because lack of good statistical estimates confounds reports made at the city level'. Federal outlays data systematically understate the amount of federal funding to cities, Anton, Cawley and Kramer (1980) contend, which is 'further aggravated by underreporting of expenditures by some agencies ... outlays reports of H.U.D. expenditures represent only a fraction of total H.U.D. obligations for any given year, further weakening the current usefulness of outlays data for analyzing federal aid to cities' (pp. 86–7). It should be noted, however, that if this underreporting is *systematic* (which it appears to be), then any inequalities in the distribution of aid should be reflected in our aggregate data. This mitigates some of these criticisms. A number of other points can be made about utilising the existing data on federal aid to cities.

The problems appear to be most severe for those scholars concerned to examine the impact of individual policies or programmes: the census source over-reports many of them while the outlays data either under-reports or neglects entirely some of these programmes. Fortunately, our analysis is focused on the *distribution of funds among cities* rather than on absolute levels of funding. Accordingly, we propose that these federally-generated figures on federal flows to cities can still be used as proxies or surrogate measures, that is, as indicators of the overall patterns and trends in central state aid to municipalities: whether they over-report the magnitude of the trends is less important than that they give a consistent picture of its distribution. Thus they should be adequate for testing the plausibility of our theoretical propositions. Therefore we use the figures recorded in *City Government Finances* as originating from federal sources as our indicator of the amount of aid these cities received. Stein (1981) has also confronted this problem but still relies on the federal census source for empirical analysis. It should be noted that despite many incomparabilities, we found that the aggregate federal funds to large cities in 1980 reported in the two sources correlated 0.93, a reassuring finding given the characterisations of the two sources cited above. Finally, since population size is important to the formulas used in the 1970s to allocate federal aid we use federal aid *per capita* for our dependent variable throughout.

Variables and their standardisation

Table 4.2 lists the independent city-level variables collected for this study and their sources: most of the data were collected for 1960, 1970 and 1980 from the US Bureau of the Census's annual *City Government Finances* and *County and City Data Book*. They are listed in Table A, with their respective sources.

To weight for city population the following city-level variables have been 'per capitised' (that is, divided by city population): total civilian employment; total employment in manufacturing and in wholesale and retail trade; total long-term and short-term city debt; total city expenditure; city capital outlay; federal aid; property taxes; total city revenues; number of housing units; number of new housing permits issued; number of female-headed households; value added by manufacturing; violent and property crime. The following city-level variables have been calculated per 1000 of the city population: federal, state and local government employment; death rate. There are two dummy variables: 1. form of municipal government coded as mayor–council = 1, city manager = 0; and 2. region, coded as Frostbelt city (mid-west and north-east) = 1, Sunbelt city (west and south) = 0.

The empirical analysis focuses on a twenty-year period of recent American political history (1960–80). The first section of Chapter 4 indicated the enormous expansion of the federal–city fiscal connection which occurred during these two decades, though falling off after 1977. The period up to 1978 is termed 'Old Federalism' while the post-1978 era is deemed to be that of 'New Federalism' (see Shannon, 1984; Gelfand, 1980: this overlooks Nixon's earlier use of the term 'New Federalism'). As one scholar notes of the post-1978 period, 'there has been a sharp decline in the relative importance of federal aid flows when compared to state and local own source revenues – a drop from nearly 32 per cent in 1978 to an estimated 21 per cent for 1983' (Shannon, 1984, p. 329). Thus the period under consideration in this study constitutes a historically-bounded period. In Chapter 6 some attention was given to the post-1978 trends and their implications for state–city relations.

Regression method

The regression models reported in Table 4.4 (see p. 146) were calculated using ordinary least-squares regression techniques. A number of different versions of the models were assessed using alternative measures of the city-level characteristics, and problems of multicollinearity and mean skewedness were addressed. For the equations estimated there is a sufficient sample size to offset the dangers arising from too few degrees of freedom. The procedures used in the generation of the final regression equations are as follows. First, all the variables have been included in a backward regression and sequentially removed as they fail to meet the F-value removal criterion of 1.00. This *F*-value was selected because the continued inclusion of variables with *F*-values below 1.00 works to increase the equation's mean square error and to reduce the amount of variance explained by the equation. Next, to ensure that the backward regression procedure has not eliminated any variables mistakenly, the analysis is repeated using a forward regression procedure, which begins with no variables in the equation and enters variables with *F*-values greater than 1.00 beginning with those contributing most powerfully to the variance explained. After one variable has been entered, the next one is selected using the statistics for the remaining variables not in the equation, which calculates in effect the *F*-value of those variables. This process is continued until all the variables which meet the entry criterion have been selected. Although the removal and entry criteria used by the backward and forward regression procedures are the same (*F*-value greater than 1.00) the two procedures may produce different results – though they did not in the current analysis. It should also be noted that the

Hypothesis 1: Electoral interests	Sources
Percentage population black	1
Percentage population other minorities	1, 2
National union headquarters	6
Mayor–council form of government	10

Hypothesis 2:   Programmatic objectives

1. Social needs

Percentage of population dependent (18, 65)	1, 2
Percentage of families below the poverty line	1
Female headed households per capita	1
Percentage housing stock pre-1940 in 1970	8
Percentage of population < 5 yrs education	1
Percentage of population 4 yrs + high school	1
Percentage of population 4 yrs college	1

2. Economic needs

Per capita money income	1
Percentage of workforce unemployed	1
Percentage employment in manufacturing	1
Percentage employment in wholesale/retail	1
Total population	1
Total civilian employment per capita	1, 2
Total employment in manufacturing per capita	1
Total employment in wholesale/retail per capita	1

3. Fiscal needs

City long-term debt per capita	3
City short-term debt per capita	3
City property taxes per capita	3
Total city revenues per capita	3
City total debt per capita	3
Total city expenditures per capita	3
City capital outlay per capita	2, 3

Hypothesis 3:   Public order and administrative control

Violent crime per capita	7
Property crime per capita	7
Racial rioting 1963–69	
Arrests per capita	11*
Days of rioting per capita	11*
Deaths per capita	11*
State capital	*
Federal employment per 1000	1
Federal employment as percentage of civilian employment	1

Hypothesis 4: Economic interests

Corporate headquarters	5
Value added by manufacturing in city per capita	2
Total number of new housing permits issued per capita	2

* Our coding

F-value criterion is a very conservative one. The procedure used may seem rather conservative but it has the advantage over stepwise regression analysis of equalising the opportunities for core and alternative variables to be retained or deleted.

SOURCES
1. *Census of Population*, 1950, 1960, 1970, 1980.
2. *County and City Data Book*, 1962, 1967, 1972, 1977, 1982.
3. *City Government Finances*, 1960–80
4. *City Employment*, 1960–80
5. *Fortune* magazine.
6. *AFL–CIO Directory*.
7. *FBI Uniform Crime Reports*, 1960, 1970, 1980.
8. *Census of Housing*, 1960, 1970, 1980.
9. Community Services Administration, *Geographic Distribution of Federal Funds: A Report of the Federal Government Impact by State, County and Large City* (Washington, D.C., 1968–77).
10. *Moody's Bond Record*, 1978.
11. *Facts on File, Violence in the U.S.*: vol. 1: 1956–67; Vol. 2: 1968–71.

Notes and References

1 A Theory of State–City Relations in Western Societies

1. Most recent research on urban political economy in the Unites States and Britain gives primacy to economic factors; see, for example, the review by Stone, 1984. A substantial exception, evaluated in Chapter 4, is John Mollenkopf's recent study (1983). See also Gottdiener, 1985.
2. This is a new theoretical argument, not one that has been more fully developed in other papers. It has been influenced by our reading of Ronald Cohen and Elman Service's anthropological analyses of the evolution of the state (Cohen and Service, 1978; Service, 1975), Dalton's writings in economic anthropology (1968) and historical accounts of the emergence of the European state in addition to conventional and neo-Marxist writings on state autonomy.
3. The spatial domain in which an elite has effective control is highly variable and there is no necessary conjunction between the scope of an economic elite's control and that of a political elite. In contemporary industrial societies, both socialist and democratic, political elites have used the instrument of the state to attain dominance, or parity, *within the geographic confines of the nation-state*. But there is a larger, 'global' capitalist system which is substantially autonomous of supranational political control for lack of a cohesive international political elite using the instrumentalities of a global state. And within societies there are local and regional political elites who have varying degrees of autonomy versus the national political elite, and varying degrees of autonomy from economic interests – an issue whose implications are considered briefly below and more fully in the following chapter.
4. On early modern conceptions of the state see Eckstein, 1979. Modern liberal and neo-Marxist conceptions of the state are reviewed by Carnoy, 1984. For general characterisations of the state in capitalist societies see Clark and Dear, 1984, ch. 2 and Greenberg, 1985, ch. 3.
5. This definition parallels Pettman's (1979, pp. 105–8) and is consistent with prevailing anthropological conceptions of the state; see, for example, Service, 1975, ch. 1 and Cohen and Service, 1978, introduction. For a definition which centres on functions rather than structures and claims see Jordan, 1985, pp. 1–2.
6. In some states judges are also among the policy makers. On quasi-public authorities see Sharkansky, 1979.

7. For empirical evidence on the differences in values and objectives among bureaucrats and politicians in Western democracies see Aberbach, Putnam and Rockman, 1981.

8. For the initial statement of this argument see Niskanen (1971). Subsequent analyses, for example Fiorina and Noll (1978) and Miller and Moe (1983), examine formally the effects of bargaining between budget-maximising bureaucrats and legislators concerned with maximising electoral support.

9. Margaret Levi has formulated 'The Predatory Theory of Rule' (1981) which rests on the assumption that 'the ruler is predatory in that he attempts to formulate policies that maximise his personal objectives' (p. 438). The effects of institutional constraints or ideological commitments on those objectives are not specified; to the extent that they do shape rulers' objectives, predation seems an inappropriate concept. Robert I. Rotberg characterised Haiti under François Duvalier as a 'predatory state ... defined as one in which brigandage is the predominant form of power, where effective power is exercised by praetorian specialists in violence' (1971, p. 342). But Papa Doc's Haiti was exceptional in this respect, even by the standards of Haitian history (Rotberg 1971, ch. 6).

10. The short- versus long-run distinction is prompted by Alex Hicks' comments (personal communication).

11. This paragraph is prompted by Brian Elliott's queries (personal communication) about the origins of officials' commitments to the state and follows from Weber's arguments about the sources and consequences of legitimacy in bureaucracies (1947, p. 324 ff.).

12. Both pluralists and neo-Marxists are critical of the influence of business and capital on the state, the latter more than the former. Advocates for private capital make the mirror-image criticism that business is unduly constrained by the state's fiscal demands and regulatory activities. Elkin (1985), summarising the pluralist perspective, takes a more balanced view. In the liberal democratic state 'the central concern of public officials and businessmen is not that business interests dominate policy decisions but that they always be present' (p. 199).

13. The state's impact on the private economy is a function both of its revenue-raising powers and its pattern of spending. Almost all public expenditures (with the exception of foreign aid and payments to supranational institutions) are spent in the domestic private sector: they consist of wages, pensions, welfare and other transfer payments, contracts with private suppliers, grants and interest payments on public debt – most of which are used by their recipients to finance purchases of private goods and services.

14. Our calculations from GNP data in current national currencies in International Monetary Fund, *International Finance Statistical Yearbook*, 1983 and data on general government finance from International Monetary Fund, *Government Finances Statistical Yearbook*, 1984.

15. These data refer to *central state* expenditures whereas those cited above are for expenditures by all levels of government. There are no consistent

data on the aggregate expenditures of local governments in most of these countries prior to 1950.

16. Rose (1984) has developed a 'program approach' to assessing the changing scope of state activity, including regulatory activity, and is applying it to cross-national comparison. For the present, historical trends in the expansion of state powers cannot be traced with comparable precision.

17. On the transition in origins and outlook of public officials in early Victorian Britain see Roberts, 1960, chs 5 and 6. Elsewhere in Europe, in Prussia and Russia for example, the development of an autonomous bureaucratic state preceded the industrial revolution, the state took the lead in promoting industrialisation, and the interests of private capital never enjoyed ascendency over the state as they did in nineteenth-century Britain and the United States; see Jacoby, 1973.

18. An influential general argument on the relation between the growth of 'civilisation' and cities was developed by V. Gordon Childe, best summarised in Childe, 1950. A comparative historical study of the emergence and growth of premodern cities which takes into account their political organisation is Hammond, 1972. Most accounts of the development of Western cities, however, emphasise processes of economic change; Hohenberg and Lees (1985) is typical in this respect, so is Girouard (1985), which encompasses colonial and modern Third world cities as well medieval and early modern European cities. Elliott and McCrone (1982) is atypical in its attention to the ways in which European cities have been shaped by politics and power.

19. The theoretical basis for these distinctions is developed in Eckstein, 1971 and Eckstein and Gurr, 1975, especially chs 7 and 15. They follow from arguments developed by Weber, 1947, Part III.

20. For accounts and theoretical interpretations of these processes see Strayer, 1970, Jacoby, 1973, Anderson, 1974, Tilly, 1975, Bendix, 1978 and Giddens, 1985.

21. In the United Kingdom total public expenditures during Margaret Thatcher's first Government increased by 7.2 per cent between 1979–80 and 1983–84 (King, 1985a), while in the United States aggregate federal outlays as a percentage of GNP increased from 21.7 per cent in 1979, during the Carter Administration, to 25.9 per cent four years later under the Reagan Administration (our calculation from the sources in note 14).

22. On the conditions of life in pre-industrial London see George, 1965; a useful survey of urban social problems during the Victorian period is Tobias, 1967, Part Three.

23. The relationship between the growth of social problems in nineteenth-century Britain and the establishment of the rudiments of the welfare state is examined by Roberts (1969); Bruce (1966) traces the process through the 1930s. Briggs (1965) provides detailed accounts of the costs and benefits of progress in six Victorian cities, with ample evidence on the circumstances in which municipal governments took on new responsibilities.

24. Piven and Cloward (1971) make this argument with respect to the twentieth-century expansion of welfare expenditures in the United States. Swank (1983) reports comparative empirical evidence for such a relationship among seventeen industrial democracies.

25. Local governments of most Western democracies depend substantially on local revenues irrespective of degrees of political centralisation. In centralised Sweden and the United Kingdom local revenues accounted for 72 per cent and 55 per cent respectively of local government expenditures c.1980; in West Germany and the United States, both of them federal systems, local revenues accounted for 70 per cent and 51 per cent of local expenditure in the same year (our calculations from International Monetary Fund, *Government Finances Statistical Yearbook 1981*).

2 The Autonomy of the Local State in a Period of Fiscal Crisis

1. Portions of this chapter were included in 'The State and the City: Economic Transformation and the Autonomy of the Local State in Advanced Industrial Societies', pp. 3–22 in Paul M. Johnson and William R. Thompson (eds), *Rhythms in Politics and Economics* (New York: Praeger, for the International Studies Association, 1985).

3 The Political Salience of Urban Decline: Why and How the State Responds to Urban Change

1. An earlier version of the conceptual arguments of this chapter appeared in ch. 11 of Lané (1985).

2. Most studies of relations among economic and demographic dimensions of urban growth and decline in the United States distinguish between central cities and metropolitan regions but focus principally on the metropolitan region (see, for example, Bradbury, Downs and Small, 1982). A similar approach is taken in the major urban research projects underway in Europe, including the Urban Europe Project (van den Berg *et al.*, 1982) and the ongoing work of Peter Hall and associates at the University of Reading (England), for example, Hall and Hay, 1980). There are substantial differences among these studies in how widely the urban region is defined, but in all of them it is larger than what we call the political city, that is, the politically-organised central city.

3. For a sharp debate about the responsibility of the public versus the private sector for urban change in the United States and Europe see the exchange between John D. Kasarda and Peter Marcuse in Hellstern, Spreer and Wollmann, 1982, vol. 1.

4. Many of the activists in urban squatting movements in European capitals are (ex)university students and younger people in skilled and professional occupations. Other participants are of more diverse social origins. On squatters in London see Cockburn, 1977, ch. 3 and Kearns, 1981; in Amsterdam, Priemus, 1983 and in West Berlin, Katz and Mayer, 1985.

5. The immediate region for comparison is the Standard Metropolitan Statistical Area (SMSA) of which the core county is part. As many as eight counties are included in each SMSA. The larger region of reference is the grouping of states in which the city is located: north-east, mid-Atlantic, east north central, west south central (Texas), and west.

6. In most of these comparisons limitations of the data make it impossible to distinguish among the contributions of the federal, regional and local states to state material presence.

4 The Political Salience of Urban Crisis in the United States: The Federal Response

1. Part of the second section of this chapter was included in 'Federal Responses to Urban Fiscal Strain and Decline in the United States', *British Journal of Political Science*, vol. 16, no. 4.

5 Urban Decline and the Politicisation of Central–Local Relations in Great Britain

1. There remain significant differences in structures and emphases between England and Wales on the one hand and Scotland and Northern Ireland on the other. We concentrate on government structures in England and Wales.

2. In non-urban areas these structures are paralleled by non-metropolitan county councils (47) and non-metropolitan district councils (33) which are not considered in this discussion.

3. For detailed accounts of the process leading up to the proposals and their adoption by the Conservative Party see Flynn, Leach and Vielba, 1985; Forrester, Lansley and Pauley, 1985; and Wheen, 1985. See Wheen (1985) for extracts from the Coopers and Lybrand report which questions the savings to be gained from abolition of the metropolitan authorities.

4. This paragraph is prompted by comments received from Ken Newton on an earlier draft of this chapter.

Bibliography

ABERBACH, JOEL D., PUTNAM, ROBERT D. and ROCKMAN, BERT A. (1981) *Bureaucrats and Politicians in Western Democracies* (London and Cambridge, Mass.: Harvard University Press).

ADVISORY COMMISSION ON INTERGOVERNMENTAL RELATIONS (1975) *City Financial Emergencies* (Washington, D.C.).

ALCAHY, R. and MERMELSTEIN, D. (1976) (eds) *The Fiscal Crisis of American Cities* (New York: Vintage).

ALLAMAN, P. A. and BIRCH, D. L. (1975) *Components of Employment Change for States by Industry Group* (Cambridge, Mass.: Joint Center for Urban Studies, Working Paper no. 5).

ALT, JAMES E. and CHRYSTAL, K. ALEC (1983) *Political Economics* (Brighton: Wheatsheaf Books).

ANDERSON, PERRY (1974) *Lineages of the Absolutist State* (London: New Left Books).

ANTON, THOMAS J., CAWLEY, JERRY P. and KRAMER, KEVIN L. (1980) *Moving Money* (Cambridge, Mass.: Delgeschalger, Gunn & Hain).

ARDANT, G. (1975) 'Financial Policy and Economic Infrastructure of Modern States and Nations' in Charles Tilly (ed.) *The Formation of National States in Western Europe* (Princeton, New Jersey: Princeton University Press).

ASHFORD, DOUGLAS E. (1974) 'The Effects of Central Finance on the British Local Government System', *British Journal of Political Science*, 4, pp. 305–22.

—— (ed.) (1980) *Financing Urban Government in the Welfare State* (New York: St. Martin's Press).

BADCOCK, B. (1984) *Unfairly Structured Cities* (Oxford: Basil Blackwell).

BALL, N. and LEITENBERG M. (eds) (1983) *The Structure of the Defence Industry* (London: Croom Helm).

BANFIELD, EDWARD C. (1961) *Political Influence* (Glencoe, Illinois: The Free Press).

BAYLEY, DAVID H. (1975) 'The Police and Political Development in Europe' in Charles Tilly (ed.) *The Formation of National States in Western Europe* (Princeton, New Jersey: Princeton University Press).

BENDIX, REINHARD (1978) *Kings or People: Power and the Mandate to Rule* (Berkeley, Calif.: University of California Press).

BENJAMIN, ROGER and ELKIN, STEPHEN L. (1985) (eds) *The Democratic State* (Lawrence, Kansas: University Press of Kansas).

219

BERRY, BRIAN J. L. (1973) *Growth Centers in the American Urban System* (Cambridge, Mass.: Ballinger) vols 1 & 2.

—— (1977) *The Changing Shape of Metropolitan America 1960–1970.* (Cambridge, Mass.: Ballinger).

BETZ, M. (1974) 'Riots and Welfare: Are They Related?', *Social Problems*, 21, pp. 345–55.

BINGHAM, RICHARD D., HAWKINS, BRETT and HERBERT, TED F. (1978) *The Politics of Raising State and Local Revenue* (New York: Praeger).

BLOCK, FRED (1977) 'The Ruling Class Does Not Rule: Notes on the Marxist Theory of the State', *Socialist Revolution*, 33 (May–June), pp. 6–28.

—— (1981a) 'Beyond Relative Autonomy: State Managers as Historical Subjects' *New Political Science* 2, pp. 33–49.

—— (1981b) 'The Fiscal Crisis of the Capitalist State', *Annual Review of Sociology*, 7, pp. 1–27.

BLUESTONE, B. and HARRISON, B. (1982) *The Deindustrialization of America: Plant Closings, Community Abandonment, and the Dismantling of Basic Industry* (New York: Basic Books).

BODDY, MARTIN (1983) 'Central–Local Government Relations: Theory and Practice', *Political Geography Quarterly*, 2, pp. 119–38.

BRADBURY, KATHERINE L., DOWNS, ANTHONY and SMALL, KENNETH A. (1981) *Futures for a Declining City: Simulations for the Cleveland Area* (Washington, DC: Brookings Institution).

—— (1982) *Urban Decline and the Future of American Cities* (Washington, DC: Brookings Institution).

BREHENY, M. J. and McQUAD, R. W. (1985) *Technology Industries*, Reading University Geographical Papers no. 87.

BRIGGS, ASA (1965) *Victorian Cities* (New York: Harper and Row; Harmondsworth: Penguin Books).

BROADBENT, ANDREW (1977) *Planning and Profit in the Urban Economy* (London: Methuen).

BRUCE, MAURICE (1966) *The Coming of the Welfare State* (New York: Schocken Books; London: Batsford).

BUNCE, HAROLD and GLICKMAN, NORMAN (1980) 'The Spatial Dimension of the Community Development Block Grant Program: Targeting and Urban Impacts' in N. Glickman (ed.) *The Urban Impacts of Federal Policies* (Baltimore: The Johns Hopkins University Press).

BUTLER, STUART M. (1981a) *Enterprise Zones: Greenlining the Inner Cities* (New York: Universe Books; London: Heinemann).

—— (1981b) 'Enterprise Zones: Pioneering in the Inner City' in George Sternlieb and David Listokin (eds) *New Tools for Economic Development: The Enterprise Zone, Development Bank and RFC* (Piscataway, New Jersey: Rutgers University).

BUTTON, JAMES W. (1978) *Black Violence: Political Impact of the 1960s Riots* (Princeton, New Jersey: Princeton University Press).

BYRNE, TONY (1985) *Local Government in Britain* (Harmondsworth: Penguin Books).

CAMERON, G. C. (1973) 'Economic Analysis for a Declining Urban Economy' in G. C. Cameron and L. Wingo (eds) *Cities, Regions and Public Policy* (Edinburgh: Oliver & Boyd).

—— (1980) 'The Economies of the Conurbations' in G. C. Cameron (ed.) *The Future of the British Conurbations: Policies and Prescription for Change* (London and New York: Longman).

CARNOY, MARTIN (1984) *The State and Political Theory* (Princeton, New Jersey: Princeton University Press).

CARROLL, GLENN R. and MEYER, JOHN W. (1983) 'Capital Cities in the American Urban System: The Impact of State Expansion' *American Journal of Sociology*, 88, pp. 565–78.

CASTELLS, MANUEL (1977) *The Urban Question* (Cambridge, Mass.: MIT Press; London: Edward Arnold).

—— (1983) *The City and the Grassroots* (Berkeley, Calif.: University of California Press).

CAWSON, ALAN (1982) 'Corporatism and State Theory in the Analysis of Urban Policy' in Gerd-Michael Hellstern, Frithjof Spreer and Hellmutt Wollmann (eds) *Applied Urban Research* (Bonn: Federal Research Institute for Regional Geography and Regional Planning) vol. 1.

CAWSON, A. and SAUNDERS, PETER (1983) 'Corporatism, Competitive Politics and Class Struggle' in R. King (ed.) *Capital and Politics* (London: Routledge and Kegan Paul).

CECCARELLI, PAOLO (1982) 'Politics, Parties, and Urban Movements: Western Europe' in Norman I. Fainstein and Susan S. Fainstein (eds) *Urban Policy Under Capitalism* (Beverly Hills, Calif.: Sage Publications).

CERNY, PHILIP G. (1985) 'State Capitalism in France and Britain and the International Economic Order' in Philip G. Cerny and Martin A. Schain (eds) *Socialism, the State and Public Policy in France* (New York: Methuen; London: Frances Pinter).

CHASE-DUNN, CHRISTOPHER (1984) 'Urbanization in the World-System' in Michael P. Smith (ed.) *Cities in Transformation* (Beverly Hills, Calif.: Sage Publications).

CHILDE, V. GORDON (1950) 'The Urban Revolution', *Town Planning Review*, 21, pp. 3–17.

CHIROT, DANIEL (1985) 'The Rise of the West', *American Sociological Review*, 50, pp. 181–95.

CHURCH OF ENGLAND (1985) *Faith in the City: A Call for Action by Church and Nation* (London: Church House Publishing).

CLARK, GORDON L. (1984) 'A Theory of Local Autonomy', *Annals of the Association of American Geographers*, 74, pp. 195–208.

CLARK, GORDON L. and DEAR, MICHAEL (1984) *State Apparatus: Structures and Language of Legitimacy* (London and Boston: George Allen and Unwin).

CLARKE, SUSAN E. (1982) 'Enterprise Zones: Seeking the Neighborhood Nexus', *Urban Affairs Quarterly*, 18, pp. 53–71.

COAKLEY, M. (1983) 'Portland, Me., Has Still Another Rebirth', *Chicago Tribune*, 4 September.

COCKBURN, CYNTHIA (1977) *The Local State: Management of Cities and People* (London: Pluto Press).

COHEN, RONALD and SERVICE, ELLMAN R. (eds) (1978) *Origins of the State: The Anthropology of Political Evolution* (Philadelphia: Institute for the Study of Human Issues).

CUCITI, P. (1978) *City Need and the Responsiveness of Federal Grants Programs* (Washington, DC: Report for the US House of Representatives Committee on Banking, Finance, and Urban Affairs, Subcommittee on the City).

DAHL, ROBERT (1961) *Who Governs?* (New Haven, Conn.: Yale University Press).

DALTON, GEORGE (1968) (ed.) *Primitive, Archaic and Modern Economies: Essays of Karl Polyani* (Boston, Mass.: Beacon Press).

DAVIES, H. W. E. (1980) 'Neighbourhood Revitalization: The British Experience' in Donald B. Rosenthal (ed.), *Urban Revitalization* (Beverly Hills, Calif.: Sage Publications).

—— (1981) 'The Inner City in Britain' in G. G. Schwartz (ed.), *Advanced Industrialization and the Inner Cities* (Lexington, Mass.: Lexington Books).

DEAR, MICHAEL (1981) 'A Theory of the Local State' in Alan D. Burnett and Peter J. Taylor (eds) *Political Studies from Spatial Perspectives* (New York and Chichester: Wiley).

DEARBORN, P. M. (1980) 'Urban Fiscal Studies', in J. E. Peterson and C. L. Spain (eds), *Essays in Public Finance and Financial Management* (Chatham New Jersey: Chatham House).

DEARLOVE, JOHN (1979) *The Reorganisation of British Local Government* (Cambridge: Cambridge University Press).

DEPARTMENT OF THE ENVIRONMENT (1983) *Report for the Financial Year 1982/83* (London: HMSO).

DJILAS, MILOVAN (1957) *The New Class: Analysis of the Communist System* (New York: Praeger).

DOMMEL, PAUL R. (1980) 'Distributional Impacts of General Revenue Sharing', in Norman J. Glickman (ed.), *The Urban Impacts of Federal Policies* (Baltimore, Maryland: Johns Hopkins University Press.)

DONNISON, DAVID and SOTO, PAUL (1980) *The Good City: A Study of Urban Development and Policy in Britain* (London: Heinemann).

DOWNES, BRYAN T. (1970) 'A Critical Reexamination of the Social and Political Characteristics of Riot Cities', *Social Science Quarterly*, 49, pp. 349–60.

DOWNS, ANTHONY (1973) *Opening up the Suburbs: A Strategy for America* (New Haven, Conn. and London: Yale University Press).

DUNCAN, S. S. and GOODWIN, M. (1982) 'The Local State: Functionalism, Autonomy and Class Relations in Cockburn and Saunders', *Political Geography Quarterly*, 1, pp. 77–96.

DUNLEAVY, PATRICK (1979) 'The Urban Bases of Political Alignment: Social Class, Domestic Property Ownership, or State Invervention in Consumption Processes', *British Journal of Political Science*, 9, pp. 409–43.

—— (1980) *Urban Political Analysis* (London: Macmillan).

ECKSTEIN, HARRY (1971) *The Evaluation of Political Performance: Problems and Dimensions* (Beverley Hills, Calif.: Sage Professional Papers in Comparative Politics) no. 17.

—— (1979) 'On the "Science" of the State', *Daedalus* (Fall) 108, pp. 1–20.

—— (1982) 'The Idea of Political Development', *World Politics*, 34, pp. 468–83.

ECKSTEIN, HARRY and GURR, TED ROBERT (1975) *Patterns of Authority: A Structural Basis for Political Inquiry* (New York: Wiley-Interscience)

ECONOMIC AND SOCIAL RESEARCH COUNCIL (1985) *Changing Cities* (London: ESRC).

ECONOMIST, THE (1982) *Britain's Urban Breakdown* (London: The Economist Newspaper).

EDEL, MATTHEW (1980) '"People" versus "Places" in Urban Impact Analysis' in Norman J. Glickman (ed.) *The Urban Impacts of Federal Policies* (Baltimore, Maryland: The Johns Hopkins University Press).

ELAZAR, DANIEL J. (1984) *American Federalism: A View from the States* (New York: Harper, Row).

ELKIN, STEPHEN L. (1985) 'Pluralism in Its Place: State and Regime in Liberal Democracy' in Roger Benjamin and Stephen L. Elkin (eds) *The Democratic State* (Lawrence, Kansas: University Press of Kansas).

ELLIOTT, BRIAN and McCRONE, DAVID (1982) *The City: Patterns of Domination and Conflict.* (London: Macmillan and New York: St Martin's Press).

EVANS, PETER B., RUESCHEMEYER, DIETRICH and SKOCPOL, THEDA (1985) (eds) *Bringing the State Back In* (Cambridge: Cambridge University Press).

FAINSTEIN, NORMAN I. and FAINSTEIN, SUSAN S. (1974) *Urban Political Movements* (Englewood Cliffs, New Jersey: Prentice-Hall).

FAINSTEIN, SUSAN S. *et al.* (1983) *Restructuring the City* (New York: Longman).

FARKAS, SUZANNE (1971) *Urban Lobbying: Mayors in the Federal Arena* (New York: New York University Press).

FEAGIN, JOE R. (1984) 'Sunbelt Metropolis and Development Capital: Houston in the Era of Late Capitalism' in Larry Sawers and William K. Tabb (eds) *Sunbelt/Snowbelt: Urban Development and Regional Restructuring* (New York and Oxford: Oxford University Press).

—— (1985) 'The Global Context of Metropolitan Growth: Houston and the Oil Industry', *American Journal of Sociology*, 90, pp. 1204–30.

FIORINA, MORRIS P. and NOLL, R. (1978) 'Voters, Bureaucrats and Legislators: A Rational Choice Perspective on the Growth of Bureaucracy', *Journal of Public Economics*, 9, pp. 239–54.

FLORESTANO, P. S. and MARANADO, V. L. (1981) *The State and the Metropolis* (New York: Marcel Dekker).

FLYNN, NORMAN, LEACH, STEVE and VIELBA, CAROL (1985) *Abolition or Reform? The GLC and the Metropolitan County Councils* (London: George Allen and Unwin).

FORRESTER, ANDREW, LANSLEY, STEWART and PAULEY, ROBIN (1985) *Beyond Our Ken: A Guide to the Battle for London* (London: Fourth Estate).

FOSSETT, JAMES W. (1983) *Federal Aid to Big Cities: The Politics of Dependence* (Washington, DC: Brookings Institution).

FOTHERGILL, STEPHEN and GUDGIN, GRAHAM (1982) *Unequal*

Growth: Urban and Regional Employment Change in the UK (London: Heinemann).

FREY, BRUNO S. and SCHNEIDER, FREDERICK (1978) 'An Empirical Study of Politico-Economic Interaction in the U.S.', *Review of Economics and Statistics*, 60, pp. 174–83.

FRIEDLAND, ROGER (1976) 'Class Power and Social Control: The War on Poverty', *Politics and Society*, 6, pp. 459–89.

—— (1980) 'Corporate Power and Urban Growth: The Case of Urban Renewal', *Politics and Society*, 10, pp. 203–24.

—— (1983) *Power and Crisis in the City: Corporations, Unions and Urban Policy* (London: Macmillan; New York: Schocken).

FRIEDLAND, ROGER, PIVEN, FRANCIS FOX and ALFORD, ROGER (1977) 'Political Conflict, Urban Structure and the Fiscal Crisis' in Douglas Ashford (ed.) *Comparing Public Policies: New Concepts and Methods* (Beverly Hills, Calif.: Sage Publications).

FRIEDLAND, ROGER and WONG, HERBERT (1983) 'Congressional Politics, Federal Grants, and Local Needs: Who Gets What and Why?' in Alberta M. Sbragia (ed.) *The Municipal Money Chase: The Politics of Local Government Finance* (Boulder, Col.: Westview Press).

GANZ, ALEXANDER (1985) 'Where has the Urban Crisis Gone? How Boston and Other Large Cities Have Stemmed Economic Decline', *Urban Affairs Quarterly*, 20, pp. 449–68.

GARROW, DAVID J. (1978) *Protest At Selma: Martin Luther King, Jr, and the Voting Rights Act of 1965* (New Haven, Conn.: Yale University Press).

GELFAND, MARK I. (1980) 'How Cities Arrived on the National Agenda in the United States' in Douglas E. Ashford (ed.), *Financing Urban Government in the Welfare State* (New York: St Martin's Press).

GEORGE, M. DOROTHY (1965) *London Life in the 18th Century* (New York: Capricorn).

GERMAN MARSHALL FUND (1985) 'The New Entrepreneurs of Europe', *Translantic Perspectives*, no. 13, pp. 3–8.

GIDDENS, ANTHONY (1985) *The Nation-State and Violence: Volume Two of A Contemporary Critique of Historical Materialism* (Berkeley, Calif.: University of California Press).

GIROUARD, MARK (1985) *Cities and People: A Social and Architectual History* (New Haven, Conn.: Yale University Press).

GIVEN, JAMES BUCHANAN (1977) *Society and Homicide in Thirteenth Century England* (Stanford, Calif.: Stanford University Press).

GLICKMAN, NORMAN J. (1980) (ed.) *The Urban Impacts of Federal Policies* (Baltimore, Maryland: The Johns Hopkins University Press).

GLUCK, P. and MEISTER, R. (1979) *Cities in Transition* (New York: New Viewpoints).

GOLDEN, DAVID and POTERBA, JAMES (1980) 'The Price of Popularity: The Political Business Cycle Reexamined', *American Journal of Political Science*, 24, pp. 696–714.

GOLDSMITH, MICHAEL and NEWTON, KENNETH (1983) 'Central-Local Government Relations: The Irresistible Rise of Centralised Power', *West European Politics*, 6, pp. 216–33.

GORDON, DAVID (1976) 'Capitalism and the Roots of Urban Crisis' in R. E. Alcahy and D. Mermelstein (eds) *The Fiscal Crisis of American Cities* (New York: Vintage).

GOTTDIENER, M. (1985) (ed.) 'Symposium: Whatever Happened to the Urban Crisis?' *Urban Affairs Quarterly*, 20, pp. 419–86.

GOULD, FRANK (1983) 'The Growth of Public Expenditures: Theory and Evidence from Six Advanced Democracies' in Charles Lewis Taylor (ed.) *Why Governments Grow: Measuring Public Sector Size* (Beverly Hills, Calif.: Sage Publications).

GREENBERG, EDWARD S. (1985) *Capitalism and the American Political Ideal* (Armonk, New Jersey: M. E. Sharpe).

GREENBERG, M. and VALENTE, N. (1975) 'Recent Economic Trends in the Major Northeastern Metropolises' in G. Sternlieb and J. Hughes (eds) *Post-Industrial America* (New Brunswick, New Jersey: Rutgers University Center for Urban Policy).

GREENSTONE, JACK D. and PETERSON, PAUL E. (1973) *Race and Authority in Urban Politics* (Chicago: University of Chicago Press).

GREENWOOD, ROYSTON (1982) 'Pressure from Whitehall', in Richard Rose and Edward Page (eds), *Fiscal Stress in Cities* (Cambridge: Cambridge University Press).

GUDE, S., HEINZ, W. and ROTHAMMER, P. (1981) 'Urban Policy in the Federal Republic of Germany' in G. G. Schwartz (ed.) *Advanced Industrialization and the Inner Cities* (Lexington, Mass.: D. C. Heath).

GURR, TED ROBERT (1976) *Rogues, Rebels, and Reformers: A Political History of Urban Crime and Conflict* (Beverly Hills, Calif.: Sage Publications).

—— (1977) 'Crime Trends in Modern Democracies since 1945', *International Annals of Criminology*, 16, pp. 41–86.

—— (1979) 'Political Protest and Rebellion in the 1960s: The United States in World Perspective' in Hugh Davis Graham and Ted Robert Gurr (eds) *Violence in America: Historical and Comparative Perspectives* (Beverly Hills, Calif.: Sage Publications).

—— (1980) 'On the Outcomes of Violent Conflict' in Ted Robert Gurr (ed.) *Handbook of Political Conflict: Theory and Research* (New York: The Free Press; London: Macmillan).

GURR, TED ROBERT, GRABOSKY, PETER N. and HULA, RICHARD C. (1977) *The Politics of Crime and Conflict: A Comparative History of Four Cities* (Beverly Hills, Calif.: Sage Publications).

GUTERBOCK, THOMAS M. (1980) 'The Political Economy of Urban Revitalization: Competing Theories', *Urban Affairs Quarterly*, 15, pp. 429–38.

GUYOT, DOROTHY H. (1983) 'Newark: Crime and Politics in a Declining City' in Anne Heinz, Herbert Jacob and Robert L. Lineberry (eds) *Crime in City Politics* (New York and London: Longman).

GYFORD, JOHN (1983) 'The New Urban Left: A Local Road to Socialism?', *New Society*, 21 April.

—— (1985) *The Politics of Local Socialism* (London: George Allen & Unwin).

HALE, G. E. and PALLEY, MARION LIEF (1981) *The Politics of Federal Grants* (Washington, DC: Congressional Quarterly Press).

HALL, PETER (1975) *Urban and Regional Planning* (Harmondsworth: Penguin Books).

—— (ed.) (1981) *The Inner City in Context: The Final Report of the Social Science Research Council Inner Cities Working Party* (London: Heinemann).

HALL, PETER and HAY, DENNIS (1980) *Growth Centres in the European Urban System* (London: Heinemann).

HAMBLETON, ROBIN (1978) *Policy Planning and Local Government* (London: Hutchinson; Montclair, New Jersey: Allanheld, Osmun).

HAMMOND, MASON (1972) *The City in the Ancient World* (Cambridge, Mass.: Harvard University Press).

HARLOE, MICHAEL (1981) (ed.) *New Perspectives in Urban Change and Conflict* (London: Heinemann).

HARRISON, PAUL (1983) *Inside the Inner City* (Harmondsworth: Penguin Books).

HARVEY, DAVID (1973) *Social Justice and the City* (London: Edward Arnold; Baltimore, Maryland: The Johns Hopkins University Press).

—— (1975) 'The Political Economy of Urbanization in Advanced Capitalist Societies: The United States' in G. Gappert and H. M. Rose (eds) *The Social Economy of Cities* (Beverly Hills, Calif.: Sage Publications).

HECLO, HUGH (1974) *Modern Social Policies in Britain and Sweden: From Relief to Income Maintenance* (New Haven, Conn.: Yale University Press).

HELLSTERN, G.-M., SPREER, R. and WOLLMANN, H. (1982) (eds) *Applied Urban Research: Proceedings of the European Meeting on Applied Urban Research, Essen* (Bonn: Bundesforschungsanstalt für Landeskunde und Raumordnung) vols 1–3.

HENIG, JEFFREY R. (1985) *Public Policy and Federalism: Issues in State and Local Politics* (New York: St Martin's Press).

HICKS, ALEXANDER (1981) 'State Policy Determination: Structure *cum* Choice' (Paper read to the 1981 Annual Meetings of the American Political Science Association).

—— (1984) 'Elections, Keynes, Bureaucracy and Class: Explaining U.S. Budget Deficits, 1961–1978', *American Sociological Review*, 49, pp. 165–82.

HILL, RICHARD CHILD (1977) 'State Capitalism and the Urban Fiscal Crisis in the United States', *International Journal of Urban and Regional Research*, 1, pp. 76–100.

—— (1983) 'Market, State and Community: National Urban Policy in the 1980s', *Urban Affairs Quarterly*, 19, pp. 5–20.

—— (1984) 'Economic Crisis and Political Response in the Motor City' in Larry Sawers and William K. Tabb (eds), *Sunbelt/Snowbelt: Urban Development and Regional Restructuring* (New York and Oxford: Oxford University Press).

HOBSBAWM, E. J. (1959) *Primitive Rebels: Studies in Archaic Forms of Social Movement in the Nineteenth and Twentieth Centuries* (New York: W. W. Norton).

HOHENBERG, PAUL M. and LEES, LYNN HOLLEN (1985) *The Making of Urban Europe 1000–1950* (Cambridge, Mass.: Harvard University Press).

HOWITT, ARNOLD M. (1984) *Managing Federalism: Studies in Intergovernmental Relations* (Washington, DC: Congressional Quarterly).

IRIS, MARK (1983) 'American Urban Riots Revisited', *American Behavioral Scientist*, 26, pp. 333–52.

JACKSON, KENNETH T. (1985) *Crabgrass Frontier: The Suburbanization of the United States* (New York: Oxford University Press).

JACOB, HERBERT and LINEBERRY, ROBERT L. *et al.* (1982) *Governmental Responses to Crime: Crime and Governmental Responses in American Cities* (Washington, DC: National Institute of Justice, US Department of Justice).

JACOBS, JANE (1984) *Cities and the Wealth of Nations: Principles of Economic Life* (New York: Random House).

JACOBY, HENRY (1973) *The Bureaucratization of the World* (Berkeley, Calif.: University of California Press).

JENNINGS, E. T., Jr (1979) 'Urban Riots and Welfare Policy Change: A Test of the Piven–Cloward Theory' in Helen Ingram and D. Mann (eds), *Why Policies Succeed or Fail* (Beverly Hills, Calif.: Sage Publications).

JOHNSTON, R. J. (1982) *Geography and the State* (London: Macmillan).

JONES, BRYAN D. (1983) *Governing Urban America: A Policy Focus* (Boston: Little, Brown).

JORDAN, BILL (1985) *The State: Authority and Autonomy* (Oxford: Basil Blackwell).

JUDD, DENNIS R. (1984) *The Politics of American Cities: Private Power and Public Policy* (Boston: Little, Brown) 2nd edn.

KASARDA, JOHN D. (1976) 'The Changing Occupational Structure of the American Metropolis: Apropos the Urban Problem', in Barry Schwartz (ed.), *The Changing Face of the Suburbs* (Chicago: University of Chicago Press).

—— (1980) 'The Implications of the Contemporary Redistribution Trends for National Urban Policy', *Social Science Quarterly*, 61, pp. 373–400.

—— (1982) 'Adapting Policy to New Urban Realities' (Paper read to the Conference on the Future of the City, University of Chicago, June 18–19).

KATZNELSON, IRA (1976) 'The Crisis of the Capitalist City: Urban Politics and Social Control', in Willis D. Hawley (ed.), *Theoretical Perspectives on Urban Politics* (Englewood Cliffs, N. J.: Prentice-Hall).

—— (1981) *City Trenches* (New York: Pantheon Books).

KATZNELSON, IRA, GILLIE, KATHLEEN and WEIR, MARGARET (1982) 'Race and Schooling: Reflections on the Social Bases of Urban Movements' in Norman I. Fainstein and Susan E. Fainstein (eds) *Urban Policy Under Capitalism* (Beverly Hills, Calif.: Sage Publications).

KATZ, STEVEN and MAYER, MARGIT (1985) 'Gimme Shelter: Self-help Housing Struggles Within and Against the State in New York City and West Berlin', *International Journal of Urban and Regional Research*, 9, pp. 15–46.

KEARNS, KEVIN C. (1981) 'Urban Squatter Strategies: Social Adaptation to Housing Stress in London', *Urban Life* 10 (July), pp. 123–153.

KENNETT, STEPHEN and HALL, PETER (1981) 'The Inner City in Spatial Perspective' in Peter Hall (ed.) *The Inner City in Context: The Final Report of the Social Science Research Council Inner Cities Working Party* (London: Heinemann).

KETTLE, M. and HODGES, L. (1982) *Uprising! The Police, the People and the Riots in Britain's Cities* (London: Pan).

KING, DESMOND S. (1985a) *A Statist Analysis of Central State Penetration of*

Municipalities: State Autonomy Under Capitalism (Unpublished PhD thesis, Northwestern University).

KING, DESMOND S. (1985b) 'The New Right and the Public Sector: Theoretical Assumptions and the Experience of the Thatcher and Reagan Administrations', paper presented to the annual meeting of the European Consortium for Political Research, Barcelona.

KING, DESMOND S. and GURR, TED ROBERT (1983) 'State Fiscal Crisis and Urban Decline in Western Societies' (Paper read to the American Political Science Association annual meeting, Chicago).

KIRBY, ANDREW (1979) '"Managerialism" and Local Authority Housing: A Review', *Public Administration Bulletin*, 30 (August), pp. 47–60.

—— (1982) 'The External Relations of the Local State in Britain: Some Empirical Examples' in Kevin R. Cox and R. J. Johnston (eds) *Conflict, Politics and the Urban Scene* (New York: St Martin's Press; London: Edward Arnold).

KIRK, GWYNETH (1980) *Urban Planning in a Capitalist Society* (London: Croom Helm).

KIRWAN, R. M. (1980) 'The Fiscal Context' in G. C. Cameron (ed.) *The Future of the British Conurbations: Policies and Prescription for Change* (London: Longman).

KONRAD, GEORGE and SZELENYI, IVAN (1979) *The Intellectuals on the Road to Class Power* (New York: Harcourt Brace Jovanovich; Brighton: Harvester).

KRASNER, STEPHEN D. (1978) *Defending the National Interest: Raw Materials, Investments and U.S. Foreign Policy* (Princeton, New Jersey: Princeton University Press).

—— (1984) 'Approaches to the State: Alternative Conceptions and Historical Dynamics', *Comparative Politics*, 16, pp. 223–46.

KRAUSHAAR, R. (1981) 'Policy Without Protest: The Dilemma of Organizing for Change in Britain' in M. Harloe (ed.) *New Perspectives in Urban Change and Conflict* (London: Heinemann).

KRISTOL, IRVING (1979) *Two Cheers for Capitalism* (New York: New American Library, Mentor Books).

LANE, FREDERIC C. (1966) *Venice and History: The Collected Papers of Frederic C. Lane* (Baltimore, Maryland: The Johns Hopkins University Press).

LANÉ, JAN-ERIK (1985) (ed.) *State and Market: The Politics of the Public and the Private* (London: Sage Publications for the European Consortium for Political Research).

LANE, ROGER (1980) 'Urban Police and Crime in Nineteenth-Century America' *Crime and Justice: An Annual Review of Research*, 2, pp. 1–44.

LAURENCE, SUSAN and HALL, PETER (1981) 'Deprivation in the Inner City' in Peter Hall (ed.) *The Inner City in Context: The Final Report of the Social Science Research Council Inner Cities Working Party* (London: Heinemann).

LEVI, MARGARET (1981) 'The Predatory Theory of Rule', *Politics and Society*, 10, pp. 431–65.

LEVINE, C. H., RUBIN, I. S. and WOLOHOJIAN, G. G. (1981) *The Politics of Retrenchment* (Beverly Hills, Calif.: Sage Publications).

LEVINE, MYRON A. (1983) 'The Reagan Urban Policy: Efficient Growth and Public Sector Minimization', *Journal of Urban Affairs*, 5.

LONG, NORTON E. (1971) 'The City as Reservation', *Public Interest*, 25, pp. 22–38.

McADAM, DOUG (1984) *Political Process and the Development of Black Insurgency 1930–1970* (Chicago: University of Chicago Press).

McCALLUM, J. D. (1980) 'Statistical Trends of the British Conurbations' in G. C. Cameron (ed.) *The Future of the British Conurbations: Policies and Prescriptions for Change* (London: Longman).

McEVEDY, COLIN (1972) *The Penguin Atlas of Medieval History* (New York: Penguin Books).

McKAY, DAVID H. and COX, ANDREW W. (1979) *The Politics of Urban Change* (London: Croom Helm).

MacPHERSON, C. B. (1977) 'Do We Need a Theory of the State?', *European Journal of Sociology*, 18, pp. 223–44.

MARENIN, OTWIN (1985) 'Police Performance and State Rule: Control and Autonomy in the Exercise of Coercion', *Comparative Politics*, 17, pp. 101–22.

MEEHAN, EUGENE J. (1980) 'Urban Development: An Alternative Strategy' in D. B. Rosenthal (ed.), *Urban Revitalization* (Sage Urban Affairs Annual Review, 18, pp. 279–301).

MEYER, JOHN W. (1980) 'The World Polity and the Authority of the Nation–State' in Albert Bergesen (ed.) *Studies of the Modern World-System* (New York: Academic Press).

MILIBAND, RALPH (1983) 'State Power and Class Interests', *New Left Review*, 138, pp. 57–68.

MILLER, GARY and MOE, TERRY M. (1983) 'Bureaucrats, Legislators and the Size of Government', *American Political Science Review*, 77, pp. 297–322.

MOLLENKOPF, JOHN (1983) *The Contested City* (Princeton, New Jersey: Princeton University Press).

MOLOTCH, HARVEY (1976) 'The City as a Growth Machine: Toward a Political Economy of Place', *American Journal of Sociology*, 82, pp. 309–32.

—— (1979) 'Capital and Neighborhood in the United States: Some Conceptual Links', *Urban Affairs Quarterly*, 14, pp. 289–312.

MONKKONEN, ERIC H. (1981) *Police in Urban America, 1860–1920* (New York and Cambridge: Cambridge University Press).

—— (1985) 'What Urban Crisis? A Historian's Point of View', *Urban Affairs Quarterly*, 20, pp. 429–48.

MUMFORD, LEWIS (1961) *The City in History: Its Origins, Its Transformations and Its Prospects* (New York: Harcourt Brace Jovanovich; Harmondsworth: Penguin Books).

NATHAN, RICHARD P. and ADAMS, CHARLES (1976) 'Understanding Central City Hardship', *Political Science Quarterly*, 91, pp. 47–62.

NEW STATESMAN (1986) 'City Stranglehold on Local Democracy', 3 January 1986.

NEW YORK TIMES (1985) 'Home of Rolls-Royce Slides Into a Recession', 29 July.

NEWTON, KENNETH and KARRAN, T. J. (1985) *The Politics of Local Expenditure* (London: Macmillan).

NISKANEN, WILLIAM (1971) *Bureaucracy and Representative Government* (Chicago: Aldine).

NORDLINGER, ERIC A. (1981) *On the Autonomy of the Democratic State*

(Cambridge, Mass.: Harvard University Press).

—— (1986) 'Taking the State Seriously' in Myron Weiner and Samuel P. Huntington (eds) *Understanding Political Development* (Boston: Little, Brown).

NOYELLE, T. J. and STANBACK, T. M. (1984) *The Economic Transformation of the Cities* (Totowa, New Jersey: Rowman & Allenheld).

O'CONNOR, JAMES (1973) *The Fiscal Crisis of the State* (New York: St Martin's Press; London: Macmillan).

OECD (1983) *Managing Urban Change*, 2 vols (Paris: OECD).

PAHL, RAYMOND E. (1970) 'Urban Social Theory and Research' in R. E. Pahl (ed.) *Whose City?* (London: Longman).

—— (1975) (ed.) *Whose City?* (Harmondsworth: Penguin Books) 2nd edn.

PARKINSON, MICHAEL and DUFFY, JAMES (1984) 'Government's Response to Inner-City Riots: The Minister for Merseyside and the Task Force', *Parliamentary Affairs*, 37, pp. 76–96.

PATTERSON, JAMES T. (1969) *The New Deal and the States: Federalism in Transition* (Princeton, New Jersey: Princeton University Press).

PERRY, D. and WATKINS, A. (1977) *The Rise of the Sunbelt Cities* (Beverly Hills, Calif.: Sage Publications).

PETERSON, PAUL E. (1981) *City Limits* (Chicago: University of Chicago Press).

PETTENGILL, R. and UPPAL, J. (1974) *Can Cities Survive?* (New York: St. Martin's Press).

PETTMAN, RALPH (1979) *State and Class: A Sociology of International Affairs* (New York: St Martin's Press).

PICKVANCE, C. G. (1976) 'On the Study of Urban Social Movements', in C. G. Pickvance (ed.) *Urban Sociology: Critical Essays* (London: Tavistock).

PIERCE, NEAL (1985) '"Urban Villages" in the Suburbs', *Denver Post*, 18 August.

PIVEN, FRANCES FOX and CLOWARD, RICHARD A. (1971) *Regulating the Poor: The Functions of Social Welfare* (New York: Vintage; London: Tavistock).

POGGI, GIANFRANCO (1978) *The Development of the Modern State: A Sociological Introduction* (Stanford, Calif.: Stanford University Press; London: Hutchinson).

POLANYI, KARL (1944) *The Great Transformation* (New York: Rinehart).

PRIEMUS, HUGO (1983) 'Squatters in Amsterdam: Urban Social Movement, Urban Managers or Something Else?' *International Journal of Urban and Regional Research*, vol. 7, no. 3, pp. 417–27.

REES, GARETH and LAMBERT, JOHN (1985) *Cities in Crisis* (London: Edward Arnold).

REX, JOHN and MOORE, ROBERT (1967) *Race, Community, and Conflict* (Oxford: Oxford University Press).

RHODES, R. A. W. (1984) 'Continuity and Change in British Central- -Local Relations: "The Conservative Threat", 1979–83', *British Journal of Political Science*, 14, pp. 261–83.

RICHARDSON, JAMES F. (1970) *The New York Police: Colonial Times to 1901* (New York: Oxford University Press).

ROBERTS, DAVID (1969) *Victorian Origins of the British Welfare State* (New

York: Archon Books).

ROSE, RICHARD (1984) *The Growth of Government: The Programmatic Approach* (Beverly Hills, Calif.: Sage Publications).

ROTBERG, ROBERT, I. (1979) *Haiti: The Politics of Squalor* (Boston: Houghton Mifflin).

ROSS, JOHN and GREENFIELD, JAMES (1980) 'Measuring the Health of Cities', in Charles Levine and Irene Rubin (eds), *Fiscal Stress and Public Policy* (Beverly Hills, Calif.: Sage).

SAMPSON, ANTHONY (1984) *The Changing Anatomy of Britain* (New York: Vintage Books).

SAUNDERS, PETER (1979) *Urban Politics: A Sociological Interpretation* (London: Hutchinson).

—— (1981) *Social Theory and the Urban Question* (London: Hutchinson).

SAUNDERS, PETER (1985) 'Corporatism and Urban Service Provision' in Wyn Grant (ed.) *The Political Economy of Corporatism* (London: Macmillan).

SBRAGIA, ALBERTA M. (1983) (ed.) *The Municipal Money Chase: The Politics of Local Government Finance* (Boulder, Col.: Westview Press).

SCARMAN, LORD (1982) *The Scarman Report: The Brixton Disorders 10–12 April 1981* (Harmondsworth: Penguin Books).

SCHOTT, KERRY (1984) *Policy, Power and Order: The Persistence of Economic Problems in Capitalist States* (New Haven, Conn.: Yale University Press).

SCHWARTZ, B. (1976) (ed.) *The Changing Face of the Suburbs* (Chicago: University of Chicago Press).

SERVICE, ELMAN R. (1975) *Origins of the State and Civilization: The Process of Cultural Evolution* (New York: Norton).

SHANNON, J. (1984) 'New Federalism in the 1980s', in J. H. Carr (ed.) *Crisis and Constraints in Municipal Finance* (New York: Chatham).

SHARKANSKY, IRA (1979) *Wither the State? Politics and Public Enterprise in Three Countries* (Chatham, New Jersey: Chatham House).

SHARPE, L. J. (1981) (ed.) *The Local Fiscal Crisis in Western Europe* (Beverly Hills, Calif. and London: Sage Publications).

SHEFTER, MARTIN (1977) 'New York City's Fiscal Crisis: The Politics of Inflation and Retrenchment', *The Public Interest*, 48, pp. 98–127.

SHORT, JOHN R. (1984) *The Urban Arena: Capital, State and Community in Contemporary Britain* (London: Macmillan).

SILVER, ALLAN (1967) 'The Demand for Order in Civil Society: A Review of Some Theories in the History of Urban Crime, Police, and Riot', in David J. Bordua (ed.) *The Police: Six Sociological Essays* (New York: Wiley).

SIMMIE, JAMES and JAMES, NICHOLAS (1986) 'The Money Map of Defence', *New Society*, 31 January 1986.

SJOBERG, GIDEON (1964) 'The Rise and Fall of Cities: A Theoretical Perspective', *International Journal of Comparative Sociology*, 4, pp. 107–20.

SKOCPOL, THEDA (1980) 'Political Response to Capitalist Crisis: Neo-Marxist Theories of the State and the Case of the New Deal', *Politics and Society*, 10, pp. 155–201.

SKOGAN, WESLEY G. (1977) 'The Changing Distribution of Big-City Crime', *Urban Affairs Quarterly*, 13, pp. 33–48.

SKOWRONEK, STEPHEN (1982) *Building a New American State: The*

Expansion of National Administrative Capacities, 1877–1920 (Cambridge: Cambridge University Press).

SMITH, MICHAEL PETER (1979) *The City and Social Theory* (New York: St. Martin's Press; Oxford: Blackwell).

—— (1984) (ed.) *Cities in Transformation: Class, Capital, and the State* (Beverly Hills, Calif.: Sage Publications).

SPILERMAN, SEYMOUR (1976) 'Structural Characteristics of Cities and the Severity of Racial Disorders', *American Sociological Review*, 41, pp. 771–92.

STEGGART, G. X. (1975) *Community Action Groups and City Governments* (Cambridge, Mass.: Ballinger).

STEIN, ROBERT M. (1981) 'The Allocation of Federal Aid Monies: The Synthesis of Demand-Side and Supply-Side Explanations', *American Political Science Review*, 75, pp. 334–43.

STERNLIEB, G. and HUGHES, J. (1975) (eds) *Post-Industrial America* (New Brunswick, New Jersey: Rutgers University Center for Urban Policy).

STONE, CLARENCE N. (1984) 'City Politics and Economic Development: Political Economy Perspectives', *Journal of Politics*, 46, pp. 286–99.

STRAYER, JOSEPH R. (1970) *On the Medieval Origins of the Modern State* (Princeton, New Jersey: Princeton University Press).

SWANK, DUANE H. (1983) 'Between Incrementalism and Revolution: Group Protest and the Growth of the Welfare State', *American Behavioral Scientist*, 26, pp. 291–310.

TABB, WILLIAM K. (1982) *The Long Default* (New York: Monthly Review Press).

—— (1984) 'Economic Democracy and Regional Restructuring: An Internationalization Perspective' in Larry Sawers and William K. Tabb (eds) *Sunbelt/Snowbelt: Urban Development and Regional Restructuring* (New York and Oxford: Oxford University Press).

THERBORN, GORAN (1984) 'The Prospects of Labour and the Transformation of Advanced Capitalism', *New Left Review*, no. 145, pp. 5–38.

THOMSON, ANDREW (1982) 'Local Government as an Employer' in Richard Rose and Edward Page (eds) *Fiscal Stress in Cities* (Cambridge: Cambridge University Press).

TILLY, CHARLES (1975) 'Reflections on the History of European State-Making' in Charles Tilly (ed.) *The Formation of National States in Western Europe* (Princeton, New Jersey: Princeton University Press).

TILLY, CHARLES, TILLY, LOUISE and TILLY, RICHARD (1975) *The Rebellious Century 1830–1930* (Cambridge, Mass.: Harvard University Press; London: Dent).

TOBIAS, J. J. (1967) *Crime and Industrial Society in the Nineteenth Century* (London: B. T. Batsford).

TUFTE, EDWARD (1978) *The Political Control of the Economy* (Princeton, New Jersey: Princeton University Press).

VAN ALSTYNE, WILLIAM W. (1985) 'The Second Death of Federalism', *Michigan Law Review*, 83 (June), pp. 1709–33.

VAN DEN BERG, L., DREWETT, R., KLAASEN, L. H., FOSSI, A. and VIJVERBERG, C. H. T. (1982) *Urban Europe: A Study of Growth and Decline* (New York: Pergamon Press; Oxford: Pergamon).

VAN DER WEILEN, HENNY (1983) 'The Public Sector's Interaction with the Market Sector: The Netherlands' in Charles Lewis Taylor (ed.) *Why Governments Grow: Measuring Public Sector Size* (Beverly Hills: Sage Publications).

VISHER, MARY G. and REMOE, SVEND O. (1984) 'A Case Study of a Cuckoo Nestling: The Role of the State in the Norwegian Oil Sector', *Politics & Society*, 13, pp. 321–41.

VON BEYME, KLAUS (1985) 'The Role of the State and the Growth of Government', *International Political Science Review*, 6, pp. 11–34.

WEBER, MAX (1947) *The Theory of Social and Economic Organization* (New York: The Free Press).

—— (1958) *The City*, trans. and ed. Don Martindale and Gertrud Neuwirth (New York: The Free Press; London: Heinemann).

WEBMAN, JERRY A. (1981) 'Centralization and Implementation: Urban Renewal in Great Britain and France', *Comparative Politics*, 13, pp. 127–48.

—— (1982) *Reviving the Industrial City: The Politics of Urban Renewal in Lyon and Birmingham* (New Brunswick, New Jersey: Rutgers University Press; London: Croom Helm).

WEIR, MARGARET and SKOCPOL, THEDA (1985) 'State Structures and the Possibilities for "Keynesian" Responses to the Great Depression in Sweden, Britain, and the United States' in Peter B. Evans, Dietrich Rueschemeyer and Theda Skocpol (eds) *Bringing the State Back In* (Cambridge: Cambridge University Press).

WHEEN, FRANCIS (1985) *The Battle for London* (London: Pluto Press).

WILENSKY, HAROLD L. (1976) *The 'New Corporatism', Centralization and the Welfare State* (London: Sage Professional Papers in Contemporary Sociology) 2, no. 20.

WINTER, WILLIAM O. (1969) *The Urban Polity* (New York: Dodd, Mead).

WIRTH, FREDERICK (1985) 'The Dependent City? External Influences upon Local Government', *Journal of Politics*, 47, pp. 83–112.

WOLMAN, HAROLD (1982) 'Local Autonomy and Intergovernmental Finances in Britain and the United States' in Richard Rose and Edward Page (eds), *Fiscal Stress in Cities* (Cambridge: Cambridge University Press).

YOUNG, KEN and MILLS, LIZ (1982) 'The Decline of Urban Economies' in Richard Rose and Edward Page (eds) *Fiscal Stress in Cities*, (Cambridge: Cambridge University Press).

ZUKIN, SHARON (1980) 'A Decade of the New Urban Sociology', *Theory and Society*, 9, pp. 575–601.

Index